CookingLight®
Cooking *through the* Seasons

Cooking Light.

Cooking *through the* Seasons

an everyday guide to enjoying the freshest food

Oxmoor House.

©2010 by Oxmoor House, Inc.
P.O. Box 360220, Des Moines, IA 50336-0220

ISBN-13: 978-0-8487-3319-3
ISBN-10: 0-8487-3319-3
Library of Congress Control Number: 2009937173

Printed in the United States of America
First Printing 2010

Be sure to check with your health-care provider before making any changes in your diet.

Oxmoor House, Inc.
VP, Publishing Director: Jim Childs
Editorial Director: Susan Payne Dobbs
Brand Manager: Allison Long Lowery

Cooking Light **Cooking Through the Seasons**
Senior Editor: Heather Averett
Project Editor: Diane Rose
Senior Designer: Melissa Jones Clark
Director, Test Kitchens: Elizabeth Tyler Austin
Assistant Director, Test Kitchens: Julie Christopher
Test Kitchens Professionals: Allison E. Cox, Julie Gunter,
    Kathleen Royal Phillips, Catherine Crowell Steele,
    Ashley T. Strickland
Photography Director: Jim Bathie
Senior Photo Stylist: Kay E. Clarke
Associate Photo Stylist: Katherine Eckert Coyne
Production Manager: Tamara Nall

Contributors
Copy Editor: Jacqueline B. Giovanelli
Proofreader: Jasmine Hodges
Indexer: Mary Ann Laurens
Interns: Georgia Dodge, Perri K. Hubbard,
    Allison Leigh Sperando, Christine Taylor
Food Stylists: Ana Kelly, Iris O'Brien

Cooking Light
Editor: Scott Mowbray
Creative Director: Carla Frank
Acting Design Director: Ellene Wundrok
Deputy Editor: Phillip Rhodes
Food Editor: Ann Taylor Pittman
Special Publications Editor: Mary Simpson Creel, M.S., R.D.
Nutrition Editor: Kathy Kitchens Downie, R.D.
Associate Food Editors: Timothy Q. Cebula, Julianna Grimes
Associate Editors: Cindy Hatcher, Brandy Rushing
Test Kitchens Director: Vanessa T. Pruett
Assistant Test Kitchens Director: Tiffany Vickers Davis
Senior Food Stylist: Kellie Gerber Kelley
Test Kitchens Professionals: Mary Drennen Ankar,
    SaBrina Bone, Deb Wise
Art Director: Fernande Bondarenko
Deputy Art Director: J. Shay McNamee
Senior Photographer: Randy Mayor
Senior Photo Stylist: Cindy Barr
Photo Stylist: Leigh Ann Ross
Copy Chief: Maria Parker Hopkins
Assistant Copy Chief: Susan Roberts
Research Editor: Michelle Gibson Daniels
Editorial Production Director: Liz Rhoades
Production Editor: Hazel R. Eddins
Administrative Coordinator: Carol D. Johnson
Cookinglight.com Editor: Kim Cross

To order additional publications, call 1-800-765-6400
    or 1-800-491-0551.

For more books to enrich your life, visit oxmoorhouse.com

To search, savor, and share thousands of recipes,
    visit myrecipes.com

Cover: Heirloom Tomato and Avocado Stack (page 174) and
    Classic Apple Pie (page 294)
Back Cover: Strawberry Layer Cake (page 74) and Brussels
    Sprouts with Currants and Pine Nuts (page 272)

why cook seasonally?

When you use fresh fruits and vegetables in your recipes, you don't have to do much to make them taste good. Sometimes just pulling them out of your market basket and rinsing them is all you need to do. From summer's garden-fresh corn to winter's juicy citrus fruits, there are plenty of colorful, delightful, and, above all, delicious items to choose from throughout the year.

Choosing the season's best foods for taste and freshness alone is reason enough to cook seasonally. But here's another: Fresh, in-season produce maximizes nutrients and adds variety to your meals, too. Take vitamin C–packed strawberries, for instance. They're an excellent source of potassium and fiber, and they also offer folate, a B vitamin known for its role in reducing the risk of birth defects. And don't forget about autumn's famed crisp, crunchy apples. They're a good source of fiber, which helps lower cholesterol and control blood sugar.

Cooking with in-season fruits and vegetables can also save you money. Out-of-season produce is costly and generally lacks flavor. Our recommendation is to skip it and choose fruits and vegetables that are in season. When produce is at its peak, there's an abundance of it—and you can find it for a bargain. In the summer, enjoy tomatoes, cucumbers, fresh herbs, bell peppers, and more. During autumn and winter, look to winter squashes; dark, leafy greens; citrus fruits; and sweet potatoes. And in spring, try berries, asparagus, artichokes, and fresh peas.

Let *Cooking Light* **Cooking Through the Seasons** be your guide to exploring and enjoying new varieties and flavors of fresh produce all year long.

The *Cooking Light* Editors

contents

spring

the spring kitchen

Along with the first blooms of spring arrives a bounty of fresh produce for you to enjoy. Head down to your local farmers' market or U-pick and peruse the season's best offerings—asparagus, artichokes, green peas, and fava beans, to name a few—and showcase them in your next springtime meal.

Settle down to dinner with favorites like Pasta Primavera (recipe on page 30), Braised Chicken with Baby Vegetables and Peas (recipe on page 54), or Cream of Asparagus Soup (recipe on page 69), and delight in the simple pleasures of fresh ingredients at their finest. Or try your hand at something new, and pair Carrot-Pineapple Slaw (recipe on page 62) with grilled pork chops for a sweet and savory meal. To make a statement at your next spring soiree, highlight some of the season's unique ingredients with dishes that have a little kick, like Seared Tuna and Radish Salad with Wasabi Dressing (recipe on page 39) and Grilled Chicken, Mango, and Jicama Salad with Tequila-Lime Vinaigrette (recipe on page 56). Impress your guests and serve White Sangria (recipe on page 24), a refreshing twist on the classic Spanish libation.

For the most satisfying treats, make use of spring's peak fruits like strawberries, pineapple, coconut, and rhubarb. Timeless dishes such as Strawberry Layer Cake (recipe on page 74) and Lattice-Topped Rhubarb Pie (recipe on page 93) are sure to please any sweet tooth, and Piña Colada Cheesecake Bars (recipe on page 82) offer a new take on a traditional dessert favorite. Whether you're preparing dinner for the family or planning a get-together with friends, make the most of this season's harvest while you can.

Whether shopping at your local farmers' market or the produce section of your favorite supermarket, take advantage of the bounty of spring with the fresh flavors of quintessential favorites such as asparagus, green peas, spring onions, strawberries, and more.

fruits

Bananas

Blood Oranges

Coconuts

Grapefruit

Kiwifruit

Lemons

Limes

Mangoes

Navel Oranges

Papayas

Passionfruit

Pineapples

Strawberries

Tangerines

Valencia Oranges

....

vegetables

Artichokes

Arugula

Asparagus

Avocados

Baby Leeks

Beets

Belgian Endive

Broccoli

Cauliflower

Dandelion Greens

Fava Beans

Green Onions

Green Peas

Kale

Lettuce

Mushrooms

Radishes

Red Potatoes

Rhubarb

Snap Beans

Snow Peas

Spinach

Sugar Snap Peas

Sweet Onions

Swiss Chard

....

herbs

Chives

Dill

Garlic Chives

Lemongrass

Mint

Parsley

Thyme

spring

From goat cheese and Dijon mustard to vinaigrettes and angel hair pasta, here are some ideas for staples, seasonings, and other ingredients ideally suited for springtime brunches, patio lunches, and alfresco dinners.

Dijon Mustard: Beyond serving mustard as a condiment, straight-up on sandwiches, or as a pretzel dip, we like to use it to add a zip of flavor as well as to bind sauces and vinaigrettes.

Extra-Virgin Olive Oil: When using olive oil for its flavor, particularly if tossing it with vegetables or adding it to pasta, a higher-priced extra-virgin olive oil will usually produce a much better result than a mid-priced one. It's definitely worth the splurge.

Goat Cheese: With a characteristic acidic flavor, goat cheese ranges from soft and spreadable to dry and crumbly. Soft goat cheese comes in cones, discs, or logs—sometimes rolled in herbs.

Herbs: Chives, dill, and mint are examples of spring herbs that add depth and freshness to spring recipes. Grow herbs in containers on your back porch and pick

them when you're ready to prepare your meal, or simply purchase them from your local supermarket.

Lemons: It might be fair to say that we use lemons in our Test Kitchens more than any other fruit as a flavoring ingredient. Whether we use juice, lemon zest (rind), or slices, the acidity of lemon adds to the final balance of flavor in all types of food, from savory to sweet.

Pasta: Pasta is one of the most versatile and popular types of grain products, and it's one we like to use in the spring. Some of our favorites include angel hair and fettuccine.

Pimiento Peppers: Tossing asparagus and other veggies with sweet pimiento peppers is a great springtime application. One of our all-time comfort favorites is pimiento cheese sandwiches!

Pine Nuts: Certainly, pine nuts are essential to a good pesto, providing the resinous foundation upon which a

pyramid of flavors is built. But pine nuts can also be a snack food that tastes great roasted and lightly salted, or a sweet and welcome crunch tucked into a rice dish or sprinkled in a salad.

Spring Onions: Also known as green onions or scallions, these wild alliums add flavor and color. Served raw, onions have a sweet, delicate flavor that is excellent in potato or rice salads and in salsa with chiles. Cooked spring onions are ideal for fast recipes such as pasta, omelets, pancakes, and stir-fries.

Vinaigrettes: Bottled vinaigrettes such as balsamic and sun-dried tomato are great accompaniments for spring salads and vegetables. Just a hint of vinaigrette provides an amazing flavor boost.

best ways to cook

Boiling and steaming are two cooking techniques that help to make the most of spring's seasonal ingredients.

Boiling

We use boiling to prepare everything from pasta and green vegetables to stewed meats. This essential technique is a virtually fat-free cooking method that requires little more than a heavy-bottomed pot or saucepan to distribute the heat. Heating water in a pan sounds elementary and a procedure an average cook can master without special skills, but learning the specifics of boiling will help you become a better cook.

Boiling cooks food at a relatively high temperature—212° is the boiling point for water at sea level. When liquids boil, bubbles break through and pop on the surface while the whole batch of liquid churns vigorously.

What Boiling Does

In the case of pasta, churning, boiling water keeps the food in motion, prevents sticking, and cooks quickly so the pasta doesn't get soggy. In a process called blanching, green vegetables tossed into boiling water cook as quickly as possible so they retain their flavor and brightness. If they simmered gently in a covered pot, their color would dull, and they would lose much of their texture. Boiling causes speedy evaporation, a useful process for reducing sauces where the volume of the liquid decreases and flavors are concentrated.

Boiling Liquid

When ingredients are boiled, they're done so in water, sometimes containing salt and oil or butter for flavor and texture. The food is usually added to the liquid once it reaches a boil.

Best Bets for Boiling

This intense cooking method is well suited for pasta, some grains, and green vegetables. Boiling is also useful for reducing sauces.

Steaming

Steaming is a staple preparation for a number of international cuisines. It's relatively quick, easy to master, and offers a healthful way to cook since steaming achieves excellent results with no added fat and it minimizes nutrient loss during cooking. The result is light, fresh fare with textures ranging from crispy to chewy.

Once you master the basics of steaming, the possibilities are endless. Experiment with different vegetables, poultry, fish and shellfish, and dumpling fillings. And this technique isn't only for Asian dishes—try curry spices, barbecue, or Mediterranean flavors. You'll love being able to put together an entrée or healthful side with little effort and plenty of flavor.

What Steaming Does

Steaming cooks food more gently than almost any other method. Because the liquid never touches the food, it's less likely to jostle, overcook, or absorb too much water. This means food retains its shape, color, flavor, and texture. Steaming is considered a light cooking technique because it doesn't require fat. And unlike boiling, which leaches water-soluble nutrients from food, steaming retains most of the nutrients.

Best Bets for Steaming

Steaming is ideal for foods that need moisture and foods that should be soft and silken rather than crunchy or caramelized. For example, steamed Asian dumplings develop a soft-chewy texture rather than a firm or crunchy one. Almost all vegetables are good candidates (excluding mushrooms, eggplant, and other spongy vegetables or tough ones, such as greens).

When selecting a protein, choose light, delicate ingredients, such as chicken breast and most fish and shellfish. Avoid bold-flavored seafood, such as bluefish, or firm-fleshed fish, such as tuna. Also, stay away from beef or pork, which fare best by browning.

Equipment

Steaming requires little more than a pan with a well-fitting lid and a rack to support the food over the liquid in the pan. Creating a good seal with the lid is crucial for holding in steam. If the lid doesn't fit tightly, cover the pan with foil, and then top with the lid. Many cookware sets come with steamer inserts, as do woks. If you don't have these, there are other options.

A collapsible metal vegetable steamer works well for vegetables and certain shellfish—foods that can touch or stack on top of one another as they cook. If you don't have a vegetable steamer, you can improvise by placing a footed metal colander in the pan (make sure the lid will close) or setting a round cooling rack on top of two ramekins in the bottom of the pan so the food will be higher than the water level.

For foods that need to lie flat or shouldn't touch (such as salmon fillets or dumplings), try a bamboo steamer. Available at most Asian markets, these steamers come with two or three tiers that can be stacked, allowing you to cook a lot of food at one time. They also come with a lid that rests atop the uppermost tier. Set this type of steamer in a wok or large skillet with an inch of water.

howto:

Steam Safely

Three tips will ensure your safety:

1. Open the lid away from you so that the steam is released to the back of the stove away from your face.

2. Use silicone baking mitts to pick up a steaming rack. Because the rack will be damp, scalding water can soak through cloth oven mitts and cause a burn.

3. Use tongs or spatulas to remove food from the steamer. Steamed food often retains heat longer because the hot steam has permeated the food.

Strawberries

You know spring is here when you take that first bite into a plump, juicy strawberry. Enjoy the berries while you can—the season peaks in May.

To select: Choose brightly colored berries that still have their green caps attached. If fully ripe, they should have a potent strawberry fragrance.

To store: Store (in a single layer if possible) in a moisture-proof container in the refrigerator for three or four days. To freeze, place strawberries in a single layer on a cookie sheet; then put them in the freezer for a couple of hours. Once the berries are frozen, transfer them to a heavy-duty zip-top plastic bag or a freezer-safe container. This way, they won't stick together, and you can measure out small amounts anytime you need them.

To prepare: Do not wash or remove the hulls until you're ready to use the strawberries. Use an egg slicer to cut strawberries into uniform slices to use in a recipe or for garnishing.

To cook: It's best not to overwhelm the fresh flavor of strawberries. Try a mousse or a simple sweet soup—or toss the berries with fresh salad greens.

Health benefits: Strawberries are an excellent source of potassium and fiber; they also offer some folate, a B vitamin known for its role in reducing the risk of birth defects. Ten medium strawberries provide more than 100 percent of the daily value for vitamin C.

The original version of this cocktail hails from Harry's Bar in Venice. Our rendition substitutes strawberries for the traditional peaches. You can prepare the strawberry base up to one day ahead. Make sure to give it another spin in the blender just before mixing the cocktails.

Strawberry Bellinis

6   cups sliced strawberries
¼   cup powdered sugar
2   tablespoons brandy
3   cups prosecco or other sparkling wine
6   large strawberries

1. Combine first 3 ingredients in a blender. Let stand 10 minutes. Process until smooth; chill until ready to serve.

Strawberry Agua Fresca

2. Place ¼ cup strawberry mixture in each of 6 glasses. Add ½ cup prosecco to each serving, and stir to blend. Garnish each serving with 1 large strawberry. Serve immediately. **Yield: 6 servings.**

CALORIES 176; FAT 0.7g (sat 0g, mono 0.1g, poly 0.3g); PROTEIN 1.2g; CARB 21.1g; FIBER 3.7g; CHOL 0mg; IRON 0.8mg; SODIUM 2mg; CALC 29mg

At her restaurants, Chef Traci Des Jardins enjoys highlighting local, naturally raised ingredients chosen at their peak ripeness. Although she loves Mexican foods, she wants people to know that it's not about heavy, fat-laden recipes. Many Mexican-inspired recipes, such as this one, can be clean, fresh, and flavorful. Spanish for "fresh water," agua fresca is a refreshing, fruit-infused drink that is served throughout Mexico. Depending on the ripeness of the berries, adjust the amount of sugar for desired sweetness.

Strawberry Agua Fresca

4   cups water
⅓   cup sugar
6   cups hulled strawberries
¼   cup fresh lime juice (about 2 limes)

1. Combine water and sugar, stirring until sugar dissolves. Place strawberries in a blender, and process until smooth. Combine sugar mixture, strawberry puree, and juice; stir well. **Yield: 8 cups (serving size: 1⅓ cups).**

CALORIES 71; FAT 0.4g (sat 0g, mono 0.1g, poly 0.2g); PROTEIN 0.8g; CARB 17.8g; FIBER 2.3g; CHOL 0mg; IRON 0.5mg; SODIUM 4mg; CALC 21mg

For extra zip, rub the rim of each empty glass with a lime wedge, then coat the rims with salt and chili powder.

Mango-Avocado Margarita

- 2 cups ice cubes
- 1 cup chopped peeled mango (about 1 large)
- 6 tablespoons chopped ripe peeled avocado
- 6 tablespoons fresh lime juice
- ¼ cup tequila
- ¼ cup orange juice
- 2 tablespoons sugar
- 2 tablespoons Triple Sec (orange-flavored liqueur)
- 4 lime wedges (optional)

1. Place first 8 ingredients in a blender; process until smooth.
2. Divide mixture evenly among 4 glasses. Serve drinks with lime wedges, if desired. Serve immediately.
Yield: 4 servings (serving size: 1 cup).

CALORIES 162; FAT 4g (sat 1.1g, mono 2.1g, poly 0.7g); PROTEIN 1.1g; CARB 23g; FIBER 1.7g; CHOL 0mg; IRON 0.1mg; SODIUM 2mg; CALC 10mg

howto:

Prepare Avocados

Add avocados' buttery texture and mild, nutty flavor to sandwiches and salads, or use them to make fresh guacamole or Mango-Avocado Margarita (recipe on page 20). To easily dice, start with an 8- to 10-inch chef's knife. Insert it into the top where the stem was (it will be a darker area), and gently press down until you reach the pit. Then follow the tips below.

1. Rotate the fruit so the knife travels around the pit, cutting the entire avocado. Remove knife; slowly and gently twist the sides away from each other to separate.

2. Strike the pit, and pierce it with the blade. Then twist and remove the knife; the pit will come with it.

3. Pierce the flesh in horizontal and vertical rows. Don't cut through the skin. Remove flesh with spoon. To prevent browning, sprinkle with lemon juice.

Mint tea, made with spearmint, is the traditional drink of Morocco and North Africa. A few leaves of fresh or dried lemon verbena add a lovely citrus flavor. Be sure to use Chinese green tea, such as Gunpowder Green, Young Hyson, or Formosa Oolong. For a lighter minty flavor, remove the mint sprigs before chilling. This tea is traditionally very sweet, but use less sugar, if desired.

Iced Mint Tea

8   cups boiling water
1   tablespoon loose Chinese green tea
25   fresh mint sprigs (about 1½ ounces)
½   cup sugar

1. Combine water and tea in a medium bowl; cover and steep 2½ minutes. Strain tea mixture through a fine sieve into a bowl, and discard tea leaves. Add mint; steep 5 minutes. Add sugar; stir until sugar dissolves. Cool completely. Serve over ice. **Yield:** 8 cups (serving size: 1 cup).

CALORIES 52; FAT 0.1g (sat 0g, mono 0g, poly 0.1g); PROTEIN 0.2g; CARB 13.3g; FIBER 0.4g; CHOL 0mg; IRON 0.3mg; SODIUM 9mg; CALC 18mg

This easy-to-make drink is based on the bar specialty at the Fish Trap restaurant in Cruz Bay, St. John, U.S. Virgin Islands.

Frozen Lemonade with Coconut Rum

1½ cups ice cubes, crushed
3   tablespoons frozen lemonade concentrate
2   tablespoons coconut rum (such as Malibu)
Lime wedge (optional)

1. Place ice, concentrate, and rum in a blender; blend until slushy. Garnish with lime wedge, if desired. **Yield:** 1 serving (serving size: about 1 cup).

CALORIES 172; FAT 0.1g (sat 0g, mono 0g, poly 0.1g); PROTEIN 0.2g; CARB 25.8g; FIBER 0.1g; CHOL 0mg; IRON 0.4mg; SODIUM 2mg; CALC 4mg

Prepare this Spanish libation the day before for best flavor and add the chilled sparkling water just before serving. We use white Rioja wine, but any dry white wine will work.

White Sangria

⅓   cup brandy
⅓   cup peach schnapps
1½ tablespoons sugar
2   (750-milliliter) bottles white Rioja wine, chilled
1   lemon, thinly sliced
1   small navel orange, quartered and sliced
1   green apple, cored and sliced
1   ripe peach, peeled and sliced
1   (12-ounce) bottle sparkling water, chilled

1. Combine first 3 ingredients in a large pitcher; stir to dissolve sugar. Stir in wine and next 4 ingredients. Chill at least 2 hours or until cold.
2. Stir in sparkling water. Yield: 12 servings (serving size: about 1 cup).

CALORIES 163; FAT 0g; PROTEIN 0.1g; CARB 10.8g; FIBER 0.2g; CHOL 0mg; IRON 0.5mg, SODIUM 7mg; CALC 11mg

Smoked Salmon Dip

Make this dip ahead, and serve it on whole wheat crackers or toasted baguette slices.

Smoked Salmon Dip

1 (8-ounce) tub light cream cheese
2 tablespoons chopped fresh dill
1 tablespoon fresh lemon juice
4 ounces smoked salmon, chopped, divided
Dill sprigs (optional)

1. Place first 3 ingredients in a food processor. Add half of salmon; process until smooth. Fold in remaining half of salmon. Garnish with dill sprigs, if desired. **Yield:** 12 servings (serving size: 2 tablespoons).

CALORIES 56; FAT 3.5g (sat 2.1g, mono 0g, poly 0g); PROTEIN 4g; CARB 1.4g; FIBER 0g; CHOL 9mg; IRON 0.2mg; SODIUM 89mg; CALC 30mg

Chipotle-Lime Crab Crisps

americanfavorite

These appetizers combine sweet crab, Parmesan cheese, jicama, bell pepper, cilantro, and mayonnaise highlighted with fiery chipotles. A little crab goes a long way in these appetizers.

—Bob Gadsby, Great Falls, MT

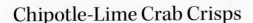

Chipotle-Lime Crab Crisps

48 baked tortilla chips
½ cup reduced-fat mayonnaise
1 teaspoon chopped canned chipotle chile in adobo sauce
1 tablespoon fresh lime juice
¾ pound lump crabmeat, shell pieces removed
¼ cup (1 ounce) grated fresh Parmesan cheese
2 tablespoons finely chopped peeled jicama
2 tablespoons thinly sliced green onions
2 tablespoons finely chopped red bell pepper
2 tablespoons finely chopped fresh cilantro
1 tablespoon finely chopped celery
1 medium avocado, peeled and diced

1. Preheat oven to 350°.
2. Arrange tortilla chips in a single layer on 2 baking sheets.
3. Combine mayonnaise, chile, and juice, stirring with a whisk.
4. Combine crab and next 6 ingredients in a medium bowl. Add mayonnaise mixture, stirring until well combined. Spoon about 1 tablespoon crab mixture onto each chip. Bake at 350° for 5 minutes or until thoroughly heated; top chips evenly with avocado. **Yield:** 16 servings (serving size: 3 crisps).

CALORIES 85; FAT 3.3g (sat 0.6g, mono 1.5g, poly 0.8g); PROTEIN 5.1g; CARB 9.1g; FIBER 1.2g; CHOL 18mg; IRON 0.4mg; SODIUM 211mg; CALC 44mg

If you plan to dye Easter eggs, cook extras for this dish. Stuffed eggs are often served warm in France, and this recipe is similar to one from the Périgord region.

French-Style Stuffed Eggs

8   large eggs
⅓   cup minced reduced-fat ham
1   tablespoon minced green onions
1   tablespoon minced fresh parsley
1   tablespoon low-fat mayonnaise
1   teaspoon mustard
¼   teaspoon chopped fresh thyme
⅛   teaspoon salt
⅛   teaspoon freshly ground black pepper
2   (1-ounce) slices white bread, torn into large pieces
Cooking spray
Thyme leaves (optional)

1. Place eggs in a large saucepan. Cover with water to 1 inch above eggs; bring just to a boil. Remove from heat; cover and let stand 12 minutes. Drain and rinse with cold running water until cool.

2. Peel eggs; slice in half lengthwise. Remove yolks; discard 4 yolks. Place remaining 4 yolks in a medium bowl. Add ham and next 7 ingredients, and stir until combined.

3. Place bread in a food processor; pulse 10 times or until coarse crumbs measure 1 cup.

4. Spoon about 1 teaspoon yolk mixture into each egg white half. Top each half with 1 tablespoon breadcrumbs. Coat breadcrumbs with cooking spray.

5. Preheat broiler.

6. Place eggs on a baking sheet; broil 1 minute or until breadcrumbs are toasted. Garnish with thyme leaves, if desired. **Yield:** 16 servings (serving size: 1 egg half).

CALORIES 38; FAT 1.6g (sat 0.5g, mono 0.6g, poly 0.2g); PROTEIN 3.3g; CARB 2.3g; FIBER 0.1g; CHOL 54mg; IRON 0.4mg; SODIUM 127mg; CALC 14mg

Boil Eggs

Follow these steps to get the best results when boiling eggs. First, place the eggs in a large saucepan. Cover with water to 1 inch above the eggs; bring to a full boil. Immediately cover the pan and remove it from heat; let stand according to how you'd like the eggs prepared. After the eggs have cooked, drain and rinse them with cold running water until they're cool enough to handle.

Medium-boiled eggs: Let stand 4½ minutes. The yolk is solid, but it's still dark orange-yellow, moist, and dense in the middle. Serve on top of a salad.

Hard-boiled eggs: Let stand 12 minutes. The yolk will be solid, light yellow, and crumbly, with no green ring around the yolk, which is a sign of overcooking. Use for deviled eggs or in egg salad or enjoy as a handy snack.

Make the leek mixture and cook the potatoes a day ahead. Or use store-bought diced cooked potatoes (such as Simply Potatoes), whisk the eggs, combine everything, and bake the morning of the brunch.

Frittata with Spinach, Potatoes, and Leeks

1	teaspoon butter
2	cups thinly sliced leek (about 2 large)
1	(10-ounce) package fresh spinach
1/3	cup fat-free milk
2	tablespoons finely chopped fresh basil
1/2	teaspoon salt
1/4	teaspoon black pepper
4	large eggs
4	large egg whites
2	cups cooked, peeled red potato (about 3/4 pound)

Cooking spray

1 1/2	tablespoons dry breadcrumbs
1/2	cup (2 ounces) shredded provolone cheese

1. Preheat oven to 350°.
2. Melt butter in a Dutch oven over medium heat. Add leek; sauté 4 minutes. Add spinach; sauté 2 minutes or until spinach wilts. Place mixture in a colander, pressing until barely moist.
3. Combine milk, basil, salt, pepper, eggs, and egg whites; stir well with a whisk. Add leek mixture and potato. Pour into a 10-inch round ceramic baking dish or pie plate coated with cooking spray. Sprinkle with breadcrumbs and top with cheese. Bake at 350° for 25 minutes or until center is set.
4. Preheat broiler.
5. Broil frittata 4 minutes or until golden brown. Cut into wedges. **Yield:** 6 servings (serving size: 1 wedge).

CALORIES 185; FAT 7.1g (sat 3g, mono 1.5g, poly 0.6g); PROTEIN 12.5g; CARB 18.9g; FIBER 2.8g; CHOL 150mg; IRON 3mg; SODIUM 429mg; CALC 176mg

choiceingredient

Spinach

When choosing spinach, pick dark leaves without too much of a stem. One pound of spinach (or a 12-ounce package) should be enough for two servings.

Spinach provides the best taste if eaten immediately, but it may be refrigerated for up to three days. Spinach also comes canned and frozen; it freezes quite well. Since it is usually grown in sandy soil, it needs to be thoroughly washed before it is consumed. Submerge the leaves in lukewarm water and then rinse a few times with cold water for best results. Even prewashed and bagged spinach may need a brief rinsing.

There are a variety of ways to enjoy this vegetable. It can be served raw in a fresh, crisp salad or cooked (try boiling, sautéing, or blanching). For fullest flavor, cook only until it begins to turn limp. It also works well as an ingredient in casseroles, quiches, and soups. Dishes that use spinach as a main ingredient may be followed by the phrase à la florentine.

Fresh spinach, although available year-round, is especially popular in the spring. It is a rich source of vitamins A and C, calcium, iron, and potassium.

Field Salad with Snow Peas, Grapes, and Feta

5	tablespoons white wine vinegar
5	tablespoons fresh orange juice
2	tablespoons extra-virgin olive oil
2 ½	teaspoons sugar
½	teaspoon salt
¼	teaspoon freshly ground black pepper
8	cups gourmet salad greens
2	cups snow peas, trimmed and cut lengthwise into thin strips

2 cups seedless red grapes, halved
½ cup (2 ounces) crumbled feta cheese

1. Combine first 6 ingredients in a small bowl; stir well with a whisk. Combine remaining ingredients in a large bowl. Drizzle dressing over salad; toss well. **Yield: 6 servings.**

CALORIES 151; FAT 7.9g (sat 2.6g, mono 4.2g, poly 0.7g); PROTEIN 4.3g; CARB 18.6g; FIBER 3g; CHOL 11mg; IRON 2mg; SODIUM 354mg; CALC 123mg

While fava beans are best, frozen lima beans or green peas can be used in a pinch. If using frozen beans or peas, just toss them into the pasta water during the last minute of cooking and drain with the pasta. If you can't find orecchiette, use seashell pasta.

Orecchiette with Fresh Fava Beans, Ricotta, and Chopped Mint

2   pounds unshelled fava beans (about 1 cup shelled)
1   pound uncooked orecchiette pasta ("little ears" pasta)
1   teaspoon extra-virgin olive oil
¾   teaspoon salt
1   cup part-skim ricotta cheese
½   cup (2 ounces) grated fresh Parmesan cheese
½   cup coarsely chopped fresh mint
½   teaspoon freshly ground black pepper
Mint sprigs (optional)

1. Remove beans from pods, and discard pods. Cook beans in boiling water 1 minute. Remove beans with a slotted spoon. Plunge beans into ice water; drain. Remove tough outer skins from beans; discard skins. Set beans aside.
2. Cook pasta according to package directions, omitting salt and fat. Drain pasta, reserving 1 cup pasta water. Place pasta in a large bowl; add oil and salt. Toss well.
3. Combine 1 cup reserved pasta water, ricotta cheese, Parmesan cheese, chopped mint, and pepper. Add beans and cheese mixture to pasta mixture; toss to combine. Garnish with mint sprigs, if desired. **Yield:** 6 servings (serving size: about 1 cup).

CALORIES 507; FAT 8.8g (sat 4.1g, mono 2.5g, poly 1.3g); PROTEIN 29.2g; CARB 85.5g; FIBER 4.7g; CHOL 25mg; IRON 6.2mg; SODIUM 540mg; CALC 255mg

Pasta Primavera

2   cups green beans, trimmed and halved crosswise
2   cups broccoli florets
½   cup (1-inch) slices asparagus (about 2 ounces)
6   ounces uncooked fettuccine
1   tablespoon olive oil
1   cup chopped onion
2   teaspoons minced fresh garlic
⅛   teaspoon crushed red pepper
½   cup fresh or frozen green peas
1   cup grape tomatoes, halved
⅔   cup half-and-half
1   teaspoon cornstarch
¾   teaspoon salt
¼   cup chopped fresh basil
¼   cup (1 ounce) shaved Parmigiano-Reggiano cheese

1. Cook green beans in boiling water 1 minute. Add broccoli and asparagus; cook 2 minutes or until vegetables are crisp-tender. Remove vegetables from pan with a slotted spoon; place in a large bowl. Return water to a boil. Add pasta; cook 10 minutes or until al dente. Drain and add to vegetable mixture.
2. Heat oil in a large nonstick skillet over medium-high heat. Add 1 cup onion, and sauté 2 minutes. Add garlic and red pepper; sauté 3 minutes or until onion begins to brown. Add peas, and sauté 1 minute. Add tomatoes; sauté 2 minutes. Combine half-and-half and cornstarch, stirring with a whisk. Reduce heat to medium. Add half-and-half mixture and salt to pan; cook 1 minute or until sauce thickens, stirring constantly. Pour sauce over pasta mixture; toss gently to coat. Sprinkle with basil and cheese. Serve immediately. **Yield:** 4 servings (serving size: 2 cups pasta mixture, 1 tablespoon basil, and 1 tablespoon cheese).

CALORIES 338; FAT 10.8g (sat 4.7g, mono 4.4g, poly 0.8g); PROTEIN 13.7g; CARB 49.6g; FIBER 7.1g; CHOL 20mg; IRON 2.9mg; SODIUM 607mg; CALC 205mg

WINENOTE

Pasta Primavera is a burst of spring. The wine that accompanies it should be, too. **Sauvignon blanc** is a good option since the fresh "green" quality mirrors vegetables perfectly. But because this is a cream-based pasta primavera, opt instead for a **pinot blanc**. Rounder and more mellow than sauvignon blanc, pinot blanc at its best soars with freshness and vivacity, and is loaded with floral and citrus character.

Pasta Primavera

Pappardelle with Lemon, Baby Artichokes, and Asparagus

12   ounces uncooked pappardelle (wide ribbon pasta)
2 ¼ cups cold water, divided
¼   cup fresh lemon juice (about 2 lemons)
24   baby artichokes (about 2 pounds)
3   tablespoons extra-virgin olive oil, divided
1   pound asparagus, trimmed and cut diagonally
     into (1-inch) pieces
2   tablespoons chopped fresh flat-leaf parsley
1   tablespoon grated lemon rind
1   teaspoon chopped fresh thyme
½   teaspoon salt
½   teaspoon black pepper
1 ¼ cups (5 ounces) grated fresh Parmigiano-
     Reggiano cheese

1. Cook pasta according to package directions, omitting salt and fat. Drain pasta, reserving ½ cup cooking liquid. Set pasta aside; keep warm.
2. Combine 2 cups water and juice in a bowl. Working with 1 artichoke at a time, cut off stem to ¼-inch from base; peel stem. Remove bottom and tough outer leaves, leaving tender heart and bottom; trim 1 inch from top of artichoke. Cut each artichoke in half lengthwise. Place halves in lemon water.
3. Heat 1 tablespoon oil in a large skillet over medium heat. Drain artichokes well; pat dry. Add artichokes to pan. Cover and cook 8 minutes, stirring occasionally; uncover. Increase heat to medium-high; cook 2 minutes or until artichokes are golden, stirring frequently. Place artichokes in a large bowl.
4. Place pan over medium heat; add remaining ¼ cup water and asparagus to pan. Cover; cook 5 minutes or until crisp-tender. Add asparagus, parsley, and rind to artichokes; toss well. Add pasta, reserved cooking liquid, remaining 2 tablespoons oil, thyme, salt, and pepper to artichoke mixture; toss well. Place 2 cups pasta mixture into each of 6 shallow bowls; top each serving with about 3 tablespoons cheese. **Yield:** 6 servings.

CALORIES 411; FAT 12.6g (sat 4g, mono 6.4g, poly 1.3g); PROTEIN 20.2g; CARB 59.5g; FIBER 12.2g; CHOL 15mg; IRON 3.9mg; SODIUM 644mg; CALC 217mg

Baby Artichokes

Baby artichokes contain the same succulent, nutty, and complex flavor as globe artichokes but require less preparation. They grow lower on the same stalk as globe artichokes but receive less sunlight, so at full maturity they're still small, ranging in size from that of a walnut to a large egg.

To select: A tightly closed, unblemished head ensures freshness. Once open, an artichoke is not good.

To store: You may keep baby artichokes in a plastic bag in the refrigerator for several days. The appearance of the artichoke changes little over time, but texture and flavor will decline. Cleaned and blanched, artichokes can be frozen up to three months.

To prepare: Trim and peel the stems; then snap off the outer leaves. Halve, quarter, or leave the artichokes whole; place them in a bowl of cold lemon water (so they don't turn brown) until you cook them.

To cook: Grill, steam, roast, or sauté baby artichokes.

Health benefits: Artichokes are nutrient dense with magnesium, chromium, manganese, potassium, phosphorus, iron, and calcium. They are also a good source of fiber, vitamin C, and folate.

Pink peppercorns lend pretty color to this entrée and impart a sweet note to the salsa.

Pink Peppercorn Mahimahi with Tropical Salsa

1¼ cups chopped pineapple
½ cup chopped red onion
¼ cup chopped fresh cilantro
2 tablespoons flaked sweetened coconut
2 tablespoons fresh lime juice
1 jalapeño pepper, finely chopped
2 teaspoons pink peppercorns, crushed and divided
½ cup panko (Japanese breadcrumbs)
3 tablespoons finely chopped macadamia nuts
½ teaspoon sea salt, divided
½ cup light coconut milk
2 tablespoons low-sodium soy sauce
4 (6-ounce) mahimahi or other firm white fish fillets
1½ tablespoons olive oil
Cooking spray

1. Preheat oven to 400°.
2. Combine first 6 ingredients and 1 teaspoon peppercorns in a bowl; set aside.
3. Combine panko, nuts, remaining 1 teaspoon peppercorns, and ¼ teaspoon salt in a shallow dish. Combine milk and soy sauce in another shallow dish. Sprinkle fish with remaining ¼ teaspoon salt. Dip one side of fish in milk mixture; dredge dipped side in panko mixture.
4. Heat oil in a large ovenproof nonstick skillet coated with cooking spray over medium-high heat. Add fish, crust side down, to pan; cook 3 minutes. Turn fish over, and bake at 400° for 10 minutes or until fish flakes easily when tested with a fork or until desired degree of doneness. Serve with salsa. **Yield:** 4 servings (serving size: 1 fillet and ½ cup salsa).

CALORIES 331; FAT 13.6g (sat 3.8g, mono 7.6g, poly 1g); PROTEIN 34.5g; CARB 18.3g; FIBER 2.5g; CHOL 124mg; IRON 2.8mg; SODIUM 743mg; CALC 49mg

This version of stir-fry rice is a fine use for leftover salmon. You can make it even simpler by cooking rice and salmon a day ahead. Just warm both in the microwave before completing the dish.

Spring Pilaf with Salmon and Asparagus

4 cups water
4 (6-ounce) salmon fillets (about 1 inch thick)
1 tablespoon butter
2 cups (1-inch) diagonally cut asparagus
3 cups hot cooked long-grain rice
1 cup fresh or frozen peas, thawed
½ cup vegetable broth
2 tablespoons chopped fresh flat-leaf parsley
2 tablespoons chopped fresh chives
1 tablespoon fresh lemon juice
½ teaspoon salt
¼ teaspoon freshly ground black pepper

1. Bring water to a boil in a large skillet; add salmon (skin side up). Return to a boil. Reduce heat, cover, and simmer 10 minutes or until fish flakes easily when tested with a fork. Remove fish with a slotted spoon and discard water; cool fish slightly. Remove and discard skin; break fish into large pieces.
2. Return pan to heat; melt butter over medium-high heat. Add asparagus; cook 6 minutes or until tender, stirring occasionally. Stir in rice, peas, and broth, and cook 1 minute. Add salmon, parsley, and remaining ingredients; stir well to combine. Cook 2 minutes or until thoroughly heated. **Yield:** 6 servings (serving size: 1⅓ cups).

CALORIES 391; FAT 12.8g (sat 3.4g, mono 4.3g, poly 4g); PROTEIN 24.7g; CARB 42.9g; FIBER 2.7g; CHOL 61mg; IRON 3.2mg; SODIUM 385mg; CALC 43mg

Spring Pilaf with Salmon and
Asparagus

Pineapple

While pineapple is available year-round, its peak season runs from March through July. And although the fruit is native to South America, Hawaii is now the leading producer.

To select: Choose the largest, plumpest pineapple you can find. It should have a strong color and be slightly soft to the touch with crisp, dark leaves. Avoid pineapples that have soft or dark areas on the skin (which is a sign of over-ripeness), or yellow or brown-tipped leaves. One medium pineapple will yield about three cups of chunks.

To store: These succulent tropical gems don't ripen off the plant, so those you buy will be immediately ready to eat. They can be stored in the refrigerator, tightly wrapped, for up to three days before cutting plus three more days after cutting.

To prepare: Using a sharp knife, cut off the base and leaves, then stand the pineapple on one end and shave off strips of skin from top to bottom. To remove the eyes, cut a wedge-shaped groove on either side, taking away as little flesh as possible. To core, cut it into quarters after peeling, then stand each quarter on end and cut downward to remove the core.

Health benefits: Pineapple is a wonderful source of vitamin C, which protects you from heart disease, cancer, and cataracts; it also contains manganese, which helps keep your bones strong. Plus, pineapple contains an enzyme that helps relieve indigestion—making it a dessert your tummy will appreciate.

Serve with coconut rice. Round out the menu with a romaine lettuce salad tossed with lime dressing.

Spicy Tilapia with Pineapple-Pepper Relish

2	teaspoons canola oil
1	teaspoon Cajun seasoning
¼	teaspoon kosher salt
¼	teaspoon ground red pepper
4	(6-ounce) tilapia fillets
1½	cups chopped fresh pineapple chunks
⅓	cup chopped onion
⅓	cup chopped plum tomato
2	tablespoons rice vinegar
1	tablespoon chopped fresh cilantro
1	small jalapeño pepper, seeded and chopped
4	lime wedges

1. Heat oil in a large nonstick skillet over medium-high heat. Combine Cajun seasoning, salt, and pepper in a small bowl. Sprinkle fish evenly with spice mixture. Add fish to pan, and cook 2 minutes on each side or until fish flakes easily when tested with a fork or until desired degree of doneness.

2. Combine pineapple and next 5 ingredients in a large bowl, stirring gently. Serve pineapple mixture with fish. Garnish with lime wedges. **Yield:** 4 servings (serving size: 1 fillet, about ½ cup relish, and 1 lime wedge).

CALORIES 228; FAT 5.5g (sat 1.2g, mono 2.2g, poly 1.4g); PROTEIN 34.9g; CARB 11.2g; FIBER 1.5g; CHOL 85mg; IRON 1.2mg; SODIUM 328mg; CALC 29mg

Although the addition of tuna makes this dish an entrée, you can omit it and serve it as a salad with other grilled fish or meats.

Grilled Tuna with White Bean and Charred Onion Salad

Tuna:

1   tablespoon grated lemon rind
2   tablespoons fresh lemon juice
½   teaspoon Dijon mustard
½   teaspoon olive oil
¼   teaspoon freshly ground black pepper
1   garlic clove, minced
4   (6-ounce) tuna steaks

Cooking spray

Salad:

1   medium Vidalia or other sweet onion, cut into
     ¼-inch-thick slices
3   tablespoons red wine vinegar
1   tablespoon olive oil
¼   teaspoon salt
¼   teaspoon freshly ground black pepper
¼   teaspoon Dijon mustard
1   garlic clove, minced
½   cup chopped seeded peeled cucumber
¼   cup chopped flat-leaf parsley
1   tablespoon capers
1   (15-ounce) can cannellini beans,
     rinsed and drained
6   cups mixed salad greens

1. Prepare grill.

2. To prepare tuna, combine first 6 ingredients in a large zip-top plastic bag. Add tuna to bag; seal. Marinate in refrigerator 30 minutes, turning once. Remove tuna from bag; discard marinade. Place tuna on a grill rack coated with cooking spray; grill 2 minutes on each side or until desired degree of doneness.

3. To prepare salad, place onion slices on a grill rack coated with cooking spray; grill 5 minutes on each side or until tender. Cool and chop.

4. Combine vinegar and next 5 ingredients in a large bowl, stirring with a whisk until blended. Add onion, cucumber, parsley, capers, and beans to vinegar mixture; toss to coat. Arrange 1½ cups salad greens on each of 4 plates. Top each serving with about ½ cup onion mixture and 1 tuna steak.

Yield: 4 servings.

CALORIES 383; FAT 12.7g (sat 2.7g, mono 5.5g, poly 3.3g); PROTEIN 44g; CARB 21.9g; FIBER 6.6g; CHOL 63mg; IRON 4.6mg; SODIUM 515mg; CALC 110mg

Chef, restaurant owner, and author Michel Nischan's family garden inspires his cooking. He covets fresh-from-the-vine, just-dug fare for his kitchens, both at home and his restaurant. Dressing Room—A Homegrown Restaurant, reflects Nischan's commitment to local, natural, and organic ingredients, which he has carried over into this recipe as well. In this particular salad Nischan focuses on the fresh ingredients of spring: snow peas, lettuce, radishes, and mint. The tuna is seared, but you can serve it raw if you purchase sushi-grade fish.

Seared Tuna and Radish Salad with Wasabi Dressing

Salad:

½   cup fresh snow peas
1   cup torn Bibb lettuce
1   cup thinly sliced radishes (about 4 ounces)
2   tablespoons chopped fresh mint
2   tablespoons chopped fresh cilantro
2   tablespoons radish sprouts
1½   tablespoons fresh lemon juice
1½   tablespoons mirin (sweet rice wine)
1   teaspoon canola oil
4   (6-ounce) sushi-grade tuna steaks
½   teaspoon kosher salt

Dressing:

3   tablespoons silken tofu
1½   tablespoons wasabi powder
1   tablespoon rice vinegar
1   tablespoon fresh lemon juice
1   tablespoon mirin (sweet rice wine)
5   tablespoons water

1. To prepare salad, cook snow peas in boiling water 3 minutes or until crisp-tender. Drain and rinse with cold water; drain. Thinly slice snow peas

crosswise. Combine peas and next 7 ingredients in a medium bowl; set aside.

2. Heat oil in a large nonstick skillet over medium-high heat. Sprinkle fish with salt. Add fish to pan; cook 2 minutes on each side or until desired degree of doneness. Let stand 2 minutes. Cut into ¼-inch-thick slices.

3. To prepare dressing, place tofu and next 4 ingredients in a food processor, and process until smooth. With processor on, slowly pour water through food chute; process until well blended. Serve fish over salad; drizzle with dressing just before serving.

Yield: 4 servings (serving size: 5 ounces fish, ¾ cup salad, and 2 tablespoons dressing).

CALORIES 280; FAT 3.6g (sat 0.5g, mono 1g, poly 1g); PROTEIN 41.8g; CARB 10.7g; FIBER 1.1g; CHOL 77mg; IRON 2.2mg; SODIUM 428mg; CALC 64mg

Chimichurri is a thick herb sauce commonly made with parsley and oregano and served with grilled meat in Argentina. Mint gives this version a more delicate taste, making it perfect for seafood. Serve over a bed of rice to soak up the flavorful sauce.

Cornmeal-Crusted Scallops with Mint Chimichurri

1½ cups loosely packed fresh mint leaves

¾   cup sliced green onions

2   tablespoons water

1½ tablespoons fresh lime juice

1   tablespoon honey

1   teaspoon minced seeded serrano chile

½   teaspoon salt

½   teaspoon freshly ground black pepper

1   garlic clove

3   tablespoons yellow cornmeal

1½ pounds sea scallops

1   tablespoon olive oil

Green onion strips (optional)

1. Place first 9 ingredients in a food processor; process until finely chopped. Set aside.

2. Place cornmeal in a shallow dish. Dredge scallops in cornmeal. Heat oil in a large nonstick skillet over medium-high heat. Add scallops; cook 3 minutes on each side or until done. Serve with chimichurri, and garnish with onion strips, if desired.

Yield: 4 servings (serving size: about 4 ounces sea scallops and 2 tablespoons chimichurri).

CALORIES 237; FAT 4.9g (sat 0.6g, mono 2.6g, poly 0.9g); PROTEIN 29.6g; CARB 17.3g; FIBER 2.1g; CHOL 56mg; IRON 1.4mg; SODIUM 576mg; CALC 68mg

Mint

Bursting with fragrance and color, mint adds dimension to both sweet and savory dishes. While mint leaves impart delicious complexity to a simple green salad, its coolness also balances the fire in spicy dishes, which is why it's an important seasoning in Middle Eastern, Asian, and Latin cuisines. Its clean, refreshing taste and cooling effect make it a welcome addition to beverages during warmer months. Many people are familiar with classic mint-infused cocktails such as the julep and the mojito, but mint also refreshes nonalcoholic beverages, such as limeade. And, of course, the sprightly herb is at home in a variety of desserts.

Mint grows wild throughout the world. It's easy to cultivate, so you can have it on hand to flavor icy beverages, main dish salads and entrées, or stunning sweets. There are approximately 500 mint varieties, with spearmint and peppermint being the two most common.

If you're buying mint at the market, look for bright green, crisp leaves with no signs of wilting. Place the stems in a glass containing a couple inches of water, and cover leaves loosely with plastic wrap or a zip-top plastic bag (do not seal the bag). Refrigerate for up to one week, changing the water every other day.

Fresh mint can also be frozen for later use. Simply rinse the leaves, pat dry, and freeze in a zip-top plastic bag (the leaves will darken once they're frozen, but that doesn't affect the flavor). Later, pull out what you need, and return the rest to the freezer. You may prefer to freeze whole or chopped mint leaves in ice-cube trays with water, which preserves the green color. After they freeze, remove cubes from the trays, and store in zip-top plastic bags. Add these minty ice cubes to drinks; or thaw, drain, and use in recipes calling for mint.

Buy peeled, cored fresh pineapple for the salsa. Enjoy the rest of it in a fresh fruit salad.

Shrimp Saté with Pineapple Salsa

Salsa:

¾ cup finely chopped pineapple

¼ cup finely chopped red onion

1 tablespoon minced seeded jalapeño pepper

1 tablespoon chopped fresh cilantro

1 tablespoon cider vinegar

1 teaspoon honey

Saté:

2 tablespoons chopped fresh mint

2 tablespoons fresh lime juice

¼ teaspoon salt

¼ teaspoon chili powder

24 large shrimp, peeled and deveined
(about 1½ pounds)

Cooking spray

4 fresh cilantro sprigs (optional)

1. Prepare grill.

2. To prepare salsa, combine first 6 ingredients in a medium bowl.

3. To prepare saté, combine mint, juice, salt, and chili powder in a large bowl; add shrimp, tossing gently to coat. Thread 3 shrimp onto each of 8 (6-inch) skewers. Place shrimp on a grill rack coated with cooking spray; grill 1½ minutes on each side or until shrimp turn pink. Serve with salsa. Garnish with cilantro sprigs, if desired.

Yield: 4 servings (serving size: 2 skewers and ¼ cup salsa).

CALORIES 208; FAT 3g (sat 0.6g, mono 0.4g, poly 1.2g); PROTEIN 34.9g; CARB 8.7g; FIBER 0.7g; CHOL 259mg; IRON 4.3mg; SODIUM 403mg; CALC 98mg

Shrimp and Crab Salad Rolls

We loved the kick provided by the horseradish. For a milder flavor, use one teaspoon horseradish. Look for it in the condiment section near mustards. If you can't find crabmeat, double the amount of coarsely chopped cooked shrimp to three cups.

Shrimp and Crab Salad Rolls

3 tablespoons chopped green onions
3 tablespoons light mayonnaise
1 tablespoon prepared horseradish
2 teaspoons Dijon mustard
¼ teaspoon hot sauce
8 ounces coarsely chopped cooked shrimp (about 1½ cups chopped)
8 ounces lump crabmeat, drained and shell pieces removed
4 small whole wheat hoagie rolls, split and toasted
4 small Boston lettuce leaves

1. Combine first 5 ingredients in a large bowl, and stir well. Add chopped cooked shrimp and lump crabmeat, stirring to combine. Line each hoagie roll with 1 lettuce leaf. Place ⅔ cup shrimp mixture in each bun. **Yield:** 4 servings.

CALORIES 327; FAT 8.8g (sat 1.1g, mono 1.8g, poly 4.1g); PROTEIN 29.7g; CARB 35.4g; FIBER 5.4g; CHOL 172mg; IRON 4.2mg; SODIUM 766mg; CALC 152mg

Shrimp Saté with Pineapple Salsa

Prepare Fresh Favas

When shopping for favas, select small pods; those that bulge with beans are past their prime. Two pounds unshelled beans yield about 1 cup shelled. Shelling and cooking fava beans involves three simple steps. Once the three steps are complete, the beans are ready to use in any recipe.

1. Remove beans from their pods.

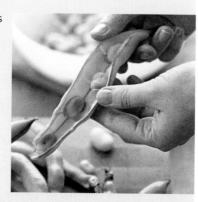

2. Cook shelled beans in boiling water for 1 minute. Drain and plunge beans into ice water; drain.

3. Remove the tough outer skins from beans by pinching the outer skin between your thumb and forefinger; discard skins.

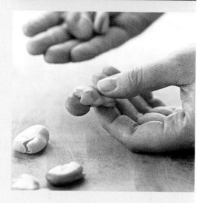

Removing the skins from fresh-shelled favas is a necessary task that's worth the effort. The prepared beans have a firm texture and a nutty flavor.

Fava Bean and Grilled Shrimp Salad in Radicchio Cups

1½ cups shelled fava beans (about 2 pounds unshelled)
1 pound peeled and deveined medium shrimp
2 tablespoons extra-virgin olive oil, divided
½ teaspoon salt, divided
¼ teaspoon freshly ground black pepper, divided
Cooking spray
2 tablespoons fresh lemon juice
1 garlic clove, minced
3 tablespoons chopped fresh flat-leaf parsley
4 radicchio leaves

1. Cook beans in boiling water 1 minute. Drain and plunge beans into ice water; drain. Remove tough outer skins from beans; discard skins. Place beans in a large bowl; set aside.
2. Prepare grill.
3. Thread shrimp evenly onto 6 (12-inch) skewers; brush with 1 teaspoon oil. Sprinkle shrimp evenly with ¼ teaspoon salt and ⅛ teaspoon pepper. Place skewers on a grill rack coated with cooking spray; grill 1½ minutes on each side or until shrimp are done. Cool slightly; remove shrimp from skewers. Add shrimp to beans.
4. Combine remaining 5 teaspoons oil, remaining ¼ teaspoon salt, remaining ⅛ teaspoon pepper, juice, and garlic in a small bowl, stirring with a whisk. Drizzle juice mixture over shrimp mixture; toss to coat. Stir in parsley.
5. Place 1 radicchio leaf on each of 4 salad plates; spoon 1 cup shrimp mixture into each leaf. **Yield:** 4 servings.

CALORIES 378; FAT 9.6g (sat 1.5g, mono 5.4g, poly 1.8g); PROTEIN 38g; CARB 35.4g; FIBER 14.3g; CHOL 172mg; IRON 6.8mg; SODIUM 474mg; CALC 125mg

Radishes

Spring is a good time to rediscover radishes since it's the time of year that they are at their peak. A cousin of mustard, radishes that are harvested in the spring are actually surprisingly mild. However, those harvested in the summer have a much sharper taste.

When purchasing radishes, always look for bunches with the leaves still attached. The greens guarantee the roots' freshness. Wilted leaves are a sure sign of mealy radishes and are a red flag to keep looking. Once you select your radishes chop off the greens, wash the radishes well, and store them between paper towels in a zip-top plastic bag. The greens have a mild, aromatic flavor, and can go raw in salads or cooked in soups. Store the radish roots in breathable plastic bags in your hydrator. If the radishes become spongy after a few days, crisp them by placing them in a bowl of ice water for up to one hour.

Look beyond the crudité tray and welcome these versatile, colorful roots into slaws, soups, salads, and sauces.

Southeast Asian salads are traditionally eaten out of hand, with lettuce leaves for wrappers. To make slicing the steak easier, chill it in the freezer for 10 minutes beforehand.

Thai Beef and Radish Salad

1   tablespoon chile paste with garlic
2   teaspoons minced peeled fresh ginger
1   garlic clove, minced
1   pound (½-inch-thick) boneless sirloin steak, cut diagonally across grain into thin slices
1 ½ tablespoons fresh lime juice
1   tablespoon fish sauce
2   teaspoons sugar
Cooking spray
2   cups sliced radishes
¼   cup chopped fresh cilantro
2   tablespoons chopped fresh mint
1   serrano chile, seeded and finely chopped
8   Bibb lettuce leaves

1. Combine chile paste, ginger, and garlic in a large zip-top plastic bag; add steak, tossing to coat. Marinate in refrigerator 30 minutes, turning once. **2.** Combine lime juice, fish sauce, and sugar, stirring with a whisk; set dressing aside. **3.** Heat a large nonstick skillet over medium-high heat; coat pan with cooking spray. Remove steak from bag; discard marinade. Add steak to pan; cook 2 minutes or until desired degree of doneness, turning once. Cut steak into 1-inch pieces; place in a medium bowl. Add radishes, cilantro, mint, and serrano. Pour lime juice mixture over beef mixture, tossing to coat. Spoon about ⅓ cup salad into each lettuce leaf, and serve immediately. **Yield:** 4 servings (serving size: 2 filled lettuce leaves).

CALORIES 223; FAT 10.2g (sat 3.9g, mono 4.2g, poly 0.4g); PROTEIN 25.7g; CARB 6.8g; FIBER 1.4g; CHOL 76mg; IRON 3.1mg; SODIUM 471mg; CALC 35mg

Thai Beef and Radish Salad

Radish Slaw with New York Deli Dressing

4   cups shredded radishes (about 40 radishes)
2   cups finely chopped yellow bell pepper
1 ½ cups shredded carrot
½   cup white wine vinegar
4   teaspoons sugar
1   tablespoon chopped fresh dill
1   tablespoon mustard oil or olive oil
½   teaspoon salt
½   teaspoon black pepper

1. Combine first 3 ingredients in a large bowl. Combine white wine vinegar and remaining ingredients, stirring with a whisk. Drizzle dressing over slaw; toss well to combine. Serve immediately. **Yield:** 10 servings (serving size: ¾ cup).

CALORIES 46; FAT 1.8g (sat 0.2g, mono 0.9g, poly 0.4g); PROTEIN 0.9g; CARB 7.4g; FIBER 1.6g; CHOL 0mg; IRON 0.5mg; SODIUM 136mg; CALC 20mg

The bright, fresh taste and textures of this salad complement grilled beef, chicken, or fish as well. If using wooden skewers, soak them in water 30 minutes before grilling.

Grilled Lamb Kebabs with Warm Fava Bean Salad

4   cups shelled fava beans
     (about 8 pounds unshelled)
1½   teaspoons extra-virgin olive oil
1   tablespoon chopped fresh mint
1   teaspoon grated lemon rind
2   tablespoons fresh lemon juice
1   teaspoon salt, divided
½   teaspoon freshly ground black pepper, divided
2   tablespoons water
1½   pounds leg of lamb, trimmed and cut
     into 1-inch cubes
Cooking spray
6   lemon wedges

1. Cook fava beans in boiling water 1 minute or until tender. Drain, and rinse with cold water. Drain. Remove tough outer skins from beans; discard skins.

2. Combine olive oil, chopped mint, lemon rind, lemon juice, ½ teaspoon salt, and ¼ teaspoon freshly ground black pepper in a medium bowl, stirring with a whisk. Heat 2 tablespoons water in a medium saucepan over medium-high heat, and add beans to pan. Cook 2 minutes or until beans are thoroughly heated. Add beans to juice mixture, and toss to coat.

3. Prepare grill.

4. Thread lamb onto 12 (8-inch) skewers. Coat lamb with cooking spray; sprinkle evenly with remaining ½ teaspoon salt and remaining ¼ teaspoon pepper. Place skewers on a grill rack coated with cooking spray; grill 7 minutes or until lamb is done, turning occasionally. Serve with fava bean salad and lemon wedges. **Yield:** 6 servings (serving size: 2 kebabs, ½ cup salad, and 1 lemon wedge).

CALORIES 284; FAT 10.3g (sat 4.3g, mono 4.5g, poly 0.7g); PROTEIN 24.8g; CARB 23g; FIBER 6.3g; CHOL 53mg; IRON 3.1mg; SODIUM 442mg; CALC 51mg

Fava Beans

These large, emerald green, slightly nutty-flavored beans are traditional in Mediterranean and Asian cuisines. Fava beans are also known as broad beans.

To select: Look for long, plump, heavy pods that are bright green and unblemished; flat pods typically yield small beans.

To store: Keep the pods in a bag in the refrigerator up to a week; store peeled beans only a day or two. You can freeze blanched, peeled beans for a couple of months.

To prepare: First, open the pods and remove the beans. Boil briefly, and then remove the tough outer skin from each bean.

To cook: Once blanched and peeled, the beans add crunch to any dish. If you prefer a softer texture, sauté or cook the blanched beans in boiling water until tender.

Health benefits: Fava beans contain L-dopa, a precursor to the neurotransmitter dopamine and a drug used to treat Parkinson's disease. Some patients have described improvements in their symptoms after consuming fava beans.

The author of the best seller *The Omnivore's Dilemma*, Michael Pollan, chooses high-quality grass-fed meats from local producers for his recipe repertoire. He loves the simple pleasures of cooking and eating, and in the spring, that traditionally means lamb. The mustardy rub enhances the flavor of the lamb in this spring-inspired dish.

Garlic-Herb Roasted Rack of Lamb

2 tablespoons chopped fresh thyme
1 tablespoon chopped fresh flat-leaf parsley
2 tablespoons fresh lemon juice
1 tablespoon Dijon mustard
1 garlic clove, minced
1 (1½-pound) French-cut rack of lamb (8 ribs)
½ teaspoon salt
¼ teaspoon freshly ground black
  pepper
Cooking spray

1. Preheat oven to 425°.
2. Combine first 5 ingredients in a small bowl; stir with a whisk.
3. Sprinkle lamb evenly with salt and freshly ground pepper; rub lamb evenly with herb mixture. Place on a jelly-roll pan or broiler pan coated with cooking spray. Bake at 425° for 35 minutes or until a thermometer registers 145° (medium-rare). Cover with foil; let stand 10 minutes before serving. Slice rack into 8 pieces. **Yield:** 4 servings (serving size: 2 chops).

CALORIES 293; FAT 15.7g (sat 5.6g, mono 6.3g, poly 1.4g); PROTEIN 34.2g; CARB 1.3g; FIBER 0.3g; CHOL 112mg; IRON 3.1mg; SODIUM 463mg; CALC 29mg

This recipe from Dinners at the Farm in Connecticut combines spring produce with lamb, a meat typically associated with the season. You may need to call ahead to order lamb shoulder from your regular butcher. Look for a producer of grass-fed lamb in your area.

Lamb Shoulder Braised with Spring Vegetables, Green Herbs, and White Wine

1½ tablespoons butter

4 cups chopped onion (about 1 pound)

6 garlic cloves, crushed

2 pounds lamb shoulder, trimmed and cut into 1½-inch pieces

3 cups fruity white wine (such as riesling)

1 teaspoon salt

½ teaspoon freshly ground black pepper

1 tablespoon chopped fresh oregano

1 tablespoon chopped fresh flat-leaf parsley

2 teaspoons chopped fresh rosemary

½ pound small red potatoes, halved

½ pound turnips, peeled and cut into 1-inch cubes

½ pound carrots, peeled and cut into 1-inch pieces

½ pound asparagus, trimmed and cut into 2-inch pieces

1. Melt butter in a Dutch oven over medium-high heat. Add onion to pan; sauté 4 minutes. Add garlic; sauté 1 minute. Spoon onion mixture into a large bowl. Add half of lamb to pan; sauté 4 minutes or until browned. Remove from pan; add to onion mixture. Repeat procedure with remaining lamb.
2. Add wine to pan, scraping pan to loosen browned bits. Return lamb mixture to pan; add salt and pepper. Combine oregano, parsley, and rosemary. Add half of herb mixture to pan; bring to a boil. Cover, reduce heat, and simmer 1½ hours or until lamb is tender. Add potatoes, turnips, and carrots to pan. Cover and cook 40 minutes or until tender. Add asparagus; cook 5 minutes or until asparagus is tender. Stir in remaining herb mixture. **Yield:** 8 servings (serving size: 1¼ cups).

CALORIES 325; FAT 12.6g (sat 5.3g, mono 4.7g, poly 1.1g); PROTEIN 34.3g; CARB 17.2g; FIBER 3.6g; CHOL 110mg; IRON 4.2mg; SODIUM 448mg; CALC 75mg

WINENOTE

This succulent lamb shoulder surrounded by roasted root vegetables is fantastic with an earthy **pinot noir.** Try one that's rich and full bodied to mirror the richness of the lamb.

choiceingredient

Coconut

Fresh coconuts have hard green outer shells, which are removed before they get to the market. What you'll see is a smaller, round brown shell that is covered with hairy fibers. Choose a coconut that is heavy and filled with liquid—shake it near your ear to listen for the liquid inside. The more liquid you hear, the fresher the coconut.

To crack a coconut, drive an ice pick or long nail through one of the three smooth eyes at the end. Drain the liquid, and either use it immediately or cover and refrigerate for up to a few hours. Put the coconut on a hard surface (the floor or porch), and crack it open with a hammer. Break the shell apart using your hands or a hammer. Cut the white meat away from the shell with a knife; peel brown skin from the meat.

Although we think the flavor of fresh coconut is superior to that of processed coconut, sometimes convenience wins and we use packaged flaked coconut. Processed coconut is almost always sweetened, although you can find it unsweetened in some health-food stores. The bags contain dry coconut shreds or flakes; the canned flakes are moister than the bagged flakes.

Red curry powder is a blend of coriander, cumin, chiles, and cardamom. Use it to give this quick stir-fry a hint of Thai flavor.

Coconut Curried Pork, Snow Pea, and Mango Stir-Fry

2   (3½-ounce) bags boil-in-bag long-grain rice
1   (1-pound) pork tenderloin, trimmed
1   tablespoon canola oil
1   teaspoon red curry powder
1   cup snow peas
⅓   cup light coconut milk
1   tablespoon fish sauce
1   teaspoon red curry paste (such as Thai Kitchen)
1   cup bottled mango, cut into ½-inch pieces
½   cup sliced green onions, divided
2   tablespoons shredded coconut
4   lime wedges (optional)

1. Prepare rice according to package directions, omitting salt and fat; drain.
2. Cut pork into 1-inch cubes. Heat oil in a large nonstick skillet over medium-high heat. Sprinkle pork evenly with curry powder. Add pork and snow peas to pan; stir-fry 3 minutes.
3. Combine coconut milk, fish sauce, and curry paste, stirring well. Add milk mixture to pan; bring to a simmer. Stir in mango and ¼ cup onions; cook 1 minute or until thoroughly heated. Remove from heat. Place 1 cup rice on each of 4 plates; top each serving with 1¼ cups pork mixture. Sprinkle each serving with 1 tablespoon of remaining ¼ cup onions and 1½ teaspoons shredded coconut. Serve with lime wedges, if desired. **Yield:** 4 servings.

CALORIES 429; FAT 9.7g (sat 3.5g, mono 3.9g, poly 1.6g); PROTEIN 29.7g; CARB 54.8g; FIBER 2.3g; CHOL 74mg; IRON 4mg; SODIUM 454mg; CALC 38mg

Look for a whole chicken, cut up. If you prefer the fuller flavor of dark meat, use four chicken leg quarters instead.

Braised Chicken with Baby Vegetables and Peas

2 tablespoons butter, divided
2 bone-in chicken breast halves, skinned
2 bone-in chicken thighs, skinned
2 chicken drumsticks, skinned
½ teaspoon salt
¼ teaspoon freshly ground black pepper
2 (14-ounce) cans fat-free, less-sodium chicken broth
1 cup dry white wine

½ teaspoon chopped fresh thyme
12 baby turnips, peeled (about 8 ounces)
12 baby carrots, peeled (about 8 ounces)
12 pearl onions, peeled (about 8 ounces)
6 fresh flat-leaf parsley sprigs
2 bay leaves
2 tablespoons all-purpose flour
¾ cup fresh green peas
2 tablespoons chopped fresh flat-leaf parsley

1. Melt 1 tablespoon butter in a Dutch oven over medium-high heat. Sprinkle chicken evenly with salt and pepper. Add chicken to pan, and sauté 5 minutes on each side or until browned. Remove from pan.

2. Add broth to pan; cook 1 minute, scraping pan to loosen browned bits. Add wine and next 6 ingredients; stir. Add chicken to pan, nestling into vegetable mixture; bring to a boil. Cover, reduce heat, and simmer 20 minutes or until chicken is done. Discard bay leaves and parsley sprigs. Remove chicken and vegetables from pan. Keep warm.

3. Place a zip-top plastic bag inside a 2-cup glass measure. Pour cooking liquid into bag; let stand 10 minutes (fat will rise to the top). Seal bag; carefully snip off 1 bottom corner of bag. Drain drippings back into pan, stopping before fat layer reaches opening; discard fat. Bring liquid to a boil; cook until reduced to 1½ cups (about 5 minutes).

4. Melt remaining 1 tablespoon butter in a small skillet. Add flour, stirring until smooth. Add flour mixture to cooking liquid; cook 2 minutes or until slightly thick, stirring constantly. Return chicken and vegetable mixture to pan; stir in peas. Cook 3 minutes or until thoroughly heated. Sprinkle with chopped parsley. **Yield:** 4 servings (serving size: ¾ cup vegetables, ⅓ cup sauce, 1 chicken breast half or 1 chicken thigh and 1 drumstick, and 1½ teaspoons parsley).

CALORIES 324; FAT 11.4g (sat 5.1g, mono 3.4g, poly 1.5g); PROTEIN 32.6g; CARB 22.1g; FIBER 5.2g; CHOL 100mg; IRON 3.3mg; SODIUM 818mg; CALC 89mg

Green Peas

Green peas, also known as English or garden peas, are best served when fresh picked.

To select: The best way to guarantee freshness is to purchase peas from the grower. If possible, purchase and cook peas on the same day. Look for crisp, medium-sized bright green pods; avoid full, oversized pods, which tend to hold starchy peas. Be sure to sample a few peas before buying. The texture should be crisp, and the taste slightly sweet.

To store: Shell and chill green peas as soon as possible. If you can't cook and eat fresh peas within two or three days, blanch and freeze them up to two months.

To prepare: Green pea pods will open like a zipper when pressure is applied to the middle of the pod. Simply rake the peas out.

To cook: Boil, steam, or braise peas until tender.

Health benefits: Green peas are one of the important foods to include in your diet if you feel fatigued and sluggish. They provide nutrients that help support the energy-producing cells and systems of the body.

Jicama

Jicama is an edible root that resembles a turnip. It has a thin brown skin and crisp, juicy white flesh that's mild in flavor (think of a cross between a water chestnut and a pear). Jicama is native to Mexico, where it's sometimes referred to as yam bean, Mexican turnip, or Mexican potato. The plant is a member of the bean family, and its vine can grow up to 20 feet in length. (The root is the only edible portion of the plant, though; its leaves and seeds contain a mild toxin.)

Find jicama year-round in the produce section of many supermarkets and Latin American markets. Select firm, dry jicama roots. Skin should not appear shriveled, bruised, or blemished.

Remove skin with a sharp vegetable peeler, then cut the white flesh into cubes or strips, according to your recipe. Because jicama doesn't brown or become soggy after cutting, it makes a nice addition to crudité platters and salads. It's also good added raw to sushi rolls in place of cucumber for crunch, or included in stir-fries, as it performs best with quick-cooking methods that allow it to maintain crispness.

There are a couple of steps you can do ahead: Prepare the citrusy vinaigrette and refrigerate, and bake the tortilla strips and store in an airtight container. If time is tight, substitute baked tortilla chips for the tortilla strips.

Grilled Chicken, Mango, and Jicama Salad with Tequila-Lime Vinaigrette

Chicken:
¼ cup fresh orange juice
¼ cup low-sodium soy sauce
2 teaspoons minced garlic
¾ teaspoon chili powder
6 (6-ounce) skinless, boneless chicken breast halves

Vinaigrette:
¼ cup chopped fresh cilantro
¼ cup fresh orange juice
2 tablespoons fresh lime juice
2 tablespoons tequila
2 tablespoons extra-virgin olive oil
1½ teaspoons honey
¼ teaspoon freshly ground black pepper
⅛ teaspoon ground red pepper
Dash of salt

Tortilla Strips:
4 (6-inch) yellow corn tortillas, cut into (½-inch-wide) strips
Cooking spray
½ teaspoon ground cumin
¼ teaspoon salt
¼ teaspoon paprika
Dash of ground red pepper

Remaining Ingredients:
½ teaspoon salt
1 cup (3 x ¼-inch) strips peeled jicama
1 cup thinly sliced peeled mango (about 1 large)
1 (5-ounce) bag mixed baby greens

1. To prepare chicken, combine first 5 ingredients in a large zip-top plastic bag. Seal and marinate in refrigerator 2 hours, turning bag occasionally.

2. To prepare vinaigrette, combine cilantro and next 8 ingredients in a small bowl; stir with a whisk. Chill until ready to use.

3. Preheat oven to 350°.

4. To prepare tortilla strips, place strips in a large bowl. Coat with cooking spray; toss. Combine cumin, ¼ teaspoon salt, paprika, and dash of red pepper. Sprinkle over strips; toss well. Spread strips in a single layer on a baking sheet. Bake at 350° for 8 minutes or until almost crisp. Remove from oven; cool. (Tortilla strips will crisp as they cool.)

5. Prepare grill.

6. Remove chicken from bag, discarding marinade. Sprinkle chicken with ½ teaspoon salt. Place chicken on a grill rack coated with cooking spray, and grill 5 minutes on each side or until done. Cut chicken into ½-inch slices. Combine jicama, mango, and greens in a large bowl. Pour vinaigrette over jicama mixture, and toss to coat. Place 1⅓ cups jicama mixture on each of 6 plates, and top each serving with 1 sliced chicken breast half. Top evenly with tortilla strips. **Yield:** 6 servings.

CALORIES 330; FAT 7.3g (sat 1.3g, mono 3.9g, poly 1.1g); PROTEIN 41.9g; CARB 20.1g; FIBER 3g; CHOL 99mg; IRON 2.3mg; SODIUM 737mg; CALC 71mg

Chicken Scaloppine with Sugar Snap Pea, Asparagus, and Lemon Salad

3   cups julienne-cut trimmed sugar snap peas (about 1 pound)

2   cups (1-inch) slices asparagus (about 1 pound)

6   (6-ounce) skinless, boneless chicken breast halves

¾   teaspoon salt, divided

½   teaspoon freshly ground black pepper

Cooking spray

1   cup fat-free, less-sodium chicken broth

⅓   cup dry white wine

1   tablespoon butter

1   tablespoon chopped fresh mint

2½   tablespoons extra-virgin olive oil

1   teaspoon grated lemon rind

1½   tablespoons fresh lemon juice

6   lemon wedges

1. Steam peas and asparagus, covered, 4 minutes or until crisp-tender. Rinse pea mixture with cold water; drain. Chill.

2. Place each chicken breast half between 2 sheets of heavy-duty plastic wrap; pound to ¼-inch thickness using a meat mallet or small heavy skillet. Sprinkle chicken evenly with ½ teaspoon salt and pepper. Heat a large nonstick skillet over medium-high heat. Coat pan with cooking spray. Add 2 breast halves to pan; sauté 2 minutes on each side or until done. Remove from pan. Repeat procedure twice with remaining chicken. Add broth and wine to pan; bring to a boil, scraping pan to loosen browned bits. Cook until reduced to ½ cup (about 5 minutes). Remove from heat; stir in butter.

3. Combine remaining ¼ teaspoon salt, mint, oil, rind, and juice, stirring well with a whisk. Drizzle oil mixture over pea mixture; toss gently to coat. Serve pea mixture with chicken and sauce. Garnish with lemon wedges. **Yield:** 6 servings (serving size: 1 chicken breast half, about 1 cup pea mixture, 4 teaspoons sauce, and 1 lemon wedge).

CALORIES 315; FAT 10g (sat 2.6g, mono 5.2g, poly 1.4g); PROTEIN 43.3g; CARB 10.3g; FIBER 3.7g; CHOL 104mg; IRON 4.1mg; SODIUM 495mg; CALC 98mg

Chicken Breasts Stuffed with Goat Cheese, Caramelized Spring Onions, and Thyme

1½ teaspoons olive oil
1⅓ cups thinly sliced spring onions (about 1 pound)
¾ teaspoon salt, divided
¼ teaspoon freshly ground black pepper
¾ cup (3 ounces) crumbled goat cheese
1 tablespoon chopped fresh flat-leaf parsley
1 tablespoon fat-free milk
1½ teaspoons chopped fresh thyme
6 (6-ounce) skinless, boneless chicken breast halves
Cooking spray
½ cup dry white wine
1 cup fat-free, less-sodium chicken broth

1. Heat oil in a large skillet over medium heat. Add onions, ¼ teaspoon salt, and pepper to pan; cook 12 minutes, stirring frequently. Cover, reduce heat, and cook 8 minutes, stirring occasionally. Uncover and cook 5 minutes or until golden, stirring occasionally. Cool slightly. Combine onion mixture, ¼ teaspoon salt, cheese, parsley, milk, and thyme in a small bowl, stirring with a fork.

2. Cut a horizontal slit through thickest portion of each chicken breast half to form a pocket; stuff 1½ tablespoons cheese mixture into each pocket. Sprinkle chicken evenly with remaining ¼ teaspoon salt.

3. Return pan to medium-high heat. Coat pan with cooking spray. Add chicken to pan; sauté 5 minutes; turn chicken over. Cover, reduce heat, and cook 10 minutes or until chicken is done.

4. Remove chicken from pan; let stand 10 minutes. Add wine to pan; bring to a boil, scraping pan to loosen browned bits. Cook until reduced by half (about 2 minutes). Add broth, and cook until reduced to ¼ cup (about 9 minutes). Serve with chicken. **Yield:** 6 servings (serving size: 1 chicken breast half and 2 teaspoons sauce).

CALORIES 274; FAT 9.5g (sat 4.3g, mono 3.2g, poly 1.2g); PROTEIN 39.3g; CARB 6.6g; FIBER 2.2g; CHOL 105mg; IRON 2.8mg; SODIUM 530mg; CALC 123mg

Spring Onions

Spring onions are basically more developed green onions but not yet fully mature onions. They are also known as scallions or salad onions and can vary in thickness and length. You will find white, yellow, or red varieties, but baby Vidalia onions are most common.

To select: Look for healthy dark green tops on the onions. Dry, wilted, or slimy tops are signs of age. Also check the bulbs as you would a regular onion; they should not feel soft.

To store: Keep spring onions in a plastic bag in the crisper drawer of the refrigerator, and use them up to one week from purchase. We do not recommend freezing spring onions.

To prepare: Treat spring onions just as you would green onions. Cut off root ends and any limp or damaged parts of the green tops. Remove the outer layers of skin before you slice or chop.

To cook: Spring onions can be eaten raw; or you can sauté, bake, blanch, or grill them.

Health benefits: The regular consumption of onions has been shown to lower high cholesterol levels and high blood pressure, both of which help prevent atherosclerosis and diabetes and reduce the risk of heart attack or stroke.

Grilled Chicken with Mango-Pineapple Salsa

Salsa:

⅔ cup diced peeled ripe mango (1 medium)

⅔ cup diced fresh pineapple

2 tablespoons minced red onion

1 tablespoon minced seeded jalapeño pepper

1½ teaspoons chopped fresh cilantro

1½ teaspoons fresh lime juice

⅛ teaspoon salt

⅛ teaspoon freshly ground black pepper

Chicken:

4 (6-ounce) skinless, boneless chicken breast halves

¼ cup pineapple juice

3 tablespoons chopped fresh cilantro

3 tablespoons low-sodium soy sauce

2 tablespoons honey

1 teaspoon fresh lime juice

Dash of crushed red pepper

Cooking spray

1. To prepare salsa, combine first 8 ingredients. Cover; refrigerate 30 minutes.

2. To prepare chicken, place each chicken breast half between 2 sheets of heavy-duty plastic wrap; pound to ½-inch thickness using a meat mallet or small heavy skillet. Combine pineapple juice and next 5 ingredients in a large zip-top plastic bag. Add chicken to bag; seal. Marinate in refrigerator 30 minutes.

3. Prepare grill.

4. Remove chicken from bag, reserving marinade. Place chicken on a grill rack coated with cooking spray; grill 3 minutes on each side or until done.

5. Place reserved marinade in a small saucepan; bring to a boil. Reduce heat, and cook until reduced to ¼ cup (about 5 minutes). Drizzle over chicken. Serve salsa with chicken. **Yield:** 4 servings (serving size: 1 chicken breast half, 1 tablespoon sauce, and ¼ cup salsa).

CALORIES 222; FAT 3.4g (sat 0.9g, mono 1.1g, poly 0.7g); PROTEIN 26.9g; CARB 21.1g; FIBER 1.3g; CHOL 70mg; IRON 1.4mg; SODIUM 537mg; CALC 27mg

If you can't find baby artichokes, use six large globe artichokes instead and cook them a bit longer, just until tender.

Oven-Roasted Chicken Breasts with Artichokes and Toasted Breadcrumbs

5   quarts water, divided
⅓   cup kosher salt
6   bone-in chicken breast halves, skinned
¼   cup fresh lemon juice
18   baby artichokes
2   tablespoons olive oil, divided
¼   teaspoon freshly ground black pepper
1   tablespoon canola oil
1   cup dry white wine
1   (14-ounce) can fat-free, less-sodium chicken broth
1½   ounces French bread baguette
2   tablespoons chopped fresh flat-leaf parsley

1. Combine 3 quarts water and salt in a Dutch oven, stirring until salt dissolves. Add chicken to salt mixture. Cover and refrigerate 2 hours.
2. Combine remaining 2 quarts water and juice. Cut off stem of each artichoke to within 1 inch of base; peel stem. Remove bottom leaves and tough outer leaves, leaving tender heart and bottom. Cut each artichoke in half lengthwise; place in lemon water.
3. Heat 1 tablespoon olive oil in a large skillet over medium-high heat. Drain artichokes; pat dry. Add artichokes to pan. Cover and cook 10 minutes or until tender. Uncover and cook an additional 5 minutes or until browned, stirring frequently. Keep warm.
4. Preheat oven to 450°.
5. Remove chicken from salt mixture; discard salt mixture. Pat chicken dry; sprinkle evenly with pepper.
6. Heat canola oil in a large ovenproof skillet over medium-high heat. Wrap handle of pan with foil. Add chicken to pan, meat side down; sauté 1 minute. Bake at 450° for 10 minutes. Turn chicken over;

bake an additional 12 minutes or until done. Keep warm.
7. Place a zip-top plastic bag inside a 2-cup glass measure. Pour drippings into bag; let stand 10 minutes (fat will rise to the top). Seal bag; carefully snip off 1 bottom corner of bag. Drain drippings back into pan, stopping before fat layer reaches opening; discard fat.
8. Add wine to drippings in pan; bring to a boil, scraping pan to loosen browned bits. Reduce heat; simmer until reduced to 1 cup (about 5 minutes). Add broth to pan; simmer until reduced to 1½ cups (about 10 minutes).
9. Reduce oven temperature to 350°. Place bread in food processor; pulse 10 times or until coarse crumbs measure 1 cup. Combine remaining 1 tablespoon olive oil and breadcrumbs in a bowl; toss to coat. Arrange crumbs in a single layer on a baking sheet; bake at 350° for 5 minutes or until golden. Add parsley; toss to combine. Serve chicken with artichokes and sauce. Top with breadcrumbs. Serve immediately. **Yield:** 6 servings (serving size: 1 chicken breast half, 6 artichoke halves, ¼ cup sauce, and about 2½ tablespoons breadcrumbs).

CALORIES 293; FAT 10.5g (sat 1.8g, mono 5.8g, poly 2.2g); PROTEIN 32.5g; CARB 19.3g; FIBER 7.5g; CHOL 73mg; IRON 3.2mg; SODIUM 835mg; CALC 82mg

Serve warm, at room temperature, or chilled for maximum versatility. Leftovers make an easy and satisfying lunch.

Potato, Chicken, and Fresh Pea Salad

1   pound fingerling potatoes, cut crosswise into 1-inch pieces
2   cups fresh sugar snap peas
2   cups chopped skinless, boneless rotisserie chicken breast
½   cup finely chopped red bell pepper
½   cup finely chopped red onion
2   tablespoons extra-virgin olive oil
2   tablespoons white wine vinegar
1   tablespoon fresh lemon juice
1   tablespoon Dijon mustard
1   teaspoon minced fresh tarragon
1   teaspoon salt
½   teaspoon freshly ground black pepper
1   garlic clove, minced

1. Place potatoes in a large saucepan; cover with cold water. Bring to a boil. Reduce heat, and simmer 10 minutes or until almost tender. Add peas; cook 2 minutes or until peas are crisp-tender. Drain; place vegetables in a large bowl. Add chicken, bell pepper, and onion.
2. Combine oil and remaining ingredients, stirring with a whisk. Drizzle over salad; toss gently to combine. **Yield:** 4 servings (serving size: about 1½ cups).

CALORIES 316; FAT 9.3g (sat 1.7g, mono 5.8g, poly 1.3g); PROTEIN 26.4g; CARB 29.2g; FIBER 3.6g; CHOL 60mg; IRON 2.4mg; SODIUM 680mg; CALC 50mg

Carrot-Pineapple Slaw

The sweet notes in this salad make it a delicious match for grilled pork tenderloin or pork chops.

Carrot-Pineapple Slaw

1   cup diced fresh pineapple
½   cup raisins
1   (10-ounce) package matchstick-cut carrots
2   tablespoons canola oil
2   tablespoons fresh lemon juice
2   tablespoons maple syrup
1   tablespoon fresh pineapple juice
2   tablespoons chopped fresh flat-leaf parsley
¼   teaspoon salt
⅛   teaspoon black pepper

1. Combine first 3 ingredients in a large bowl. Combine oil and next 3 ingredients, stirring with a whisk. Add oil mixture to carrot mixture; toss well. Add parsley, salt, and pepper; toss well. Cover and chill. **Yield:** 6 servings (serving size: about 1 cup).

CALORIES 130; FAT 4.9g (sat 0.4g, mono 2.8g, poly 1.5g); PROTEIN 1g; CARB 22.7g; FIBER 2.3g; CHOL 0mg; IRON 0.6mg; SODIUM 132mg; CALC 32mg

Slice a Pineapple

Fresh pineapple is a treat, but the fruit's prickly exterior may tempt you to reach for the precut varieties. Use this quick-and-easy guide to enjoy the fruit fresh in next to no time.

1. A sharp chef's knife is key. Lay the pineapple horizontally on a cutting board, and cut off the leafy top (the plume) and the base.

2. Stand the pineapple upright on the cutting board; cut down the sides to remove the rind. Remove as little of the flesh as possible.

3. While the pineapple is upright, cut it into thirds by carefully slicing downward to remove the fibrous core. Discard the core.

This seasonal dish features fresh asparagus stalks drizzled with a delicate vinaigrette of extra-virgin olive oil, lemon juice, and grated lemon rind. The salad is finished with a garnish of twice-baked breadcrumbs tossed in browned butter, which adds crispness and a pleasant nuttiness that complements the asparagus.

Warm Asparagus Salad

2 ounces day-old French bread or other firm white bread, sliced
1 garlic clove, peeled and halved
1 tablespoon unsalted butter
1 tablespoon white wine vinegar
2 teaspoons extra-virgin olive oil
1 teaspoon grated lemon rind
2 teaspoons fresh lemon juice
1 medium shallot, peeled and minced
¼ teaspoon salt
¼ teaspoon freshly ground black pepper
1 cup water
1½ pounds asparagus
1 teaspoon grated lemon rind (optional)

1. Preheat oven to 375°.
2. Place bread in a single layer on a baking sheet. Bake at 375° for 10 minutes or until toasted. Rub cut sides of garlic over one side of each bread slice. Place bread slices in a food processor; pulse 10 times or until bread is coarsely ground. Arrange breadcrumbs in a single layer on a baking sheet; bake at 375° for 5 minutes or until golden brown. Transfer breadcrumbs to a bowl.
3. Melt butter in a small saucepan over medium-high heat. Cook 1 to 2 minutes or until butter is lightly browned, shaking pan occasionally; remove from heat. Drizzle butter over toasted bread-crumbs; toss well to coat.
4. Combine vinegar, oil, 1 teaspoon rind, lemon juice, and shallot; stir well with a whisk. Stir in salt and pepper.
5. Bring 1 cup water to a boil in a large skillet. Snap off tough ends of asparagus; add asparagus to pan. Cook 5 minutes or until tender, stirring constantly. Place asparagus on a serving platter. Drizzle with vinaigrette; top with breadcrumb mixture. Garnish with 1 teaspoon grated lemon rind, if desired. Serve immediately. **Yield:** 6 servings.

CALORIES 94; FAT 3.8g (sat 1.3g, mono 2g, poly 0.4g); PROTEIN 4.1g; CARB 13.2g; FIBER 0.4g; CHOL 5mg; IRON 3mg; SODIUM 172mg; CALC 37mg

This vibrant side salad lends itself to improvisation. Start with our basics, including tomatoes, zucchini, jicama, black beans, and queso fresco with a salsa vinaigrette. From there, you might add sliced olives, corn, diced avocado, or radishes. It's delicious with grilled chicken.

Marinated Vegetable Salad with Queso Fresco

1   cup diced tomatoes
1   cup diced zucchini
1   cup diced jicama
½   cup thinly sliced green onions
2   tablespoons chopped, pickled jalapeños
1   (15-ounce) can black beans, drained and
    rinsed
½   cup bottled salsa
3   tablespoons fresh lime juice
1½ tablespoons canola oil
½   cup chopped fresh cilantro
¼   teaspoon freshly ground black pepper
2   cups torn romaine lettuce
¼   cup (1 ounce) shredded queso fresco

1. Combine first 6 ingredients in a large bowl. Combine salsa, juice, and oil, stirring with a whisk. Pour dressing over tomato mixture. Cover; chill 1 hour.
2. Add cilantro and pepper to bowl; toss gently. Serve over lettuce. Sprinkle with cheese. **Yield:** 4 servings (serving size: 1¼ cups salad and 1 tablespoon cheese).

CALORIES 174; FAT 7.1g (sat 1.3g, mono 3.5g, poly 1.8g); PROTEIN 7.3g; CARB 21.7g; FIBER 8.1g; CHOL 5mg; IRON 2mg; SODIUM 536mg; CALC 102mg

Marinated Vegetable Salad with Queso Fresco

Raw Spring Vegetable Salad with Goat Cheese

2   medium carrots
¼   cup thinly sliced spring onion
1   (8-ounce) bunch radishes with tops
1   tablespoon thinly sliced fresh basil
2   tablespoons fresh lemon juice
1   tablespoon extra-virgin olive oil
¼   teaspoon fine sea salt
¼   teaspoon freshly ground black pepper
1   (4-ounce) package goat cheese, cut into 8 slices

1. Shave carrots into ribbons with a vegetable peeler to measure 2 cups. Combine carrots and onion in a large bowl.
2. Wash radishes and radish greens thoroughly; drain and pat dry. Cut radishes into thin slices to equal 1¾ cups; thinly slice radish greens to equal 1 cup. Add radishes, radish greens, basil, and next 4 ingredients to carrot mixture; toss gently to coat.
3. Arrange goat cheese on a serving platter; top with salad. Serve immediately. **Yield:** 4 servings (serving size: 2 cheese slices and about 1 cup salad).

CALORIES 132; FAT 9.5g (sat 4.6g, mono 3.8g, poly 0.6g); PROTEIN 6.2g; CARB 6.4g; FIBER 2g; CHOL 13mg; IRON 1.1mg; SODIUM 309mg; CALC 73mg

This salad's vinaigrette has a nice combination of sweet, tart, and pungent flavors to balance the peppery arugula and crisp grapes. The seeds add a nutty crunch to the combination.

Arugula, Grape, and Sunflower Seed Salad

3   tablespoons red wine vinegar
1   teaspoon honey
1   teaspoon maple syrup
½   teaspoon stone-ground mustard
2   teaspoons grapeseed oil
7   cups loosely packed baby arugula
2   cups red grapes, halved
2   tablespoons toasted sunflower seed kernels
1   teaspoon chopped fresh thyme
¼   teaspoon salt
¼   teaspoon freshly ground black pepper

1. Combine first 4 ingredients in a small bowl. Gradually add oil, stirring with a whisk.

2. Combine arugula, grapes, seeds, and thyme in a large bowl. Drizzle vinegar mixture over arugula; sprinkle with salt and pepper. Toss gently to coat. **Yield:** 6 servings (serving size: about 1 cup).

CALORIES 81; FAT 3.1g (sat 0.3g, mono 0.5g, poly 2g); PROTEIN 1.6g; CARB 13.1g; FIBER 1.2g; CHOL 0mg; IRON 0.7mg; SODIUM 124mg; CALC 47mg

Arugula

This aromatic, leafy green (sometimes called rocket, roquette, or rucola) is a member of the same botanical family as watercress, cabbage, and broccoli. It's low in calories (a cup contains a mere five) and rich in lutein and vitamin A.

Arugula's flavor is often likened to peppery mustard, making it somewhat stronger than most lettuces, so it's often mixed with other greens.

You'll find arugula as loose leaves in bins or bags. Sometimes it's bundled with stems attached. Either way, look for firm, fresh, uniformly green leaves.

Arugula is highly perishable and will only last about two days after purchase. Store in the refrigerator, inside a perforated plastic bag or wrapped in moist paper towels. Rinse thoroughly and dry before using.

Most often used as a salad green, arugula boosts flavor and pairs well with vinaigrettes. It can also be wilted like spinach and served as a healthful side dish. You can even use arugula in place of basil to make a peppery pesto.

We love the way the salty-sweet browned butter highlights the asparagus in this dish.

Roasted Asparagus with Balsamic Browned Butter

40   asparagus spears, trimmed (about 2 pounds)
Cooking spray
¼   teaspoon kosher salt
⅛   teaspoon freshly ground black pepper
2   tablespoons butter
2   teaspoons low-sodium soy sauce
1   teaspoon balsamic vinegar
Cracked black pepper (optional)
Grated lemon rind (optional)

1. Preheat oven to 400°.
2. Arrange asparagus in a single layer on a baking sheet; coat with cooking spray. Sprinkle with salt and pepper. Bake at 400° for 12 minutes or until tender.
3. Melt butter in a small skillet over medium heat; cook 3 minutes or until lightly browned, shaking pan occasionally. Remove from heat; stir in soy sauce and balsamic vinegar. Drizzle over asparagus, tossing well to coat. Garnish with cracked pepper and rind, if desired. **Yield:** 8 servings (serving size: 5 spears).

CALORIES 45; FAT 3g (sat 1.8g, mono 0.9g, poly 0.2g); PROTEIN 1.9g; CARB 3.9g; FIBER 1.7g; CHOL 8mg; IRON 0.7mg; SODIUM 134mg; CALC 18mg

For a vegetarian version, use vegetable broth in place of chicken broth. Garnish with thin asparagus spears for a graceful presentation.

Cream of Asparagus Soup

3   cups (½-inch) sliced asparagus (about 1 pound)
2   cups fat-free, less-sodium chicken broth
¾   teaspoon fresh thyme, divided
1   bay leaf
1   garlic clove, crushed
1   tablespoon all-purpose flour
2   cups 1% low-fat milk
Dash of ground nutmeg
2   teaspoons butter
¾   teaspoon salt
¼   teaspoon grated lemon rind

1. Combine asparagus, broth, ½ teaspoon thyme, bay leaf, and garlic in a large saucepan over medium-high heat; bring to a boil. Reduce heat, cover, and simmer 10 minutes. Discard bay leaf. Place asparagus mixture in a blender; process until smooth.
2. Place flour in pan. Gradually add milk, stirring with a whisk until blended. Add pureed asparagus and ground nutmeg; stir to combine. Bring to a boil. Reduce heat; simmer 5 minutes, stirring constantly. Remove from heat, and stir in ¼ teaspoon thyme, butter, salt, and lemon rind. **Yield:** 4 servings (serving size: 1 cup).

CALORIES 117; FAT 3.5g (sat 2g, mono 0.8g, poly 0.2g); PROTEIN 8.9g; CARB 14g; FIBER 2.5g; CHOL 13mg; IRON 1.1mg; SODIUM 748mg; CALC 163mg

Asparagus

Asparagus, a member of the lily family, is green, white, or purple. Its peak season is April through late June.

To select: Look for stalks with smooth skin; uniform color; and a dry, compact tip. Fibrous stems and shriveled stalks are sure signs of age.

To store: It's OK to wrap the stem ends in damp paper towels for several days; to extend the life, refrigerate stalks, tips up, in a cup of shallow water. Don't freeze fresh asparagus.

To prepare: Trim fibrous ends from asparagus spears. You can cook asparagus as is, or peel the skin with a vegetable peeler to make stalks more tender.

To cook: It is best broiled, steamed, grilled, roasted, or sautéed for a few minutes or until crisp-tender.

Health benefits: Eating asparagus is a great way to help protect yourself against heart disease, since it contains lots of folate, as well as vitamins E, A, and C. Asparagus also contains potassium, which helps lower blood pressure and possibly even cholesterol.

Serve warm or at room temperature for a first course or with a salad for a light meal.

Fresh Pea Soup with Mint

2   teaspoons butter
1   cup coarsely chopped green onions
4   cups shelled fresh green peas (about 4 pounds unshelled)
3   cups fat-free, less-sodium chicken broth
2   cups water
1   tablespoon fresh lemon juice
¼   teaspoon salt
¼   teaspoon freshly ground black pepper
1   tablespoon extra-virgin olive oil
2   tablespoons thinly sliced mint
Cracked black pepper (optional)

1. Melt butter in a large saucepan over medium heat. Add onions to pan; cook 3 minutes, stirring occasionally. Add peas, broth, and 2 cups water; bring to a boil. Reduce heat, and simmer 10 minutes or until peas are very tender, stirring occasionally. Remove from heat; let stand 15 minutes. Stir in juice, salt, and ¼ teaspoon pepper.

2. Place half of pea mixture in a blender; process until smooth. Pour pureed soup mixture into a large bowl. Repeat procedure with remaining pea mixture. Pour half of pureed soup mixture through a sieve over a large bowl, reserving liquid; discard solids. Return liquid to pureed soup mixture. Ladle about ¾ cup soup mixture into each of 6 bowls; drizzle each with ½ teaspoon oil. Sprinkle each serving with 1 teaspoon mint. Garnish with cracked pepper, if desired. **Yield:** 6 servings.

CALORIES 161; FAT 5.3g (sat 1.4g, mono 2.9g, poly 0.7g); PROTEIN 8.6g; CARB 20.8g; FIBER 7.7g; CHOL 3.3mg; IRON 2.6mg; SODIUM 311mg; CALC 56mg

I simply love the taste of this unique little vegetable. The recipe has a bit of lemony tang, and I opt for a Vidalia onion to complement that flavor. The easy preparation ensures that the dish comes out the same every time you make it.

—Nikki LoRé, Rochester, NY

Braised Baby Artichokes

6	cups water
2	tablespoons fresh lemon juice, divided
12	baby artichokes (about 1½ pounds)
1	large Vidalia or other sweet onion, peeled and quartered
1	cup fat-free, less-sodium chicken broth
¼	cup extra-virgin olive oil
1	teaspoon dried marjoram
1	teaspoon freshly ground black pepper
½	teaspoon salt
2	garlic cloves, peeled

1. Combine 6 cups water and 1 tablespoon juice in a large bowl. Working with 1 artichoke at a time, cut off stem of artichoke to within 1 inch of base; peel stem. Remove bottom leaves and tough outer leaves from artichoke, leaving tender heart and bottom. Trim about 1 inch from top of artichoke. Place artichoke in lemon water. Repeat procedure with remaining artichokes. Drain and set aside.

2. Place onion in center of a Dutch oven. Arrange artichokes in a single layer around onion. Add broth and remaining ingredients to pan; bring to a boil. Cover, reduce heat, and simmer 18 minutes or just until onion is tender (artichokes will be very tender). Stir in remaining 1 tablespoon juice. Remove artichokes and onion from pan with a slotted spoon; set aside, and keep warm. Bring broth mixture to a boil; cook 4 minutes or until slightly thickened. Pour sauce over artichoke mixture. **Yield:** 4 servings (serving size: 3 artichokes and 1 onion quarter).

CALORIES 198; FAT 14.1g (sat 2g, mono 10g, poly 2g); PROTEIN 5.3g; CARB 18.5g; FIBER 7.8g; CHOL 0mg; IRON 0.3mg; SODIUM 565mg; CALC 17mg

Use white balsamic vinegar to maintain the vegetables' vibrant hue. Look for baby carrots with tops, which have tender texture and subtly sweet flavor. Small carrots packed and sold as "baby" carrots are actually whittled-down mature vegetables.

Roasted Baby Spring Vegetables

3 tablespoons white balsamic vinegar
1 tablespoon chopped shallots
1 pound baby carrots with tops
1 tablespoon olive oil
½ teaspoon salt
¼ teaspoon freshly ground black pepper
12 fingerling potatoes, halved lengthwise (about 1¼ pounds)
1 (6-ounce) bag radishes, halved (about 1¾ cups)
2 cups (2-inch) slices asparagus (about 1 pound)
1 tablespoon chopped fresh flat-leaf parsley
1 tablespoon chopped fresh chives

1. Preheat oven to 500°.
2. Combine vinegar and shallots in a small bowl; set aside.
3. Trim green tops from carrots; discard tops. Combine carrots and next 5 ingredients in the bottom of a roasting pan, tossing gently to combine. Bake at 500° for 20 minutes or until vegetables begin to brown, stirring occasionally. Remove pan from oven; add shallot mixture and asparagus, tossing to combine. Return pan to oven; bake 5 minutes. Stir in parsley and chives. **Yield:** 7 servings (serving size: 1 cup).

CALORIES 127; FAT 2.2g (sat 0.3g, mono 1.4g, poly 0.3g); PROTEIN 3.9g; CARB 24.6g; FIBER 3.9g; CHOL 0mg; IRON 2.7mg; SODIUM 232mg; CALC 52mg

The season for fresh baby peas is short; if you miss it, frozen will work in this dish.

Fresh Peas with Pancetta

3 slices pancetta, chopped (about 1 ounce)
¾ cup finely chopped white onion
1 garlic clove, minced
3 cups shelled fresh green peas or frozen petite green peas
1 cup fat-free, less-sodium chicken broth
2 teaspoons sugar
¼ teaspoon salt
¼ cup chopped fresh flat-leaf parsley

1. Heat a large nonstick skillet over medium-high heat. Add pancetta; sauté 5 minutes or until crispy. Remove pancetta from pan, reserving drippings in pan. Add onion and garlic to pan; sauté 2 minutes or until tender. Add peas, broth, sugar, and salt to pan. Simmer 5 minutes or until peas are tender, stirring occasionally. Stir in pancetta and chopped parsley. **Yield:** 6 servings (serving size: ½ cup).

CALORIES 153; FAT 3.9g (sat 1.6g, mono 0.1g, poly 0.2g); PROTEIN 8.4g; CARB 21.6g; FIBER 6.4g; CHOL 8mg; IRON 2mg; SODIUM 425mg; CALC 44mg

You can use fresh orange juice instead of Grand Marnier in the cream cheese frosting.

Strawberry Layer Cake

Cake:

1¼   cups sliced strawberries
10   ounces all-purpose flour (about 2¼ cups)
2¼   teaspoons baking powder
⅛   teaspoon salt
1½   cups granulated sugar
½   cup butter, softened
2   large eggs
2   large egg whites
1   cup low-fat buttermilk
¼   teaspoon red food coloring
Cooking spray

Frosting:

⅓   cup (3 ounces) ⅓-less-fat cream cheese
⅓   cup butter, softened
2   tablespoons Grand Marnier
        (orange-flavored liqueur)
3   cups powdered sugar

Remaining Ingredient:

12   whole strawberries (optional)

1. Preheat oven to 350°.
2. To prepare cake, place sliced strawberries in a food processor; process until smooth.
3. Weigh or lightly spoon flour into dry measuring cups; level with a knife. Combine flour, baking powder, and salt, stirring with a whisk. Place granulated sugar and ½ cup butter in a large bowl; beat with a mixer at medium speed until well blended. Add eggs, one at a time, beating well after each addition. Beat in egg whites. Add flour mixture and buttermilk alternately to sugar mixture, beginning and ending with flour mixture. Add pureed strawberries and food coloring; beat just until blended.
4. Divide batter between 2 (8-inch) round cake pans coated with cooking spray. Bake at 350° for 30 minutes or until a wooden pick inserted in center comes out clean. Cool in pans on a wire rack 10 minutes. Remove from pans; cool completely on wire racks.
5. To prepare frosting, place cream cheese, ⅓ cup butter, and liqueur in a medium bowl; beat with a mixer at medium speed until blended. Gradually add powdered sugar, and beat just until blended.
6. Place 1 cake layer on a plate; spread with ½ cup frosting. Top with remaining cake layer. Spread remaining frosting over top and sides of cake. Cut 1 whole strawberry into thin slices, cutting to, but not through, the stem end. Fan strawberry on top of cake just before serving, if desired. Cut remaining 11 strawberries in half. Garnish cake with strawberry halves, if desired. **Yield:** 6 servings (serving size: 1 slice).

CALORIES 348; FAT 11.3g (sat 6.9g, mono 2.8g, poly 0.6g); PROTEIN 4.3g; CARB 57.7g; FIBER 0.7g; CHOL 55mg; IRON 1.1mg; SODIUM 212mg; CALC 74mg

Almond Jelly-Roll Cake with Raspberry Filling

Cake:

¾ cup granulated sugar

¼ cup almond paste

Cooking spray

3 ounces all-purpose flour (about ⅔ cup plus 2 teaspoons), divided

1 teaspoon baking powder

⅛ teaspoon salt

4 large eggs

1 teaspoon vanilla extract

¼ cup powdered sugar, divided

Remaining Ingredients:

⅔ cup seedless raspberry jam

½ cup whipping cream

¼ cup powdered sugar

Fresh raspberries (optional)

1. Preheat oven to 350°.

2. To prepare cake, place granulated sugar and almond paste in a blender or food processor; process until well blended. Set aside.

3. Coat a 15 x 10–inch jelly-roll pan with cooking spray. Line bottom of pan with wax paper. Coat paper well with cooking spray. Dust with 2 teaspoons flour, and set aside.

4. Lightly spoon remaining ⅔ cup flour into dry measuring cups; level with a knife. Combine flour, baking powder, and salt in a medium bowl, stirring with a whisk.

5. Place eggs in a large bowl, and beat with a mixer at high speed until pale and fluffy (about 4 minutes). Gradually add granulated sugar mixture and vanilla, beating at medium speed until smooth (about 3 minutes). Sift half of flour mixture over egg mixture; fold in. Repeat procedure with remaining flour mixture. Spread batter evenly into prepared pan. Bake at 350° for 10 minutes or until cake springs back when touched lightly in center. Loosen cake from sides of pan, and turn out onto a dish towel dusted with 2 tablespoons powdered sugar; carefully peel off wax paper. Sprinkle cake with 2 tablespoons powdered sugar; cool 1 minute. Starting at narrow end, roll up cake and towel together. Place, seam side down, on a wire rack; cool completely (about 30 minutes).

6. Unroll cake carefully; remove towel. Spread jam over cake, leaving a ½-inch margin around the outside edges. Reroll cake; place, seam side down, on a platter.

7. Place cream and ¼ cup powdered sugar in a medium bowl; beat with a mixer at high speed until stiff peaks form. Cut cake into 8 slices with a serrated knife. Top each slice with whipped cream and raspberries, if desired. **Yield:** 8 servings (serving size: 1 slice cake and 1 tablespoon whipped cream).

CALORIES 321; FAT 10.1g (sat 4.4g, mono 3.8g, poly 1g); PROTEIN 5.2g; CARB 53.9g; FIBER 0.6g; CHOL 126mg; IRON 1.1mg; SODIUM 139mg; CALC 71mg

Roll a Jelly-Roll Cake

Jelly-roll cakes are thin, flat cakes that have been filled with jams, jellies, frosting, whipped cream, or any filling you prefer, and rolled into a log. While they may look complicated, they're really not. They're a relatively quick and easy dessert that offers myriad opportunities for experimentation.

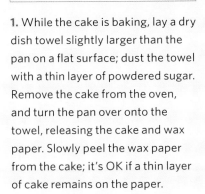

1. While the cake is baking, lay a dry dish towel slightly larger than the pan on a flat surface; dust the towel with a thin layer of powdered sugar. Remove the cake from the oven, and turn the pan over onto the towel, releasing the cake and wax paper. Slowly peel the wax paper from the cake; it's OK if a thin layer of cake remains on the paper.

2. Roll the towel and the cake together, pressing gently. Be sure to move slowly and carefully throughout the entire rolling process. The towel will end up coiled inside the cake.

3. Cool the cake on a wire rack, seam side down. After an hour, unroll and remove towel. The cake will be slightly wavy. Carefully spread the filling as directed, and reroll the cake.

Five-Spice Toasted-Coconut Cake Roll with Tropical Fruit Compote

Cake:

½	cup sifted cake flour
¾	cup granulated sugar, divided
¾	teaspoon five-spice powder
6	large egg whites
½	teaspoon cream of tartar

Dash of salt

1	teaspoon fresh lemon juice
1	teaspoon vanilla extract
½	teaspoon coconut extract
⅓	cup flaked sweetened coconut
2	tablespoons powdered sugar
1	pint mandarin orange with passionfruit sorbet (such as Edy's Whole Fruit Sorbet), softened

Compote:

1	cup (½-inch) cubed peeled ripe mango
1	cup (½-inch) cubed fresh pineapple
1	cup (½-inch) cubed peeled kiwifruit
2	tablespoons brown sugar
2	tablespoons dark rum

Remaining Ingredient:

¼	cup flaked sweetened coconut, toasted

1. Preheat oven to 325°.

2. To prepare cake, line bottom of a 15 x 10–inch jelly-roll pan with wax paper.

3. Lightly spoon flour into a dry measuring cup; level with a knife. Combine flour, 6 tablespoons granulated sugar, and five-spice powder, stirring with a whisk.

4. Place egg whites in a large bowl; beat with a mixer at high speed until foamy. Add cream of tartar and salt, and beat until soft peaks form. Add 6 tablespoons granulated sugar, 2 tablespoons at a time, beating until stiff peaks form. Beat in juice and extracts.

5. Sift ¼ cup flour mixture over egg white mixture; fold in. Repeat procedure with remaining flour mixture, ¼ cup at a time. Spread batter into prepared pan. Sprinkle with ⅓ cup coconut. Bake at 325° for 20 minutes or until cake springs back when lightly touched.

6. Place a clean dish towel over a large wire rack; dust with powdered sugar. Loosen cake from sides of pan; turn out onto towel. Carefully peel off wax paper; cool 3 minutes. Starting at narrow end, roll up cake and towel together. Place, seam side down, on wire rack; cool cake completely. Unroll cake, and remove towel. Spread sorbet over cake, leaving a ½-inch border around outside edges. Reroll cake. Wrap cake in plastic wrap; freeze 1 hour or until firm.

7. To prepare compote, combine mango, pineapple, kiwi, brown sugar, and rum, and let stand 20 minutes. Cut cake into 16 slices, and place 2 slices on each of 8 plates. Spoon about ¼ cup compote over each serving, and sprinkle each serving with 1½ teaspoons toasted coconut. **Yield:** 8 servings.

CALORIES 245; FAT 2.1g (sat 1.6g, mono 0.1g, poly 0.1g); PROTEIN 4g; CARB 51.6g; FIBER 1.7g; CHOL 0mg; IRON 1.2mg; SODIUM 80mg; CALC 22mg

Sifting the flour mixture thoroughly three times incorporates the powdered sugar for a light, tender cupcake. Top with tiny edible pansy blossoms or rosebuds for decoration. Store extra cupcakes in an airtight container, or send them home with guests as party favors.

Lemon Angel Food Cupcakes

Cupcakes:

2 ounces cake flour (about ½ cup)

¾ cup powdered sugar

¾ cup egg whites (about 5 large eggs)

⅛ teaspoon salt

¾ teaspoon cream of tartar

½ cup granulated sugar

½ teaspoon vanilla extract

2 teaspoons grated lemon rind

Lemon Frosting:

¼ cup butter, softened

2 cups powdered sugar

1 tablespoon 1% low-fat milk

1 to 2 tablespoons freshly squeezed lemon juice

Edible flowers such as pansies or rosebuds (optional)

1. Preheat oven to 350°.

2. Place 16 paper muffin cup liners in muffin cups. Set aside.

3. Lightly spoon cake flour into dry measuring cups; level with a knife. Sift together flour and ¾ cup powdered sugar into a medium bowl; repeat procedure 2 times.

4. Beat egg whites and salt with a mixer at high speed until frothy (about 1 minute). Add cream of tartar, and beat until soft peaks form. Add ½ cup granulated sugar, 1 tablespoon at a time, beating until stiff peaks form. Sprinkle flour mixture over egg white mixture, ¼ cup at a time; fold in after each addition. Stir in vanilla and rind.

5. Divide batter evenly among prepared muffin cups. Bake at 350° for 18 minutes or until lightly browned. Remove from pan; let cool completely on a wire rack.

6. To prepare frosting, beat butter with a mixer at high speed until fluffy. Gradually add 2 cups powdered sugar; beat at low speed just until blended.

Add milk and lemon juice; beat until fluffy. Add more lemon juice as needed to adjust the consistency. Spread 2 tablespoons lemon frosting over each cupcake. Garnish with edible pansies and rosebuds, if desired. **Yield:** 16 cupcakes (serving size: 1 cupcake).

CALORIES 144; FAT 2.9g (sat 1.8g, mono 0.8g, poly 0.1g); PROTEIN 1.6g; CARB 28.9g; FIBER 0.1g; CHOL 8mg; IRON 0.3mg; SODIUM 58mg; CALC 4mg

I love oatmeal cookies, so I did my best to come up with a low-fat version.

—Christine Dohlmar, Valrico, FL

Banana-Rum-Coconut Cookies

⅔ cup packed dark brown sugar
½ cup ripe mashed banana (about 1 medium)
½ cup reduced-fat mayonnaise
1 teaspoon rum
3.4 ounces all-purpose flour (about ¾ cup)
1 cup quick-cooking oats
½ cup flaked sweetened coconut
½ cup golden raisins
½ cup chopped walnuts
1 teaspoon baking powder
¼ teaspoon ground cinnamon
⅛ teaspoon ground nutmeg
Dash of ground ginger

1. Preheat oven to 350°.
2. Place first 4 ingredients in a large bowl; beat with a mixer at medium speed until blended. Lightly spoon flour into dry measuring cups; level with a knife. Combine flour and remaining ingredients, stirring with a whisk. Stir flour mixture into banana mixture. Drop dough by 2 tablespoonfuls onto parchment paper-lined baking sheets. Bake at 350° for 19 minutes or until lightly browned. Remove from pan; cool completely on a wire rack. **Yield:** 20 cookies (serving size: 1 cookie).

CALORIES 118; FAT 3.7g (sat 1.1g, mono 0.3g, poly 1.5g); PROTEIN 1.7g; CARB 19.9g; FIBER 1.1g; CHOL 0mg; IRON 0.6mg; SODIUM 86mg; CALC 26mg

Whole Wheat Banana Bread

1   cup warm water (100° to 110°)
1   package dry yeast (about 2¼ teaspoons)
1   cup mashed ripe banana
10.5 ounces bread flour (about 2¼ cups), divided
4 ¾ ounces whole wheat flour (about 1 cup)
2   ounces soy flour (about ½ cup)
1¼   teaspoons salt
Cooking spray
1   teaspoon butter, melted

1. Combine 1 cup warm water and yeast; let stand
5 minutes. Stir in banana.
2. Lightly spoon flours into dry measuring cups;
level with a knife. Add 2 cups bread flour, wheat
flour, soy flour, and salt to yeast mixture; stir until
a soft dough forms. Turn dough out onto a floured
surface. Knead until smooth and elastic (about 8
minutes); add enough of remaining ¼ cup bread
flour, 1 tablespoon at a time, to prevent dough from
sticking to hands (dough will feel sticky).
3. Place dough in a large bowl coated with cooking
spray; turn to coat top. Cover; let rise in a warm
place (85°), free from drafts, 45 minutes or until
doubled in size. (Press two fingers into dough. If
indentation remains, dough has risen enough.)
Punch dough down; cover and let rest 5 minutes.
Roll dough into a 14 x 7–inch rectangle on a floured
surface. Roll up tightly, starting with a long edge,
pressing firmly to eliminate air pockets; pinch
seam and ends to seal. Place roll, seam side down,
in a 9 x 5–inch loaf pan coated with cooking spray.
Coat top with cooking spray. Cover; let rise in a
warm place 30 minutes or until doubled in size.
(Press two fingers into dough. If indentation
remains, dough has risen enough.)
4. Preheat oven to 400°.
5. Bake at 400° for 1 hour or until lightly browned
on bottom and sounds hollow when tapped.
Remove from pan; brush with butter. Cool completely. **Yield:** 12 servings (serving size: 1 slice).

CALORIES 153; FAT 1.5g (sat 0.4g, mono 0.5g, poly 0.2g); PROTEIN 6.3g; CARB 29.8g; FIBER 3.2g;
CHOL 1mg; IRON 2mg; SODIUM 249mg; CALC 8mg

choiceingredient

Bananas

Bananas are one of those foods that almost
everybody loves, and not just for taste and
health reasons. Their elongated shape and sunny
color lend them to whimsy from banana harmoni-
cas to fake banana noses to Chiquita Banana and
her tutti-frutti hat—not to mention all those
cartoon characters slipping on banana peels.

However, bananas have a dark side, too. Left
out for a few days, their peels develop brown spots,
their firm pulp goes soft, even squishy. Overripe
bananas may not be the best for eating out of hand,
but when it comes to cooking, they couldn't be
better—they're easier to mash, sweeter (as the
fruit ripens, its starch turns to sugar), and have a
more intense flavor. When used in Banana-Rum-
Coconut Cookies (recipe on page 80) and Whole
Wheat Banana Bread (recipe at left), overripe
bananas become superstars. Ingredients such as
brown sugar, cinnamon, rum, and nutmeg give
bananas more complex flavor and show that they
don't always have to be mellow yellow.

This uses a small amount of coconut flour, which is slightly sweet, high in fiber (3 grams per tablespoon), and gluten-free. Look for it in health-food stores or order online from Bob's Red Mill (www.bobsredmill.com). You also can substitute an equal amount of all-purpose flour. Standard lemons work well in this recipe, but Meyer lemons, which have sweeter flavor, are a good substitute.

Piña Colada Cheesecake Bars

Crust:

1   cup graham cracker crumbs
2   tablespoons coconut flour or all-purpose flour
2   tablespoons turbinado sugar
½   teaspoon ground ginger
2   tablespoons butter, melted
1   tablespoon canola oil
1   tablespoon water
Cooking spray

Filling:

1   cup 2% low-fat cottage cheese
½   cup sugar
¼   cup (2 ounces) block-style fat-free
     cream cheese, softened
1½   tablespoons grated lemon rind
1   tablespoon fresh lemon juice
1   tablespoon pineapple juice
½   teaspoon vanilla extract
Dash of salt
¾   cup egg substitute

Remaining Ingredients:

1   cup chopped fresh pineapple
¼   cup unsweetened shredded
     coconut, toasted

1. Preheat oven to 350°.
2. To prepare crust, combine first 4 ingredients in a bowl. Add butter, oil, and 1 tablespoon water; toss well. Press mixture into the bottom of an 8-inch square baking pan coated with cooking spray. Bake at 350° for 10 minutes. Cool completely on a wire rack.
3. To prepare filling, place cottage cheese and next 7 ingredients in a food processor, and process until smooth. Add egg substitute, and process until blended. Spread cheese mixture over cooled crust. Bake at 350° for 33 minutes or until set. Cool 10 minutes on a wire rack. Refrigerate 2 hours or until thoroughly chilled. Top with pineapple and coconut. Cut into 16 bars. **Yield:** 16 servings (serving size: 1 bar).

CALORIES 117; FAT 4.6g (sat 2.2g, mono 1.2g, poly 0.7g); PROTEIN 4.1g; CARB 15.4g; FIBER 0.9g; CHOL 6mg; IRON 0.5mg; SODIUM 142mg; CALC 27mg

The dense base layer is like a rich, fudgy brownie, so don't overcook it or the dessert bars will be dry. Refrigerating the mint bars allows the chocolaty top layer to set properly. You can make the dessert up to one day ahead. For a more grown-up taste, you can also use dark chocolate chips for some or all of the semisweet chocolate chips in the glaze.

Chocolate-Mint Bars

Bottom Layer:

4.5 ounces all-purpose flour (about 1 cup)

½ teaspoon salt

1 cup granulated sugar

½ cup egg substitute

¼ cup butter, melted

2 tablespoons water

1 teaspoon vanilla extract

2 large eggs, beaten

1 (16-ounce) can chocolate syrup

Cooking spray

Mint Layer:

2 cups powdered sugar

¼ cup butter, melted

2 tablespoons fat-free milk

½ teaspoon peppermint extract

2 drops green food coloring

Glaze:

¾ cup semisweet chocolate chips

3 tablespoons butter

1. Preheat oven to 350°.

2. To prepare bottom layer, lightly spoon flour into a dry measuring cup; level with a knife. Combine flour and salt; stir with a whisk. Combine granulated sugar, egg substitute, ¼ cup melted butter, 2 tablespoons water, vanilla, eggs, and chocolate syrup in a medium bowl; stir until smooth. Add flour mixture to chocolate mixture, stirring until blended. Pour batter into a 13 x 9–inch baking pan coated with cooking spray. Bake at 350° for 23 minutes or until a wooden pick inserted in center comes out almost clean. Cool completely in pan on a wire rack.

3. To prepare mint layer, combine powdered sugar, ¼ cup melted butter, and next 3 ingredients in a medium bowl; beat with a mixer until smooth. Spread mint mixture over cooled cake.

4. To prepare glaze, combine chocolate chips and 3 tablespoons butter in a medium microwave-safe bowl. Microwave at HIGH 1 minute or until melted, stirring after 30 seconds. Let stand 2 minutes. Spread chocolate mixture evenly over top of cake. Cover and refrigerate until ready to serve. Cut into 20 bars. **Yield:** 20 servings (serving size: 1 bar).

CALORIES 264; FAT 8.7g (sat 5.2g, mono 2.5g, poly 0.4g); PROTEIN 2.8g; CARB 45g; FIBER 0.5g; CHOL 38mg; IRON 0.9mg; SODIUM 139mg; CALC 12mg

Rhubarb

Technically rhubarb is a vegetable, but we usually refer to it as "the first fruit of the season." And although hothouse rhubarb can be found year-round in some parts of the country, field-grown rhubarb peaks in the spring. Many favor the field-grown plant's more assertive flavor and deeper color.

To select: Choose thick, firm stalks with no wrinkling or other signs of drying. If there are leaves on the stalks, they should be fresh and unwilted (leaves must be discarded).

To store: Refrigerate fresh rhubarb in a plastic bag for up to three days. You can also chop rhubarb, place in a heavy-duty zip-top plastic bag, and freeze for up to eight months.

To prepare: Trim and discard any leaves. Wash stalks just before using. Rhubarb is almost always cooked—usually with a good amount of sugar to tame its sour taste, similar to the way cranberries are prepared.

To cook: Rhubarb fairs well in a variety of desserts. It's actually widely known by its nickname, pie plant. It can be diced and added to a coffee cake, or cooked into a sweet-sticky jam. Regardless of how it's stewed, rhubarb eventually disintegrates into a puree.

Rhubarb, which looks like crimson celery, has a short season so stock up while you can. It freezes beautifully; just store the stalks in a heavy-duty zip-top plastic bag. You can use fresh or frozen rhubarb for this recipe. We actually preferred unthawed frozen rhubarb.

Rhubarb Custard Bars

Crust:

6.75 ounces all-purpose flour (about 1½ cups)

½   cup sugar

⅛   teaspoon salt

9   tablespoons chilled butter, cut into small pieces

Cooking spray

Filling:

1.5   ounces all-purpose flour (about ⅓ cup)

1½   cups sugar

1½   cups 1% low-fat milk

3   large eggs

5   cups (½-inch) sliced fresh or frozen rhubarb (unthawed)

Topping:

½   cup sugar

½   cup (4 ounces) block-style fat-free cream cheese

½   cup (4 ounces) block-style ⅓-less-fat cream cheese

½   teaspoon vanilla extract

1   cup frozen fat-free whipped topping, thawed

Mint sprigs (optional)

1. Preheat oven to 350°.

2. To prepare crust, lightly spoon 1½ cups flour into dry measuring cups; level with a knife. Combine 1½ cups flour, ½ cup sugar, and salt in a bowl. Cut in butter with a pastry blender or 2 knives until mixture resembles coarse meal. Press into a 13 x 9–inch baking dish coated with cooking spray. Bake at 350° for 15 minutes or until crust is golden brown.

3. To prepare filling, lightly spoon ⅓ cup flour into a dry measuring cup; level with a knife. Combine ⅓ cup flour and 1½ cups sugar in a large bowl; add milk and eggs, stirring with a whisk until well blended. Stir in rhubarb, and pour mixture over crust. Bake at 350° for 40 minutes or until set. Cool to room temperature.

4. To prepare topping, place ½ cup sugar, cheeses, and vanilla in a bowl; beat with a mixer at medium speed until smooth. Gently fold in whipped topping; spread evenly over baked custard. Cover and chill at least 1 hour. Garnish with mint sprigs, if desired. **Yield:** 36 servings (serving size: 1 bar).

CALORIES 131; FAT 4.2g (sat 2.5g, mono 1.3g, poly 0.2g); PROTEIN 2.5g; CARB 21g; FIBER 0.5g; CHOL 29mg; IRON 0.4mg; SODIUM 78mg; CALC 42mg

Fresh mint leaves steep in fat-free milk to impart the herb's essence; the taste is much better than that of mint extract. Unless milk is stabilized with a thickener such as flour or cornstarch, it will "break," or curdle, when it becomes too hot; that's why it's important to go no higher than 180° at the beginning of step one.

Chocolate-Mint Pudding

3   cups fat-free milk
½   cup packed fresh mint leaves (about ½ ounce)
⅔   cup sugar
¼   cup cornstarch
3   tablespoons unsweetened cocoa
⅛   teaspoon salt
3   large egg yolks, lightly beaten
½   teaspoon vanilla extract
2   ounces semisweet chocolate, chopped
Mint sprigs (optional)

1. Heat milk over medium-high heat in a small, heavy saucepan to 180° or until tiny bubbles form around edge (do not boil). Remove from heat; add mint. Let stand 15 minutes; strain milk mixture through a sieve into a bowl, reserving milk. Discard solids. Return milk to pan; stir in sugar, cornstarch, cocoa, and salt. Return pan to medium heat; bring to a boil, stirring constantly with a whisk until mixture thickens.

2. Place egg yolks in a medium bowl; gradually add half of hot milk mixture, stirring constantly with a whisk. Add egg mixture to pan; bring to a boil, stirring constantly. Cook 1 minute or until thick. Remove from heat; add vanilla and chocolate, stirring until chocolate melts. Pour pudding into a bowl; cover surface of pudding with plastic wrap. Chill. Garnish with mint sprigs, if desired. **Yield:** 6 servings (serving size: about ⅔ cup).

CALORIES 227; FAT 6.4g (sat 3.2g, mono 2.5g, poly 0.4g); PROTEIN 6.7g; CARB 39.4g; FIBER 1.2g; CHOL 105mg; IRON 1.1mg; SODIUM 106mg; CALC 173mg

Make Stovetop Pudding

Most puddings contain starchy ingredients, such as cornstarch or flour, while others include rice, pasta, or bread as thickeners.

1. To prepare stovetop pudding, you'll need little more than a heavy saucepan, a whisk, a rubber spatula, and a little plastic wrap.

2. Most stovetop custard recipes combine dry ingredients, such as sugar and starch. This prevents the starch from clumping when it's added to the hot milk. Separately combine the eggs with a bit of milk or cream.

3. Tempering combines a hot liquid with a cool one and protects the delicate eggs from coagulating too quickly.

4. The pudding is thick enough if it coats the back of a spoon.

5. Butter enriches the flavor and texture of pudding. Add it and other ingredients, such as flavor extracts, that can suffer from exposure to heat after the custard cooks.

6. Place plastic wrap directly on the surface of the pudding to prevent a rubbery skin from forming on the top.

Meyer Lemon and Rosemary Brûlées

1   cup whole milk
½   cup evaporated fat-free milk
1   tablespoon grated Meyer lemon rind
1   teaspoon chopped fresh rosemary
½   cup sugar
3   large egg yolks
2   large eggs
¼   teaspoon vanilla extract
2   tablespoons sugar
Rosemary sprigs (optional)

1. Combine first 4 ingredients in a medium sauce-pan. Heat mixture over medium heat to 180° or until tiny bubbles form around edge (do not boil), stirring occasionally. Remove from heat. Cover; steep 10 minutes.

2. Preheat oven to 325°.

3. Combine ½ cup sugar, egg yolks, and eggs in a medium bowl, stirring with a whisk. Strain milk mixture through a sieve into egg mixture, stirring well with a whisk. Stir in vanilla. Return mixture to pan. Cook over medium-low heat 5 minutes or until mixture coats a spoon.

4. Divide mixture evenly among 4 (6-ounce) rame-kins. Place ramekins in a 13 x 9–inch baking pan; add hot water to pan to a depth of 1 inch.

5. Bake at 325° for 30 minutes or until center barely moves when ramekin is touched. Remove ramekins from pan; cool completely on a wire rack. Cover and chill at least 1 hour or overnight.

6. Sift 2 tablespoons sugar evenly over custards. Holding a kitchen blowtorch about 2 inches from top of each custard, heat sugar, moving torch back and forth, until sugar is completely melted and caramelized (about 1 minute). Garnish with rose-mary sprigs, if desired. Serve immediately. **Yield:** 4 servings (serving size: 1 brûlée).

CALORIES 261; FAT 7.9g (sat 3.2g, mono 2.9g, poly 1g); PROTEIN 9.5g; CARB 38.6g; FIBER 0.2g; CHOL 267mg; IRON 0.9mg; SODIUM 104mg; CALC 187mg

Meyer Lemons

Meyer lemons, a cross between regular lemons and a mandarin orange, were originally dis-covered by Frank Meyer, a U.S. agricultural explorer in China in the early 1900s. Today, most Meyer lem-ons are grown in California, Texas, and Florida.

With its smooth golden skin, the Meyer lemon has a rounder shape than its traditional lemon counter-part and is slightly sweeter and less acidic. Choosing a Meyer lemon over a traditional lemon is preferable when you want a burst of lemon flavor without the acidic bite.

When choosing Meyer lemons look for an orange-yellow rind that is a tell-tale sign that the fruit was fully ripened when picked. Look for a bright, shiny fruit, too. After a few days the fruit will begin to shrivel, and the rinds will become hard and dry.

Although Meyer lemon season begins in the win-ter, it extends into the spring and helps give a burst of sweet lemon flavor to early spring dishes. Squeeze the juice over fish and chicken, or add to a salad dressing. Grate the zest over steamed vegetables, or add to sweet foods such as marmalades, lemon bars, or beverages.

Strawberry
Granita

process until smooth. Pour mixture into an 8-inch square baking dish. Cover and freeze 3 hours; stir well. Cover and freeze 5 hours or overnight.

2. Remove mixture from freezer; let stand at room temperature 10 minutes. Scrape entire mixture with a fork until fluffy. Garnish with lemon rind, if desired. **Yield:** 4 servings (serving size: 1 cup).

CALORIES 136; FAT 0.5g (sat 0g, mono 0.1g, poly 0.2g); PROTEIN 0.8g; CARB 34.4g; FIBER 2.9g; CHOL 0mg; IRON 0.5mg; SODIUM 2mg; CALC 18mg

You can vary this simple dessert by using fresh tangerine, red grapefruit, or blood orange juice in place of the orange juice.

Citrusy Rhubarb Sorbet

4 cups chopped rhubarb (about 1¼ pounds)
1 cup water
⅔ cup sugar
½ cup fresh orange juice (about 2 large oranges)
Mint sprigs (optional)
Orange rind strips (optional)

1. Combine first 4 ingredients in a medium sauce-pan; bring to a boil. Reduce heat, and simmer 20 minutes or until rhubarb is tender. Cool slightly.
2. Place rhubarb mixture in a blender, and process until smooth. Pour into a bowl, and refrigerate 2 hours or until thoroughly chilled.
3. Pour mixture into the freezer can of an ice-cream freezer, and freeze according to manufac-turer's instructions.
4. Place a freezer-safe bowl in freezer 10 minutes. Spoon sorbet into bowl; cover and freeze 4 hours or until firm. Garnish with mint and rind, if desired. **Yield:** 5 servings (serving size: about ⅔ cup).

CALORIES 135; FAT 0.2g (sat 0.1g, mono 0g, poly 0.1g); PROTEIN 1.1g; CARB 33.7g; FIBER 1.8g; CHOL 0mg; IRON 0.3mg; SODIUM 4mg; CALC 87mg

This frozen dessert requires no ice-cream maker—just freeze the mixture in a pan, and scrape with a fork. If you'd like to spruce up the granita, top with chopped or halved fresh strawberries and grated lemon zest.

Strawberry Granita

½ cup sugar
½ cup warm water
3 cups sliced strawberries
2 tablespoons fresh lemon juice
Lemon rind strips (optional)

1. Place sugar and water in a blender; process until sugar dissolves. Add strawberries and juice;

Citrusy Rhubarb Sorbet

If you don't feel like weaving the dough strips through one another for the lattice topping, just arrange 6 dough strips over the pie; lay the other 6 strips perpendicular to the first strips without weaving.

Lattice-Topped Rhubarb Pie

Crust:

7.9 ounces all-purpose flour (about 1¾ cups)

3 tablespoons sugar

⅛ teaspoon salt

¼ cup cold unsalted butter, cut into small pieces

3 tablespoons vegetable shortening

5 tablespoons ice water

Cooking spray

Filling:

6 cups (1-inch-thick) slices rhubarb (about 1½ pounds)

1 cup sugar

3 tablespoons cornstarch

1½ teaspoons grated orange rind

¼ teaspoon ground nutmeg

Remaining Ingredients:

1½ teaspoons 1% low-fat milk

1 tablespoon sugar

1. To prepare crust, lightly spoon flour into dry measuring cups; level with a knife. Combine flour, 3 tablespoons sugar, and salt in a large bowl; cut in butter and shortening with a pastry blender or 2 knives until mixture resembles coarse meal. Sprinkle surface with ice water, 1 tablespoon at a time; toss with a fork until moist and crumbly (do not form a ball).

2. Gently press two-thirds of dough into a 4-inch circle on heavy-duty plastic wrap, and cover with additional plastic wrap. Roll dough into a 12-inch circle. Press remaining dough into a 4-inch circle on heavy-duty plastic wrap, and cover with additional plastic wrap. Roll dough into a 9-inch circle. Freeze both dough portions 10 minutes or until plastic wrap can be easily removed.

3. Preheat oven to 425°.

4. Remove 1 sheet of plastic wrap from 12-inch dough circle; fit dough, plastic-wrap side up, into a 9-inch pie plate coated with cooking spray, allowing dough to extend over edge of plate. Remove top sheet of plastic wrap; fold edges under, and flute.

5. To prepare filling, combine rhubarb and next 4 ingredients, tossing well to combine. Spoon filling into crust.

6. Remove top sheet of plastic wrap from remaining dough. Cut dough into 12 (¾-inch) strips. Gently remove dough strips from bottom sheet of plastic wrap, and arrange in a lattice design over rhubarb mixture. Seal dough strips to edge of crust. Brush top and edges of dough with milk, and sprinkle with 1 tablespoon sugar. Place pie on a baking sheet covered with foil. Bake at 425° for 15 minutes. Reduce oven temperature to 375° (do not remove pie from oven), and bake an additional 30 minutes or until golden (shield crust with foil if it gets too brown). Cool on a wire rack. **Yield:** 10 servings (serving size: 1 wedge).

CALORIES 276; FAT 8.8g (sat 3.9g, mono 3.1g, poly 1.3g); PROTEIN 3g; CARB 47.3g; FIBER 2g; CHOL 12mg; IRON 1.2mg; SODIUM 34mg; CALC 69mg

Classic strawberry pie is updated with a splash of balsamic vinegar.

Spring Strawberry Pie

Crust:

1⅓ cups graham cracker crumbs

3 tablespoons butter, melted

2 tablespoons sugar

Cooking spray

Filling:

2 cups sliced strawberries

2 tablespoons balsamic vinegar

¼ cup sugar

2 tablespoons water

2 teaspoons cornstarch

1 tablespoon fresh lemon juice

6 cups small strawberries

Topping:

3 tablespoons graham cracker crumbs

1 tablespoon chopped hazelnuts or almonds

1½ teaspoons sugar

1½ teaspoons butter, melted

½ cup frozen reduced-calorie whipped topping, thawed

1. Preheat oven to 350°.

2. To prepare crust, combine first 3 ingredients in a bowl, tossing with a fork until moist. Press into bottom and up sides of a 9-inch pie plate coated with cooking spray. Bake at 350° for 15 minutes, and cool on a wire rack.

3. To prepare filling, combine strawberry slices and vinegar in a medium nonstick skillet. Place berry mixture over medium-high heat; cook 3 minutes, stirring occasionally. Stir in ¼ cup sugar. Combine water and cornstarch in a small bowl. Add to pan, and bring to a boil. Cook 1 minute, stirring constantly. Remove from heat; stir in juice. Cool completely. Arrange whole strawberries, stem sides down, in crust. Pour cooled strawberry mixture over whole strawberries. Cover loosely, and chill 4 hours.

4. To prepare topping, combine 3 tablespoons cracker crumbs, nuts, 1½ teaspoons sugar, and 1½ teaspoons melted butter in a small bowl. Place crumb mixture in a small skillet over medium heat. Cook 2 minutes or until golden brown; cool. Sprinkle crumb mixture over pie. Top each serving with whipped topping. **Yield:** 8 servings (serving size: 1 wedge and 1 tablespoon whipped topping).

CALORIES 229; FAT 8.8g (sat 4.1g, mono 2.8g, poly 1.4g); PROTEIN 2.3g; CARB 37g; FIBER 3.5g; CHOL 14mg; IRON 1.4mg; SODIUM 176mg; CALC 34mg

Prepare the crust and filling up to two days ahead; assemble the morning of your brunch. You'll have extra glaze—try it on ice cream or pound cake.

Strawberry-Almond Cream Tart

Crust:

36 honey graham crackers (about 9 sheets)
2 tablespoons sugar
2 tablespoons butter, melted
4 teaspoons water
Cooking spray

Filling:

2/3 cup light cream cheese
1/4 cup sugar
1/2 teaspoon vanilla extract
1/4 teaspoon almond extract

Topping:

6 cups small fresh strawberries, divided
2/3 cup sugar
1 tablespoon cornstarch
1 tablespoon fresh lemon juice
2 tablespoons sliced almonds, toasted

1. Preheat oven to 350°.
2. To prepare crust, place crackers in a food processor; process until crumbly. Add 2 tablespoons sugar, butter, and water; pulse just until moist. Place mixture in a 9-inch round removable-bottom tart pan coated with cooking spray, pressing into bottom and up sides of pan to ¾ inch. Bake at 350° for 10 minutes or until lightly browned. Cool completely on a wire rack.
3. To prepare filling, combine cream cheese, ¼ cup sugar, and extracts in a medium bowl; stir until smooth. Spread mixture evenly over bottom of tart shell.
4. To prepare topping, place 2 cups strawberries in food processor; process until pureed. Combine strawberry puree, ⅔ cup sugar, and cornstarch in a small saucepan over medium heat, stirring with a whisk. Bring to a boil, stirring constantly. Reduce heat to low; cook 1 minute. Remove glaze from heat, and cool to room temperature, stirring occasionally.
5. Combine remaining 4 cups strawberries and lemon juice; toss to coat. Arrange berries, bottoms up, in a circular pattern over filling. Spoon half of glaze evenly over berries (reserve remaining glaze for another use). Sprinkle nuts around edge. Cover and chill 3 hours. **Yield:** 10 servings.

Note: You can use either an 8 x 12–inch rectangular pan or a 9-inch round tart pan. The recipe also works with a 9-inch springform pan and a 10-inch pie plate.

CALORIES 289; FAT 8.9g (sat 4.2g, mono 1.7g, poly 0.5g); PROTEIN 4.5g; CARB 48.7g; FIBER 3g; CHOL 15mg; IRON 1.3mg; SODIUM 242mg; CALC 59mg

summer

the summer kitchen

For anyone who enjoys food and cooking, summer offers the finest ingredients—fresh local produce from the garden, farmers' market, and grocery—to make any dish superlative. The key is to keep things simple and let the quality of seasonal ingredients shine through.

Crowd-pleasing classics such as Fresh Cherry Cobbler (recipe on page 220), Tomato Flatbread with Goat Cheese (recipe on page 126), and Watermelon Cooler (recipe on page 114) take advantage of summer's best produce at its peak ripeness. You'll also find recipes that feature ingredients in unexpected ways. Grilled Shrimp Kebabs with Summer Fruit Salsa (recipe on page 154) and Peppered Pork Tenderloin with Blue Cheese Plums (recipe on page 163) combine the sweetness of fruits with savory flavors of the entrées. Corn's natural sweetness is a pleasing complement to the fish in Grilled Salmon with Roasted Corn Relish (recipe on page 154)—a simple weeknight meal.

There are plenty of options that mean less time in the kitchen and more time for summer fun. With the wonderful selection of fresh fruits and vegetables available this season, there's something for every occasion. Fried Green Tomato BLTs (recipe on page 146), Fresh-Squeezed Lemonade (recipe on page 113), and Black-Eyed Pea Salsa (recipe on page 121) combine for easy picnic fare. And don't forget dessert—Fresh Blueberry Sauce (recipe on page 194), when chilled, is ideal over pound cake or ice cream, but it's also equally nice served warm over pancakes or waffles for breakfast. Whatever upcoming events you may have—a poolside cookout or just a lazy day at home—fresh seasonal foods will help you make the most of summertime mealtimes.

Unlike any other season, summer is marked by the arrival of fresh corn, juicy peaches, vine-ripened tomatoes, and sweet watermelons. It's so easy, enjoyable, and affordable to indulge your cravings for fresh fruits and vegetables this time of year.

fruits

Blackberries
Blueberries
Boysenberries
Cantaloupes
Casaba Melons
Cherries
Crenshaw Melons
Grapes
Guava
Honeydew Melons
Mangoes
Nectarines
Papayas
Peaches
Plums
Raspberries
Strawberries
Watermelons

··············

vegetables

Avocados
Beets
Bell Peppers
Cabbage
Carrots
Celery
Chile Peppers
Collards
Corn
Cucumbers
Eggplant
Green Beans
Jicama
Lima Beans
Okra
Pattypan Squash
Peas
Radicchio
Radishes
Summer Squash
Tomatoes

··············

herbs

Basil
Bay Leaves
Borage
Chives
Cilantro
Dill
Lavender
Lemon Verbena
Marjoram
Mint
Oregano
Rosemary
Sage
Summer Savory
Tarragon
Thyme

summer

From crisp summer salads to grilled burgers and peach ice cream, here are some ideas for staples, seasonings, and other ingredients ideally suited for backyard barbecues, family picnics, and warm sunny days.

Bottled Sauces and Marinades: When grilling in the summer, two items are essential—bottled sauces and marinades. Whether you buy them from the store or make your own, no grilled entrée is complete without them. Flavors vary from sweet to spicy and everywhere in between. And they vary by region, too, from American to Asian and Caribbean to Mexican. Keep these on hand, and you're ready to grill!

Feta Cheese: Often referred to as a pickled cheese, feta is a classic Greek cheese that adds depth to summer salads, burgers, or even Roasted Corn, Pepper, and Tomato Chowder (recipe on page 132).

Herbed Butters: Butter, when paired with the fresh herbs of the season, is great for topping potatoes, steak, or homemade breads.

Herbs: Hands down, fresh herbs are the one thing that can add the most flavor to your summertime dishes. Cultivate your own, or purchase them from your local market. Some of our summer favorites include basil, cilantro, and oregano.

Limes: Limes enhance sweet and savory summer dishes. By adding a zing of tartness, limes offset the intense spiciness or sweetness, depending on the dish.

Pastas: Bowtie, rotini, and fusilli pastas are popular in the summer. Pasta salads highlight fresh summer produce such as tomatoes, summer squash (including zucchini), and bell peppers. Just toss and go!

Rubs: Create complex taste sensations by applying simple herb-and-spice rubs to fish, poultry, meats, and vegetables. You can prepare rubs in advance so when it's time for dinner, prep is minimal. Or, you can save more time by purchasing rubs at the store.

Salsas: From chip dunking to taco topping, salsa makes a party complete. Much like sauces and marinades, salsas are essential, whether they're store-bought or prepared fresh at home.

Vanilla: When you think about summer, you think of vanilla ice cream, right? But just about any summer dessert will benefit from a splash of vanilla, too.

White Balsamic Vinegar: Salads and dressings benefit from the light crispness of white balsamic vinegar. It's a welcome change from traditional balsamic vinegar.

Wood Chips: The type of chip you choose for barbecuing helps determine the flavor of your food. Oak and hickory complement beef, lamb, and pork, while milder woods such as applewood, pecan, and alder are perfect pairs for fish and chicken.

best ways to cook

Stir-frying and grilling are two cooking techniques that help to make the most of summer's seasonal ingredients. Nothing says summer quite like stir-fried bell peppers, grilled corn on the cob, or peaches.

Stir-Frying

Stir-frying is one of the fastest and healthiest cooking methods. It's also easy, so even a novice in the kitchen will feel confident using this technique. The secret is to have all your ingredients cut, measured, and next to the stovetop. Once the oil is heated in the wok or pan, add the bite-sized pieces of food, and simply toss and turn them over high heat. In five minutes or less, the work is done. Be sure not to crowd the wok or pan so you have plenty of room to toss the ingredients and to sauté in batches, if needed. Vegetables emerge crisp and bright, while meats cook up flavorful, tender, and well seared.

Best Bets for Stir-Frying

It's ideal for most vegetables to be cut into thin, bite-sized pieces, especially those with high moisture content, such as summer squash and bell peppers. Denser vegetables like broccoli work well, too, but they may need to either be blanched first or allowed to steam briefly with a little liquid after the initial stir-frying to become tender. Leafy greens such as spinach cook in seconds once they hit the hot oil.

Tender cuts of meat such as chicken breasts, flank steak, or pork tenderloin stir-fry beautifully when cut into thin, bite-sized strips. Avoid large or tough chunks of pork shoulder, beef stew meat, or other cuts that require long, slow cooking to become tender. Shrimp, scallops, and firm-fleshed fish such as halibut work well, but delicate, flaky fish such as flounder or tilapia can fall apart.

Grilling

Grilling is a fun, casual, versatile cooking technique that creates charred edges, tell-tale grill marks, and smoky, robust tastes with minimal effort—the heat of the fire does all the work. And all these delicious qualities come with little or no added fat, making this one of the easiest and most healthful cooking methods.

What Grilling Does

Grilling adds a whole new taste sensation to vegetables, especially when they take on a char-grilled flavor and appearance. Depending on the recipe, you can either grill the vegetables first, and then slice them, or you can slice them first. The best vegetables to grill are sturdy ones such as eggplant, yellow squash, zucchini, tomatoes, bell peppers, potatoes, and onions.

Best Bets for Grilling

It works wonders with all types of meat, poultry, and seafood, as well as vegetables, fruits, and some desserts. Grilling is a go-to option for busy cooks because small, thin cuts such as skinless, boneless chicken breasts or fish fillets grill up in a flash. Larger cuts such as bone-in pork shoulder or whole chickens also fare nicely over longer periods of time on the grill.

Fruit is perfect for grilling because it's so simple to prepare. With most fruits, you just need to halve them and place them on the grill. Firm fruits hold up best, while softer fruits may require a little more attention. Be careful, though—soft fruits can become mushy if overcooked.

extend the season
In late summer, the season's most precious jewels—sparkling raspberries, fluorescent-hued peppers, and crisp cucumbers—are here today and gone tomorrow. However, with a little planning you can extend the season by preserving and freezing summer produce.

Preserve the Best

To prepare preserves, jam, or chutney, use the best fruit you can find. Whether you're at the supermarket, the local farmers' market, or out in the berry patch, there's one rule for picking the best produce: Smell it. If it lacks fragrance, it probably lacks taste.

Preserving Primer

Here are some of the differences among the types of preserves.

Chutney: A fruit-based condiment that includes a mélange of aromatics (such as onion and ginger) and vinegar, sometimes with fiery heat. It's best with roasted or grilled meats.

Jam: A whole-fruit preserve in which the fruit is cooked until it breaks down, but the pulp is not strained out. Thinned with water, it can be used as a glaze on chicken breasts or pork loin.

Relish: A vinegary condiment, often called pickle relish. Mix a little with fat-free mayonnaise for a spread on wraps and sandwiches, or spoon onto field peas.

Contain Yourself

Refrigerator preserving is simpler than traditional canning because there's no need to process and seal the jars, but you still must store the goodies in nonreactive, airtight containers. The best containers to use are glass canning jars, found in large supermarkets and some hardware stores. You can also forgo the glass jars and use stainless steel bowls or plastic containers with tight-fitting lids. Avoid reactive metals, such as aluminum, copper, and cast iron—when they come in contact with acidic ingredients, they often give the food an unpleasant metallic flavor. Store containers in the refrigerator for two weeks to two months, depending on the recipe.

Freezing Freshness

Use your freezer as another way to extend the season. It's ideal for stocking up on seasonal foods—both fruits and vegetables. When sealed properly, both fruits and vegetables will keep in the freezer for 6 to 12 months.

Vegetable Tips

- Select vegetables at their peak of texture and flavor.

- Blanching (cooking briefly in boiling water) is essential. This process inactivates enzymes in vegetables, helping to retain color, texture, flavor, and nutrients. Blanching times will differ by vegetable. The easiest way to blanch vegetables is to place them in a wire or metal colander or blanching basket. Lower the colander or basket into boiling water, making sure the vegetables are completely immersed. Carefully remove the colander or basket from boiling water when blanching is complete.

- Use good-quality freezer containers or bags for maximum quality. A good seal is essential to keep air out and moisture in. We prefer zip-top plastic freezer bags.

Berry Tips

To freeze fresh berries such as blackberries, blueberries, and raspberries, spread them out in a single layer on a baking sheet, and freeze until firm. Then you can transfer them to smaller containers and use them for smoothies, sauces, or desserts that call for frozen berries. Measure the amount of berries by the cupful as you transfer them to containers, and record this information on a label.

Lemon verbena infuses the lightly sweetened iced tea with sunny citrus flavor. You can also use the fragrant syrup to enliven cocktails or moisten pound cake. Blanching the herb leaves brightens their color so the syrup will stay green. Avoid using a strongly flavored tea, such as Earl Grey, as it will overpower the taste of the syrup.

Lemon Verbena Iced Tea

½ cup sugar
½ cup water
1 cup fresh lemon verbena leaves
4 cups ice
6 cups brewed tea, chilled
Mint leaves (optional)
Lemon wedges (optional)

1. Combine sugar and water in a small saucepan; bring to a boil. Cook 1 minute or until sugar dissolves. Cool sugar syrup completely.
2. Cook lemon verbena leaves in boiling water 1 minute. Drain and plunge into ice water; drain.
3. Place sugar syrup and verbena leaves in a blender; process until smooth. Cover and chill overnight. Strain sugar syrup through a fine sieve into a bowl. Place ⅔ cup ice into each of 6 tall glasses; add 1 cup brewed tea and 2 tablespoons sugar syrup to each serving, stirring to combine. Garnish with mint leaves and lemon wedges, if desired. **Yield: 6 servings.**

CALORIES 67; FAT 0g; PROTEIN 0g; CARB 17.4g; FIBER 0g; CHOL 0mg; IRON 0mg; SODIUM 7mg; CALC 0mg

choiceingredient

Lemon Verbena

This lemon-scented herb, also simply called verbena, is best suited for summer beverages, particularly when combined with fresh mint. However, it's also ideal for adding a citrus burst to fish, chicken, marinades and dressings, jellies, vinegars, and fruit salads. We think nothing is more refreshing on a hot day than a tall glass of sweet tea with just the right amount of tart lemon flavor, such as Lemon Verbena Iced Tea (recipe on page 110)—especially when sipped in a rocking chair on the front porch. Sprigs can be harvested all summer long, but to continue growth you'll want to cut back your plants mid-summer for a greater bounty. Be sure to use this aromatic herb sparingly, as it is potent and can easily overpower your recipe if too much is used. As with all herbs, using lemon verbena is an easy way to add lots of flavor without adding significant amounts of fat, calories, or sodium.

Fresh-Squeezed Lemonade

This quintessential summer drink never becomes outdated. Not too tart, not too sweet, not too watery—it's the perfect recipe for lemonade. To get the most juice out of your lemons, bring the lemons to room temperature before juicing.

Fresh-Squeezed Lemonade

3   cups fresh lemon juice (about 20 lemons)
2 ¼ cups sugar
12 cups chilled water
Lemon slices (optional)

1. Combine juice and sugar in a one-gallon container; stir until sugar dissolves. Stir in water. Serve over ice. Garnish with lemon slices, if desired. **Yield:** 16 servings (serving size: 1 cup).

CALORIES 120; FAT 0g; PROTEIN 0.2g; CARB 32.1g; FIBER 0.2g; CHOL 0mg; IRON 0.1mg; SODIUM 6mg; CALC 7mg

A blackberry-lime infused summer cooler is great to bring along on a picnic or to serve at a backyard party. Pour over ice, if desired.

Blackberry Limeade

6   cups water, divided
3   cups fresh blackberries
1   cup sugar
⅔ cup fresh lime juice (about 4 limes)
8   thin lime slices
Fresh blackberries (optional)

1. Place 1 cup water and 3 cups blackberries in a blender; process until smooth. Press blackberry puree through a sieve into a large pitcher; discard seeds. Add remaining 5 cups water, sugar, and juice to pitcher; stir until sugar dissolves. Place 1 lime slice and a few blackberries, if desired, into each of 8 glasses; pour about 1 cup limeade over each serving. **Yield:** 8 servings.

CALORIES 125; FAT 0.3g (sat 0g, mono 0g, poly 0.2g); PROTEIN 0.8g; CARB 31.9g; FIBER 0.7g; CHOL 0mg; IRON 0.4mg; SODIUM 5mg; CALC 22mg

Blackberry Limeade

Make this drink ahead, and keep refrigerated for up to three days. Garnish with mint and lime slices. Add 1½ ounces vodka or white rum per serving, if desired.

Watermelon Cooler

8   cups chopped seedless watermelon
     (about 3¼ pounds)
1   cup fresh lime juice (about 6 limes)
½   cup sugar
½   cup water
Dash of salt
Mint sprigs (optional)
Lime slices (optional)

1. Place half of watermelon in a blender; process until smooth. Strain watermelon through a sieve into a pitcher; discard solids. Repeat procedure with remaining watermelon. Stir in lime juice, sugar, ½ cup water, and dash of salt. Serve over ice. Garnish with mint and lime, if desired. **Yield:** 6 servings (serving size: 1 cup).

CALORIES 136; FAT 0.3g (sat 0g, mono 0.1g, poly 0.1g); PROTEIN 1.4g; CARB 35.4g; FIBER 1g; CHOL 0mg; IRON 0.5mg; SODIUM 28mg; CALC 20mg

Watermelon

You can find fresh watermelons between May and September, but they are at their peak from mid-June to late August.

To select: Choose a firm, symmetrical, unblemished melon with a dull rind, without cracks or soft spots, that barely yields to pressure. Some people swear by the "thump" test, but experts say that method is unreliable for determining ripeness. Rather, look for a pale yellow patch, indicating where the watermelon sat on the ground while ripening on the vine.

To store: Store uncut watermelon at room temperature up to one week. If serving it chilled, refrigerate 8 to 10 hours.

To prepare: Wash and dry the rind before cutting to prevent bacterial contamination. Once sliced, cover with plastic wrap; refrigerate up to four days (longer exposure to the cold will turn the flesh mushy).

Health benefits: Watermelons are a great source of cancer-fighting lycopene, and they also provide vitamins A and C. One wedge (approximately one-sixteenth of a watermelon) has 1.4 grams of fiber and no cholesterol.

Peach Mojitos

1. Place peaches in a blender or food processor; process until smooth. Press peach puree through a fine sieve into a bowl; discard solids.
2. Combine rind, lime juice, sugar, and mint in a large pitcher; crush juice mixture with back of a long spoon. Add peach puree and rum to pitcher, stirring until sugar dissolves. Stir in club soda. Serve over crushed ice. Garnish with mint sprigs, if desired. **Yield:** 10 servings (serving size: about ⅔ cup).

CALORIES 186; FAT 0.1g (sat 0g, mono 0g, poly 0.1g); PROTEIN 0.6g; CARB 21.6g; FIBER 0.9g; CHOL 0mg; IRON 0.3mg; SODIUM 21mg; CALC 14mg

Few drinks help beat the heat like the mojito. Fizzy, sweet-tart, and minty, the classic Cuban cocktail refreshes from the first sip. Fresh peach puree forms the base of this sweet-juicy version. Use a wooden muddler to crush the mint mixture in the pitcher, if available. The procedure releases the mint's essential oils, melding them with the lime juice.

Peach Mojitos

3   cups coarsely chopped peeled ripe peaches (about 1 pound)
1   teaspoon grated lime rind
1   cup fresh lime juice (about 4 large limes)
¾   cup sugar
½   cup packed mint leaves
2   cups white rum
4   cups club soda, chilled
Crushed ice
Mint sprigs (optional)

Juicy summer fruits create a beverage that's as beautiful as it is delicious. Cava is a Spanish sparkling wine with less acidity than Champagne; you may substitute another sparkling wine, such as prosecco, if you prefer. Top each beverage with a fresh mint sprig for a fragrant garnish.

Sparkling Sangria

1   cup fresh cherries, pitted and halved
1   cup fresh blueberries
1   cup fresh raspberries
1   cup quartered small fresh strawberries
½   cup chopped fresh nectarine (about 1)
⅓   cup brandy
1   cup apricot nectar, chilled
1   (750-milliliter) bottle Cava, chilled
Mint sprigs (optional)

1. Combine first 6 ingredients in a large pitcher, and chill at least 2 hours. Stir in 1 cup nectar and wine. Serve immediately. Garnish with mint sprigs, if desired. **Yield:** 8 servings (serving size: 1 cup).

CALORIES 153; FAT 0.5g (sat 0.1g, mono 0.1g, poly 0.2g); PROTEIN 0.9g; CARB 17g; FIBER 2.7g; CHOL 0mg; IRON 0.5mg; SODIUM 2mg; CALC 13mg

Sparkling Sangria

Roast Bell Peppers

Red, yellow, and orange bell peppers are virtually identical in flavor and are inter-changeable. Green peppers aren't as sweet, so keep this in mind when making substitutions. One large bell pepper (about 8 ounces), roasted, yields about ½ cup chopped.

1. Cut bell peppers in half length-wise, and discard seeds and membranes. Place pepper halves, skin sides up, on a foil-lined baking sheet; flatten with hand.

2. Broil until skins are thoroughly blackened.

3. Immediately place peppers in a large zip-top plastic bag; seal. Let stand 20 minutes.

4. Peel peppers, and discard skins. Chop peppers, and refrigerate in an airtight container until ready to use.

For convenience, prepare the dip up to three days in advance and refrigerate in an airtight container. Serve with pita wedges and bell pepper strips.

Red Pepper Hummus

½ cup chopped roasted red bell peppers (page 118)

2 ½ tablespoons fresh lemon juice

1 tablespoon tahini (sesame seed paste)

½ teaspoon freshly ground black pepper

¼ teaspoon salt

¼ teaspoon ground cumin

1 (19-ounce) can chickpeas (garbanzo beans), rinsed and drained

1 garlic clove, quartered

1. Place all ingredients in a food processor; process until smooth. **Yield: 2 cups (serving size: ⅓ cup).**

CALORIES 94; FAT 3g (sat 0.2g, mono 1.1g, poly 1.6g); PROTEIN 3.7g; CARB 14.1g; FIBER 3.7g; CHOL 0mg; IRON 1.3mg; SODIUM 209mg; CALC 30mg

A basket of fresh produce is the inspiration for this summertime starter. Roasted garlic paste comes in a tube, which makes it easy to squeeze out just the amount you need. Look for it in the spice section of the supermarket. Use a 10-ounce package of frozen baby lima beans if you can't find fresh ones. Serve with summer vegetable crudités such as whole radishes, baby carrots, endive leaves, zucchini slices, and yellow squash strips.

Garlicky Lima Bean Spread

2   cups fresh lima beans
⅓   cup fresh parsley leaves
⅓   cup water
1   tablespoon fresh lemon juice
1   tablespoon olive oil
2   teaspoons roasted garlic paste
½   teaspoon salt
¼   teaspoon freshly ground black pepper
¼   teaspoon hot sauce

1. Sort and wash beans; drain and place in a medium saucepan. Cover with water to 2 inches above beans; bring to a boil. Cover, reduce heat, and simmer 20 minutes or until tender. Drain.
2. Place beans and remaining ingredients in a food processor; process until smooth. **Yield:** 8 servings (serving size: 3 tablespoons).

CALORIES 67; FAT 1.8g (sat 0.3g, mono 1.2g, poly 0.3g); PROTEIN 2.9g; CARB 10.2g; FIBER 2.3g; CHOL 0mg; IRON 1.2mg; SODIUM 157mg; CALC 18mg

Organic tomatoes bring the best flavor to this recipe. I pick them straight from my garden, but you can substitute canned diced tomatoes.

—Judy Holder, Elk City, OK

Black-Eyed Pea Salsa

½   teaspoon fine sea salt
1   garlic clove, minced
¼   cup rice wine vinegar
2   tablespoons roasted garlic extra-virgin olive oil (such as Consorzio)
1   teaspoon ground cumin
3   cups chopped peeled tomato (about 2 large)
½   cup finely chopped onion
2   tablespoons chopped fresh cilantro
1   (15-ounce) can black-eyed peas, rinsed and drained
1   jalapeño pepper, seeded and minced
1   (6-ounce) bag baked pita chips (such as Stacy's)

1. Combine salt and garlic in a medium bowl; mash with a fork until a paste consistency. Add vinegar, oil, and cumin, stirring with a whisk. Add tomato and next 4 ingredients; toss well. Serve with pita chips. **Yield:** 6 servings (serving size: about ¾ cup salsa and 1 ounce chips).

CALORIES 228; FAT 10.1g (sat 1.2g, mono 6.4g, poly 2g); PROTEIN 5.5g; CARB 30.6g; FIBER 4.6g; CHOL 0mg; IRON 2mg; SODIUM 573mg; CALC 12mg

The three-cheese filling is a nice complement for the spicy peppers. You can also use a milder chile, such as a cherry pepper. Shredded Cheddar cheese can take the place of Parmesan, if you like.

Grilled Pepper Poppers

½   cup (4 ounces) soft goat cheese
½   cup (4 ounces) fat-free cream cheese, softened
½   cup (2 ounces) grated fresh Parmesan cheese
½   cup finely chopped seeded tomato
2   tablespoons thinly sliced green onions
2   tablespoons chopped fresh sage
½   teaspoon kosher salt
16 jalapeño peppers, halved lengthwise and seeded (about 1½ pounds)
Cooking spray
2   tablespoons chopped fresh cilantro

1. Prepare grill to medium-high heat.
2. Combine first 7 ingredients in a bowl, stirring well. Spoon about 2 teaspoons cheese mixture into each pepper half. Place pepper halves, cheese side up, on grill rack coated with cooking spray. Grill peppers 5 minutes or until bottoms of peppers are charred and cheese mixture is lightly browned. Carefully place peppers on a serving platter. Sprinkle with cilantro. **Yield:** 16 servings (serving size: 2 pepper halves).

CALORIES 84; FAT 4.8g (sat 3.1g, mono 1.2g, poly 0.2g); PROTEIN 7.1g; CARB 3.5g; FIBER 0.9g; CHOL 11mg; IRON 0.6mg; SODIUM 334mg; CALC 117mg

Hot Chile Peppers

Fresh, locally grown hot chiles abound in warm months, so summer is a good time to explore the warm-climate cuisines of Mexico, Thailand, India, and North Africa. Although chile peppers are a global ingredient, they are indigenous to the New World, where they've been used for more than 6,000 years. Of the hundreds of varieties, some of the most common in the United States are Anaheim, banana, cayenne, habanero, jalapeño, poblano, serrano, and Thai.

Chile peppers should be firm, smooth, shiny, and strongly scented. A good rule of thumb when selecting chiles: The smaller the chile, the hotter it is. If you want to tame a chile's heat, remove the seeds and veins. Avoid wiping your eyes or nose after handling hot peppers, as the capsaicin (the compound responsible for chiles' fire) can burn your skin. In our Test Kitchens, we often wear latex gloves when handling chiles.

Peel and Seed a Cucumber

Cucumbers add a cool, refreshing crispness to salads and entrées. When shopping for cucumbers, look for blemish-free cucumbers with a dark green exterior. Softening first occurs at the ends, so feel the fruit to make sure it's fresh and firm. If you're buying from a supermarket, wash the cucumber first with a vegetable brush before cutting; most have a waxy coating. Follow these tips for seeding. If you prefer to leave the skin intact (it adds a little extra crunch), skip step one.

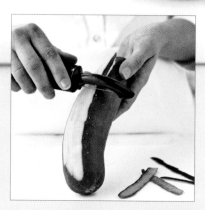

1. Remove the skin with a vegetable peeler.

2. Cut about ½ inch from each end. Slice cucumber in half lengthwise.

3. Scrape out the seeds using a spoon.

Instead of using watercress, try adding baby lettuce greens, or thinly sliced poached chicken breast.

Cucumber Tea Sandwiches with Mint-Chile Butter

6   tablespoons butter, softened
3   tablespoons chopped fresh mint
¼   teaspoon salt
1   serrano chile, seeded and finely chopped
12 (1-ounce) slices white sandwich bread
1½ cups thinly sliced English cucumber
1   tablespoon fresh lime juice
1   cup trimmed fresh watercress

1. Combine first 4 ingredients, stirring until well combined.

2. Trim crusts from bread; discard crusts. Spread each bread slice with about 1½ teaspoons butter mixture. Place cucumber in a small bowl, and drizzle with lime juice; toss to coat. Arrange cucumber slices and watercress in even layers over buttered sides of 6 bread slices; top with remaining bread slices, buttered side down. Cut sandwiches diagonally into quarters. **Yield:** 12 servings (serving size: 2 sandwich quarters).

CALORIES 89; FAT 6.2g (sat 3.6g, mono 1.5g, poly 0.2g); PROTEIN 1.2g; CARB 7.9g; FIBER 0.4g; CHOL 15mg; IRON 0.4mg; SODIUM 163mg; CALC 25mg

Serve with salad for a light lunch, or offer as an appetizer at your next outdoor party. Choose different colors of tomatoes for the most striking presentation.

Tomato Flatbread with Goat Cheese

1   package dry yeast (about 2¼ teaspoons)

¾   cup warm water (100° to 110°)

1.25 ounces all-purpose flour (about 2½ cups)

1¼   teaspoons salt

½   teaspoon freshly ground black pepper

2   tablespoons olive oil

Cooking spray

3   medium heirloom tomatoes (about 1¼ pounds), cut into ⅛-inch-thick slices

1   cup (4 ounces) crumbled goat cheese

1   tablespoon chopped fresh chives

1   tablespoon chopped fresh parsley

8   basil leaves

Freshly ground black pepper (optional)

1. Dissolve yeast in ¾ cup warm water in a small bowl; let stand 5 minutes or until bubbly. Weigh or lightly spoon flour into dry measuring cups; level with a knife. Combine flour, salt, and ½ teaspoon pepper in a large bowl; make a well in center of mixture. Add yeast mixture to flour mixture; stir just until moist. Add oil, and stir until a dough forms. Turn dough out onto a lightly floured surface. Knead until smooth and elastic (about 10 minutes). Place dough in a large bowl coated with cooking spray, turning to coat top. Cover and let rise in a warm place (85°), free from drafts, 1 hour or until doubled in size. (Press two fingers into dough. If indentation remains, dough has risen enough.)

2. Punch dough down; cover and let rest 5 minutes. Roll dough into a 16 x 11–inch rectangle; place dough on a jelly-roll pan coated with cooking spray. Cover and let rise 1 hour or until doubled in size.

3. While dough rises, arrange tomato slices in a single layer on several layers of paper towels; cover with additional paper towels. Lightly press down occasionally.

4. Preheat oven to 375°.

5. Arrange tomato slices over dough. Sprinkle evenly with cheese. Bake at 375° for 28 minutes or until lightly browned. Remove flatbread from pan; cool 5 minutes on a wire rack. Sprinkle with chives and parsley. Arrange basil over flatbread; sprinkle with additional pepper, if desired. **Yield:** 12 servings (serving size: 1 piece).

CALORIES 160; FAT 5.5g (sat 2.3g, mono 2.3g, poly 0.5g); PROTEIN 5.4g; CARB 22.2g; FIBER 1.4g; CHOL 7mg; IRON 1.7mg; SODIUM 298mg; CALC 38mg

This intriguing appetizer is savory-sweet. Ripe—but firm—peaches work best; if they're too soft, they'll make the tortillas soggy. Placing the fillings on one side of the tortilla and folding the other half over (like a taco) makes the quesadillas easier to handle. Whole wheat tortillas would also be great, offering a sweet, nutty taste. The lime-honey dipping sauce balances the richness of the buttery filling.

Peach and Brie Quesadillas with Lime-Honey Dipping Sauce

Sauce:

2 tablespoons honey

2 teaspoons fresh lime juice

½ teaspoon grated lime rind

Quesadillas:

1 cup thinly sliced peeled firm ripe peaches (about 2 large)

1 tablespoon chopped fresh chives

1 teaspoon brown sugar

3 ounces Brie cheese, thinly sliced

4 (8-inch) fat-free flour tortillas

Cooking spray

Chive strips (optional)

1. To prepare sauce, combine first 3 ingredients, stirring with a whisk; set aside.

2. To prepare quesadillas, combine peaches, 1 tablespoon chives, and sugar, tossing gently to coat. Heat a large nonstick skillet over medium-high heat. Arrange one-fourth of cheese and one-fourth of peach mixture over half of each tortilla; fold tortillas in half. Coat pan with cooking spray. Place 2 quesadillas in pan; cook 2 minutes on each side or until tortillas are lightly browned and crisp. Remove from pan; keep warm. Repeat procedure with remaining quesadillas. Cut each quesadilla into 3 wedges; serve with sauce. Garnish with chive strips, if desired. **Yield:** 6 servings (serving size: 2 quesadilla wedges and about 1 teaspoon sauce).

CALORIES 157; FAT 4g (sat 2.5g, mono 1.2g, poly 0.1g); PROTEIN 5.3g; CARB 25.5g; FIBER 0.7g; CHOL 14mg; IRON 0.9mg; SODIUM 316mg; CALC 30mg

Corn

A type of grass, corn is a New World food. May through September is peak season.

To select: A fresh husk is the number one thing to look for. Nice deep brown silk tips or ends mean it's ripe, but the whole silk shouldn't be dried up. Open the tip of the husk to see if the kernels are all the way to the end of the ear; kernels should be plump and milky when pinched.

To store: The sugars in corn begin to turn to starch as soon as it's harvested, so plan to eat it as soon as possible. You can store it in its husk in the refrigerator up to a day.

To prepare: Sweet summer corn requires minimal preparation and cooking.

To cook: Place husked ears in a pot of cold water; bring water to a boil. Once the water boils, remove from heat, and let stand 1 minute before serving. Serve it on the cob, or cut the kernels off to use in soups, salads, succotash, salsas, and other dishes.

Health benefits: One cup of corn provides 18 percent of the daily recommendation for fiber. Fiber has been shown to help lower cholesterol levels and help reduce the risk of colon cancer.

Classic blinis are nutty buckwheat flour pancakes topped with sour cream and caviar. Our version has silver-dollar-sized sweet corn pancakes crowned with cold-smoked salmon. To prevent the blinis from becoming soggy, arrange in a single layer on a platter.

Fresh Corn Blinis with Smoked Salmon and Chive Cream

½   cup reduced-fat sour cream
1   tablespoon minced fresh chives
1   ear shucked corn
1.5 ounces all-purpose flour (about ⅓ cup)
2   tablespoons fine-ground yellow cornmeal
½   cup 1% low-fat milk
1   large egg yolk
¼   teaspoon salt
¼   teaspoon black pepper
1   large egg white
Cooking spray
4   ounces cold-smoked salmon, cut into
    24 (2-inch) strips
Chopped fresh chives (optional)

1. Combine sour cream and chives in a small bowl. Cover and refrigerate.
2. Cut kernels from ear of corn. Scrape remaining pulp from cob using the dull side of a knife blade. Discard cob. Set corn aside.
3. Lightly spoon flour into a dry measuring cup; level with a knife. Combine flour and cornmeal in a medium bowl; make a well in center of mixture. Combine milk and egg yolk in a small bowl; stir well with a whisk. Add milk mixture to flour mixture, and stir with a whisk just until moist. Stir in corn, salt, and pepper.
4. Place egg white in a bowl; beat with a mixer at high speed until foamy. Gently fold egg white mixture into corn mixture.
5. Heat a large nonstick skillet over medium heat. Coat pan with cooking spray. Spoon about 1 tablespoon batter per blini onto pan, spreading to about 2-inch diameter. Cook 2 minutes or until tops are covered with bubbles and edges begin to set. Carefully turn blinis over; cook 1 minute longer. Transfer blinis to a serving platter, and arrange in a single layer; keep warm. Repeat process with remaining batter. Top each blini with 1 piece salmon and 1 teaspoon sour cream mixture. Garnish with chopped chives, if desired.
Yield: 8 servings (serving size: 3 topped blinis).

CALORIES 102; FAT 3.7g (sat 1.7g, mono 1.2g, poly 0.4g); PROTEIN 6.2g; CARB 11.2g; FIBER 0.7g; CHOL 35mg; IRON 0.7mg; SODIUM 386mg; CALC 45mg

For a bit of crunch, sauté the prosciutto in a nonstick skillet over medium-high heat for two minutes or until crisp.

Grilled Peaches over Arugula with Goat Cheese and Prosciutto

¼   cup balsamic vinegar
2   tablespoons honey
3   peaches, pitted and each cut into 6 wedges
Cooking spray
1   tablespoon extra-virgin olive oil
⅛   teaspoon freshly ground black pepper
Dash of kosher salt
10   cups trimmed arugula (about 10 ounces)
2   ounces thinly sliced prosciutto, cut into ¼-inch strips
2   tablespoons crumbled goat cheese

1. Bring vinegar to a boil in a small saucepan over medium-high heat. Reduce heat, and simmer until vinegar is reduced to 2 tablespoons (about 2 minutes). Remove from heat; stir in honey. Cool to room temperature.
2. Prepare grill to high heat.
3. Place peach wedges on grill rack coated with cooking spray; grill 30 seconds on each side or until grill marks appear but peaches are still firm. Remove from grill; set aside.
4. Combine oil, pepper, and salt in a large bowl, stirring with a whisk. Add arugula, tossing gently to coat. Arrange arugula mixture on a platter. Top with peach wedges and prosciutto. Drizzle with balsamic syrup; sprinkle with cheese. **Yield:** 6 servings (serving size: about 1⅓ cups arugula mixture, 3 peach wedges, about ⅓ ounce prosciutto, 1½ teaspoons balsamic syrup, and 1 teaspoon cheese).

CALORIES 100; FAT 4g (sat 1g, mono 2.4g, poly 0.5g); PROTEIN 3.9g; CARB 13.1g; FIBER 1.3g; CHOL 7mg; IRON 0.8mg; SODIUM 183mg; CALC 61mg

Grilling the vegetables heightens their sweetness, and blue cheese provides a pungent counterpoint in this soup. Substitute crumbled goat cheese or feta, if you prefer.

Roasted Corn, Pepper, and Tomato Chowder

3   red bell peppers, halved and seeded
3   ears shucked corn
1½ pounds tomatoes, halved, seeded, and peeled (about 4)
2   tablespoons extra-virgin olive oil
4   cups chopped onion (about 2 medium)
3   (14-ounce) cans fat-free, less-sodium chicken broth
¼   teaspoon salt
¼   teaspoon freshly ground black pepper
¼   cup (1 ounce) crumbled blue cheese
2   tablespoons chopped fresh chives

1. Prepare grill to medium-high heat.
2. Arrange bell peppers, skin side down, and corn in a single layer on a grill rack; grill 5 minutes, turning corn occasionally. Add tomatoes; grill an additional 5 minutes or until vegetables are slightly charred. Remove from heat; cool 10 minutes. Coarsely chop tomatoes and bell peppers; place in a medium bowl. Cut kernels from ears of corn; add to tomato mixture.

3. Heat oil in a large Dutch oven over medium heat. Add onion; cook 7 minutes or until tender, stirring occasionally. Stir in tomato mixture; cook 3 minutes, stirring occasionally. Increase heat to high, and stir in broth. Bring to a boil. Reduce heat, and simmer 30 minutes or until vegetables are tender. Cool 20 minutes.

4. Place one-third of tomato mixture in a blender; process until smooth. Place pureed mixture in a large bowl. Repeat procedure twice with remaining tomato mixture. Wipe pan clean with paper towels. Press tomato mixture through a sieve into pan; discard solids. Place pan over medium heat; cook until thoroughly heated. Stir in salt and black pepper. Ladle about 1½ cups soup into each of 6 bowls; top each serving with 2 teaspoons cheese and 1 teaspoon chives. **Yield:** 6 servings.

CALORIES 155; FAT 7.2g (sat 1.7g, mono 3.9g, poly 1.2g); PROTEIN 5.4g; CARB 21g; FIBER 4.4g; CHOL 4mg; IRON 1.1mg; SODIUM 620mg; CALC 45mg

Fresh Tomato Soup

americanfavorite

I love tomato soup and have found a way to enjoy it when the weather gets cooler by using plum tomatoes. They're flavorful year-round.

—Danese Blackwell, Farmington, UT

Fresh Tomato Soup

2	cups fat-free, less-sodium chicken broth
1	cup chopped onion
¾	cup chopped celery
1	tablespoon thinly sliced fresh basil
1	tablespoon tomato paste
2	pounds plum tomatoes, cut into wedges
½	teaspoon salt
¼	teaspoon freshly ground black pepper
6	tablespoons plain low-fat yogurt
3	tablespoons thinly sliced fresh basil

1. Combine first 6 ingredients in a large saucepan; bring to a boil. Reduce heat, and simmer 30 minutes. Place half of tomato mixture in a blender. Remove center piece of blender lid (to allow steam to escape); secure blender lid on blender. Place a clean towel over opening in blender lid (to avoid splatters). Blend until smooth. Pour into a large bowl. Repeat procedure with remaining tomato mixture. Stir in salt and pepper. Ladle ¾ cup soup into each of 6 bowls; top each serving with 1 tablespoon yogurt and 1½ teaspoons basil. **Yield:** 6 servings.

CALORIES 58; FAT 0.8g (sat 0.3g, mono 0.1g, poly 0.2g); PROTEIN 3.1g; CARB 11.3g; FIBER 2.8g; CHOL 1mg; IRON 1.1mg; SODIUM 382mg; CALC 49mg

The mangoes, melons, and nectarines, along with the cucumber, give the gazpacho a sweet spin. Don't seed the jalapeño if you like a soup with more zip.

Chunky Tomato-Fruit Gazpacho

2   cups finely chopped tomatoes (about ¾ pound)
2   cups finely diced honeydew melon (about ¾ pound)
2   cups finely diced cantaloupe (about ¾ pound)
1   cup finely diced mango (about 1 medium)
1   cup finely diced seeded peeled cucumber (about 1 medium)
1   cup finely diced nectarines (about 3 medium)
1   cup fresh orange juice (about 4 oranges)
½   cup finely chopped Vidalia or other sweet onion
¼   cup chopped fresh basil
3   tablespoons chopped fresh mint
3   tablespoons fresh lemon juice
1   teaspoon sugar
½   teaspoon salt
1   jalapeño pepper, seeded and finely chopped

1. Combine all ingredients in a large bowl. Cover and chill at least 2 hours. **Yield:** 7 servings (serving size: 1 cup).

CALORIES 95; FAT 0.5g (sat 0.1g, mono 0.1g, poly 0.2g); PROTEIN 2.1g; CARB 23g; FIBER 2.8g; CHOL 0mg; IRON 0.9mg; SODIUM 189mg; CALC 33mg

choiceingredient

Melons

Melons can be divided into two main categories: muskmelons and watermelons. Muskmelons include cantaloupes, honeydews, casaba, and Crenshaw melons. The two most commonly used muskmelons are cantaloupe and honeydew. Most unripe muskmelons will sweeten slightly (but not really ripen further) if you leave them in a paper bag at room temperature for a few days. But these melons will never be as sweet as those that have ripened on the vine. An exception is honeydew melon, which will stay only as sweet as it was when picked. Once they are ripe, you can store melons in the refrigerator up to five days. Wrap whole or cut melons in plastic wrap, or place in an airtight container because they absorb the flavors and odors of other foods as well as transfer their flavor and odor to other foods.

Chef Dan Barber of Blue Hill at Stone Barns in New York uses the farm's cucumber crop to prepare this gorgeous, fresh-tasting soup. The addition of avocado lends the soup a creamy touch. It's a terrific way to start a summertime dinner party.

Cucumber Soup

11   large cucumbers (about 8 pounds), divided
¼   cup honey, divided
¼   cup rice wine vinegar
1   ripe avocado, peeled and seeded
2   teaspoons chopped fresh dill
¼   teaspoon salt
¼   teaspoon freshly ground black pepper
Cracked black pepper (optional)
Dill sprigs (optional)

1. Cut 5 cucumbers into 3-inch chunks. Place half of cucumber chunks and 2 tablespoons honey in a blender or food processor, and process until smooth. Pour pureed cucumber mixture through a cheesecloth-lined sieve into a bowl. Repeat procedure with remaining chunks. Cover and chill at least 8 hours.
2. Peel, seed, and slice remaining 6 cucumbers; place slices in a bowl. Add vinegar and remaining 2 tablespoons honey; toss well to coat. Cover and chill 8 hours or overnight.
3. Working with pureed cucumber mixture in sieve, press mixture lightly with a wooden spoon or rubber spatula to squeeze out juice; discard solids.
4. Place half of marinated cucumber slices, avocado, and 1¾ cups cucumber juice in a blender or food processor; process until smooth. Pour cucumber mixture into a bowl. Repeat procedure with remaining cucumber slices and 1¾ cups cucumber juice; reserve any remaining juice for another use. Stir in chopped dill, salt, and pepper. Place 1½ cups soup into each of 6 bowls. Garnish with cracked black pepper and dill sprigs, if desired. **Yield:** 6 servings.

CALORIES 167; FAT 6g (sat 0.9g, mono 3.2g, poly 0.7g); PROTEIN 3.8g; CARB 27.3g; FIBER 5.3g; CHOL 0mg; IRON 1.6mg; SODIUM 312mg; CALC 79mg

WINENOTE

Green, vegetal flavors, like those found in this soup, call for **sauvignon blanc's** distinctive, herbaceous character. The wine's grassy, citrus qualities bring out the soup's fresh, crisp flavors.

Corn and crab, two of summer's sweetest offerings, combine well in this refreshingly light salad. The tart dressing contrasts with the sweet corn, tomatoes, and crab. Serve with a lemon wedge, if desired. Pair it with cucumber soup or a grilled sandwich.

Crab, Corn, and Tomato Salad with Lemon-Basil Dressing

1	tablespoon grated lemon rind
5	tablespoons fresh lemon juice, divided
1	tablespoon extra-virgin olive oil
1	teaspoon honey
½	teaspoon Dijon mustard
¼	teaspoon salt
⅛	teaspoon freshly ground black pepper
1	cup fresh corn kernels (about 2 ears)
¼	cup thinly sliced fresh basil leaves
¼	cup chopped red bell pepper
2	tablespoons finely chopped red onion
1	pound lump crabmeat, shell pieces removed
8	(¼-inch-thick) slices ripe beefsteak tomato
2	cups cherry tomatoes, halved

1. Combine rind, 3 tablespoons juice, and next 5 ingredients in a large bowl, stirring well with a whisk. Reserve 1½ tablespoons juice mixture. Add remaining 2 tablespoons juice, corn, and next 4 ingredients to remaining juice mixture; toss gently to coat.

2. Arrange 2 tomato slices and ½ cup cherry tomatoes on each of 4 plates. Drizzle about 1 teaspoon reserved juice mixture over each serving. Top each serving with 1 cup corn and crab mixture. **Yield:** 4 servings.

CALORIES 242; FAT 5.6g (sat 0.6g, mono 2.7g, poly 0.7g); PROTEIN 30g; CARB 17.7g; FIBER 3.6g; CHOL 128mg; IRON 1.8mg; SODIUM 613mg; CALC 161mg

This main course salad is an ideal lunch or light supper option. Plums would be a delicious substitute for the apricots.

Arugula Salad with Chicken and Apricots

2 (6-ounce) skinless, boneless chicken breast halves
1 tablespoon minced fresh parsley
2 teaspoons minced fresh tarragon
½ teaspoon salt, divided
¼ teaspoon freshly ground black pepper
Cooking spray
3 tablespoons olive oil
4 teaspoons white wine vinegar
Dash of freshly ground black pepper
4 cups baby arugula
4 cups gourmet salad greens
3 apricots (about 8 ounces), pitted and thinly sliced
⅓ cup thinly vertically sliced red onion

1. Prepare grill to medium-high heat.
2. Place chicken between 2 sheets of heavy-duty plastic wrap; pound each piece to ½-inch thickness using a meat mallet or small heavy skillet. Sprinkle chicken with parsley, tarragon, ¼ teaspoon salt, and ¼ teaspoon pepper.
3. Place chicken on grill rack coated with cooking spray; grill 4 minutes on each side or until done. Transfer to a plate; cool to room temperature.
4. Combine oil, vinegar, remaining ¼ teaspoon salt, and dash of pepper in a small bowl, stirring with a whisk.
5. Combine arugula, greens, apricots, and onion in a large bowl. Pour vinaigrette over arugula mixture; toss well to coat. Place about 2 cups arugula mixture on each of 4 plates. Cut chicken breast halves crosswise into thin slices; top each serving evenly with chicken. Serve immediately. **Yield:** 4 servings.

CALORIES 243; FAT 12.9g (sat 2.1g, mono 8.3g, poly 1.7g); PROTEIN 22.2g; CARB 10.1g; FIBER 2.9g; CHOL 54mg; IRON 2.1mg; SODIUM 364mg; CALC 86mg

WINENOTE

In this salad, arugula's peppery bite is nicely balanced by fragrant herbs, sweet apricots, and grilled chicken. A great wine with a complexly flavored salad like this is a **pinot gris**. It has a fresh, clean feel and a creamy, fruity flavor.

Sweet mangoes team with curry-marinated shrimp and crunchy vegetables for an island-inspired main dish. Customize the recipe to suit your preferences—try chicken in place of shrimp, or omit the shrimp and serve the salad cold or at room temperature as a side dish. For added flavor, use basmati or jasmine rice.

Mango Rice Salad with Grilled Shrimp

1   tablespoon minced fresh garlic
1   tablespoon minced peeled fresh ginger
1   tablespoon low-sodium soy sauce
4   teaspoons curry powder
⅛   teaspoon ground red pepper
⅛   teaspoon ground cumin
1½   pounds medium shrimp, peeled and deveined
       (about 36 shrimp)
2   cups water
⅔   cup light coconut milk
1¼   cups uncooked long-grain rice
¾   cup shredded carrot
2   cups diced peeled mango (about 2 mangoes)
1½   cups diced red bell pepper
½   cup sliced green onions
1   tablespoon chopped fresh cilantro
1   tablespoon chopped fresh parsley
2   tablespoons fresh lime juice
½   teaspoon salt
Cooking spray
Cilantro sprigs (optional)

1. Combine first 6 ingredients in a medium bowl. Add shrimp; toss to coat. Cover and chill 1 hour.
2. Bring water and coconut milk to a boil in a medium saucepan; add rice. Cover, reduce heat, and simmer 15 minutes or until the liquid is absorbed. Add carrot and next 7 ingredients; toss gently to combine.
3. Prepare grill or grill pan to medium-high heat.
4. Thread 3 shrimp onto each of 12 (6-inch) skewers. Place skewers on grill rack or grill pan coated with cooking spray; grill 3 minutes on each side or until shrimp are done. Serve kebabs over salad. Garnish with cilantro sprigs, if desired. **Yield:** 6 servings (serving size: 2 kebabs and about 1 cup salad).

CALORIES 342; FAT 4.1g (sat 1.8g, mono 0.5g, poly 1g); PROTEIN 27.4g; CARB 48.9g; FIBER 2.9g; CHOL 172mg; IRON 5.3mg; SODIUM 478mg; CALC 95mg

Cut a Mango

A mango's taste has been likened to a cross between a pineapple and a peach. This tropical fruit can add sublime sweetness to salsas, relishes, smoothies, and salads. Mangoes are shaped like a football and have a large, flat seed that make them seem awkward to cut, but it's easy to do following the tips below.

1. Use a sharp knife to trim half an inch from the top and bottom. Hold the mango in one hand, and use a vegetable peeler to slice the skin from the flesh.

2. Cut flesh from around the pit with two curved cuts down the plumpest sides, then trim remaining sides.

3. Cut the fruit's flesh according to your desire—diced or sliced.

Use a sliced loaf of good-quality Italian bread; its dense texture stands up to grilling. Sprinkle eggplant with salt; let it stand, applying pressure periodically, and rinse before grilling to leach excess moisture and bitterness.

Grilled Eggplant Sandwiches with Red Onion and Aïoli

Aïoli:

¼ cup light mayonnaise

1 tablespoon extra-virgin olive oil

1 tablespoon fresh lemon juice

1 garlic clove, minced

Sandwiches:

1 (1-pound) eggplant, cut crosswise into ¼-inch-thick slices

1 tablespoon kosher salt

1 teaspoon chopped fresh thyme

1 teaspoon chopped fresh parsley

½ teaspoon chopped fresh rosemary

Cooking spray

4 (½-inch-thick) slices red onion

8 (½-inch-thick) slices Italian bread

8 (¼-inch-thick) slices tomato

2 cups lightly packed arugula leaves

1. To prepare aïoli, combine first 4 ingredients in a small bowl, stirring well. Cover and chill.

2. To prepare sandwiches, arrange eggplant in a single layer on several layers of heavy-duty paper towels. Sprinkle both sides of eggplant with salt; cover with additional paper towels. Let stand 30 minutes, pressing down occasionally. Rinse eggplant with cold water. Drain and pat dry.

3. Prepare grill.

4. Combine thyme, parsley, and rosemary in a small bowl, stirring well. Lightly coat eggplant slices with cooking spray; sprinkle with herb mixture.

5. Arrange eggplant and onion on grill rack coated with cooking spray; grill 2 minutes on each side or until vegetables are tender and lightly browned. Remove from heat, and keep warm. Arrange bread slices in a single layer on grill rack coated with cooking spray, and grill 1 minute on each side or until toasted.

6. Spread about 2 teaspoons aïoli over 1 side of 4 bread slices; divide eggplant and onion evenly among bread slices. Place 2 tomato slices on each sandwich; top each serving with ½ cup arugula. Spread about 2 teaspoons of remaining aïoli over 1 side of remaining 4 bread slices; place on top of sandwiches. **Yield:** 4 servings (serving size: 1 sandwich).

CALORIES 352; FAT 11.7g (sat 1.3g, mono 5.9g, poly 3.6g); PROTEIN 8.2g; CARB 53.3g; FIBER 7g; CHOL 5mg; IRON 2.9mg; SODIUM 749mg; CALC 81mg

WINE NOTE

With vegetables we often think of white wine, but grilled eggplant's smoky flavor and pleasantly bitter skin marry well with medium-bodied, rustic reds. Try a **Tuscan blend.**

choice ingredient

Eggplant

A cousin to tomatoes, peppers, and potatoes, the eggplant derives its name from the first varieties to reach the West, which were white, round, and egg-sized. While colors range from creamy white to green, the shiny, vivid purple eggplant is probably most recognizable. Shapes also vary. Some are small and spherical; others are long, narrow, and curved like a banana; still others are large and bottle-shaped.

Although available year-round, eggplants are best and most abundant from July to October. Look for firm eggplants that feel heavy for their size and have smooth, shiny skins. The stem should be bright green, and the skin should spring back when pressed. Avoid eggplants with soft spots, discolorations, and scarring or wrinkling of the skin.

Eggplants are best stored in a cool, dry place (50° is ideal) for one to two days. For longer storage, place whole, unwashed eggplants in a plastic bag in the vegetable drawer of your fridge.

Shape the patties up to eight hours in advance, and cook just before serving. Use a grill pan or nonstick skillet to cook them since they may not hold up on a standard grill. If you have a mini food processor, use it to prepare the mayonnaise mixture. You can use regular hamburger buns instead of English muffins.

Chipotle Salmon Burgers

Mayonnaise:

1 tablespoon chopped fresh cilantro
3 tablespoons light mayonnaise
2 tablespoons finely chopped fresh mango
1 tablespoon finely chopped fresh pineapple
⅛ teaspoon finely grated lime rind

Burgers:

⅓ cup chopped green onions
¼ cup chopped fresh cilantro

1 tablespoon finely chopped chipotle chile, canned in adobo sauce
2 teaspoons fresh lime juice
¼ teaspoon salt
1 (1¼-pound) salmon fillet, skinned and cut into 1-inch pieces

Cooking spray

4 English muffins
4 butter lettuce leaves

1. To prepare mayonnaise, place first 5 ingredients in a food processor or blender; process until smooth. Transfer to a bowl; cover and chill.

2. To prepare burgers, place onions, ¼ cup cilantro, chile, and juice in a food processor; process until finely chopped. Add salt and salmon; pulse 4 times or until salmon is coarsely ground and mixture is well blended.

3. Divide salmon mixture into 4 equal portions; shape each portion into a (1-inch-thick) patty. Cover and chill 30 minutes.

4. Heat a grill pan over medium-high heat. Coat pan with cooking spray. Add patties to pan; cook 6 minutes on each side or until desired degree of doneness. Remove patties from pan.

5. Wipe skillet with paper towels; recoat with cooking spray. Place 2 muffins, cut sides down, in pan; cook 2 minutes or until lightly toasted. Repeat procedure with cooking spray and remaining muffins.

6. Place 1 muffin bottom on each of 4 plates; top each serving with 1 lettuce leaf and 1 patty. Spread about 1 tablespoon mayonnaise mixture over each patty; place 1 muffin top on each serving. **Yield:** 4 servings (serving size: 1 burger).

CALORIES 408; FAT 15g (sat 2.6g, mono 4.5g, poly 6.6g); PROTEIN 37.4g; CARB 28.9g; FIBER 2.9g; CHOL 94mg; IRON 3.8mg; SODIUM 595mg; CALC 124mg

One of the world's most luscious sandwiches, the lobster roll is an affordable way to stretch and enjoy this premium ingredient. The humble hot dog bun is traditional here, an important component that won't upstage the star. When choosing lobster, always purchase those stored in a clean tank. When removed from the water, they should be lively, not sluggish. You can make the mayo-based lobster filling up to a day ahead and keep it refrigerated until just before serving.

Lobster Rolls

5   tablespoons canola mayonnaise
¼   cup finely chopped celery
3   tablespoons minced fresh onion
2   tablespoons whole milk Greek-style yogurt (such as Fage)
1½ teaspoons chopped fresh dill
½   teaspoon kosher salt
⅛   teaspoon ground red pepper
1   pound cooked lobster meat, cut into bite-sized pieces (about 3 [1½-pound] lobsters)
2   tablespoons butter, melted
8   (1½-ounce) hot dog buns
8   Bibb lettuce leaves

1. Combine first 7 ingredients in a medium bowl, stirring well. Add lobster to mayonnaise mixture; toss. Cover and chill 1 hour.

2. Brush butter evenly over cut sides of buns. Heat a large skillet over medium-high heat. Place buns, cut sides down, in pan; cook 2 minutes or until toasted. Line each bun with 1 lettuce leaf; top with ⅓ cup lobster mixture. **Yield:** 8 servings (serving size: 1 sandwich).

CALORIES 272; FAT 12.3g (sat 3.3g, mono 5.1g, poly 2.9g); PROTEIN 16.3g; CARB 22.9g; FIBER 1.2g; CHOL 52mg; IRON 1.9mg; SODIUM 629mg; CALC 105mg

A Southern favorite, fried green tomatoes lend a delightful twist to this sandwich. The tomatoes take center stage over the bacon in this version.

Fried Green Tomato BLTs

8	slices 40%-less-fat bacon
⅓	cup yellow cornmeal
¼	cup finely shredded Parmesan cheese
¼	teaspoon freshly ground black pepper
12	(¼-inch-thick) slices green tomato (about 2 tomatoes)
2	teaspoons olive oil, divided
Cooking spray	
¼	cup reduced-fat mayonnaise
8	(1-ounce) slices country white bread, toasted
8	red leaf lettuce leaves

1. Cook bacon in a large nonstick skillet over medium heat until crisp. Remove bacon from pan, reserving 2 teaspoons drippings. Set bacon and drippings aside.

2. Combine cornmeal, shredded cheese, and pepper in a shallow dish. Dredge tomato slices in cornmeal mixture. Heat 1 teaspoon reserved drippings and 1 teaspoon oil in a large nonstick skillet coated with cooking spray over medium-high heat. Cook 6 tomato slices 2 minutes on each side or until lightly browned. Repeat procedure with remaining 1 teaspoon bacon drippings, remaining 1 teaspoon oil, and 6 tomato slices.

3. Spread 1 tablespoon mayonnaise over each of 4 bread slices. Top each slice with 2 lettuce leaves, 3 tomato slices, and 2 bacon slices. Top with remaining 4 bread slices. Serve immediately.

Yield: 4 servings (serving size: 1 sandwich).

CALORIES 380; FAT 13g (sat 3.9g, mono 6g, poly 2.3g); PROTEIN 14.6g; CARB 54.1g; FIBER 5.1g; CHOL 16mg; IRON 2.6mg; SODIUM 889mg; CALC 105mg

Add sizzle to your menu with these chicken sandwiches. They're a great make-ahead option for last-minute guests or a busy week-night. The chicken and sauce can be made up to two days ahead and stored in the refrigerator. Reheat the mixture in a saucepan before serving. Round out the meal with grilled corn on the cob and coleslaw.

Pulled Chicken Sandwiches

Chicken:

2   tablespoons dark brown sugar
1   teaspoon paprika
1   teaspoon chili powder
¾   teaspoon ground cumin
½   teaspoon ground chipotle chile pepper
½   teaspoon salt
¼   teaspoon ground ginger
2   pounds skinless, boneless chicken thighs
Cooking spray

Sauce:

2   teaspoons canola oil
½   cup finely chopped onion
2   tablespoons dark brown sugar
1   teaspoon chili powder
½   teaspoon garlic powder
½   teaspoon dry mustard
¼   teaspoon ground allspice
⅛   teaspoon ground red pepper
1   cup ketchup
2   tablespoons cider vinegar
1   tablespoon molasses

Remaining Ingredients:

8   (2-ounce) sandwich rolls, toasted
16   hamburger dill chips

1. Prepare grill.
2. To prepare chicken, combine first 7 ingredients in a small bowl. Rub spice mixture evenly over chicken. Place chicken on a grill rack coated with

cooking spray; cover and grill 20 minutes or until a thermometer registers 180°, turning occasionally. Let stand 5 minutes. Shred with 2 forks.
3. To prepare sauce, heat canola oil in a medium saucepan over medium heat. Add onion; cook 5 minutes or until tender, stirring occasionally. Stir in 2 tablespoons sugar and next 5 ingredients; cook 30 seconds. Stir in ketchup, vinegar, and molasses; bring to a boil. Reduce heat, and simmer 10 minutes or until slightly thickened, stirring occasionally. Stir in chicken; cook 2 minutes or until thoroughly heated.
4. Place about ⅓ cup chicken mixture on bottom halves of sandwich rolls; top each serving with 2 pickle chips and top roll half. **Yield:** 8 servings (serving size: 1 sandwich).

CALORIES 365; FAT 9.1g (sat 2.8g, mono 2.6g, poly 2.6g); PROTEIN 28.2g; CARB 42.8g; FIBER 2g; CHOL 94mg; IRON 3.4mg; SODIUM 877mg; CALC 78mg

Cherry Tomatoes

Cherry tomatoes refers to a family of tomatoes, all of which are about an inch in diameter and similar in flavor. The defining difference among the members of this family is their shape. They include the following three varieties: cherry, grape, and pear tomatoes.

Cherry tomatoes are small and round. Available in red, orange, green, or yellow, they taste similar to beefsteak and globe tomatoes but have a more pronounced sweetness. Try them in salads or quick sautés. Use as a garnish, or eat them out of hand.

Grape tomatoes have a more elliptical shape, similar to a grape, and are almost always red. They have a more intense sweetness than the cherry kind, balanced by a subtle acidity. For the best flavor, look for grape tomatoes that are no larger than an inch in diameter.

Pear tomatoes are shaped like small pears or teardrops. They are best eaten raw, but you can cook them briefly to finish a sauce or toss with pasta. Pear tomatoes are a bit smaller than the cherry variety and have a flavor similar to grape tomatoes.

Peppery arugula complements the sweetness of ripe tomatoes. Use pear tomatoes, if available, for even better flavor. Substitute fusilli for cavatappi, if desired. Serve immediately.

Cavatappi with Arugula Pesto and Cherry Tomatoes

Pesto:

5 cups trimmed arugula
½ cup (2 ounces) grated fresh Parmesan cheese
¼ cup pine nuts, toasted
1 tablespoon fresh lemon juice
¾ teaspoon salt
¼ teaspoon freshly ground black pepper
1 garlic clove, minced
⅓ cup water
2 tablespoons extra-virgin olive oil

Remaining Ingredients:

1 pound uncooked cavatappi
2 cups red and yellow cherry tomatoes, halved
   (about ¾ pound)
2 tablespoons pine nuts, toasted

1. To prepare pesto, place first 7 ingredients in a food processor; process until finely minced. With processor on, slowly pour ⅓ cup water and oil through food chute; process until well blended.
2. Cook pasta according to package directions, omitting salt and fat. Drain. Combine pesto, pasta, and tomatoes in a large bowl; toss well. Sprinkle pine nuts over pasta. Serve immediately. **Yield:** 6 servings (serving size: 1⅓ cups pasta and 1 teaspoon nuts).

CALORIES 425; FAT 13.7g (sat 2.8g, mono 6.3g, poly 3.7g); PROTEIN 14.6g; CARB 61.5g; FIBER 3.2g; CHOL 6mg; IRON 2.1mg; SODIUM 412mg; CALC 135mg

WINENOTE

There's nothing more satisfying than a light pasta dish and a glass of cold, fresh, dry Italian white wine. **Pinot grigio** fills the bill exactly, and it's a steal, too.

Peel and Seed Tomatoes

A few tricks make preparing tomatoes, when they need to be seeded for sauces, soups, salsas, and casseroles, an easy task. With this method it may seem like you're wasting a lot of tomato, but you'll finish with just the parts you need.

1. Cut a one-inch X into the bottom of each tomato. Place the tomatoes in a pan of boiling water for 30 seconds to a minute. Quickly remove each tomato with a slotted spoon, and drop into a bowl of ice and water for one minute to stop the cooking process.

2. Remove the tomatoes from the water, and peel back the flaps from the X; the skin will be easy to remove. Slice the tomatoes in half horizontally.

3. With a teaspoon or melon baller, scoop the seeds and pulp away from the flesh, and discard. Remove any remaining seeds with your hands.

Pasta, cheese, and a homemade sauce are simple components of this easy classic. The combination of tofu and ricotta creates a nice consistency.

Fresh Tomato Lasagna

Sauce:

4 ½	cups chopped onion (about 3)
2	garlic cloves, minced
6	cups chopped seeded peeled tomato (about 3½ pounds)
1	cup chopped fresh parsley
2	teaspoons dried oregano
½	teaspoon salt
½	teaspoon dried thyme
½	teaspoon dried marjoram
½	teaspoon black pepper
2	(6-ounce) cans Italian-style tomato paste

Filling:

½	teaspoon dried basil
1	(15-ounce) carton fat-free ricotta cheese
1	(12.3-ounce) package reduced-fat firm tofu, drained

Remaining Ingredients:

	Cooking spray
12	cooked lasagna noodles
2	cups (8 ounces) shredded sharp provolone cheese
½	cup (2 ounces) grated fresh Romano or Parmesan cheese

1. To prepare sauce, heat a Dutch oven over medium-high heat until hot. Add onion and garlic; cover and cook 5 minutes, stirring occasionally. Add the tomato and next 7 ingredients. Bring to a boil; cover, reduce heat, and simmer 45 minutes, stirring occasionally.

2. Preheat oven to 350°.

3. To prepare filling, combine basil, ricotta, and tofu in a bowl; mash ricotta mixture with a potato masher.

4. Spread 2 cups sauce in bottom of a 13 x 9–inch baking dish coated with cooking spray. Arrange 3 noodles over sauce; top with 1 cup filling, ½ cup provolone cheese, 2 tablespoons Romano, and 1½ cups sauce. Repeat layers twice, ending with noodles. Spread remaining sauce over noodles. Sprinkle with ½ cup provolone cheese and 2 tablespoons Romano. Bake at 350° for 45 minutes. Let stand 10 minutes before serving. **Yield:** 8 servings.

CALORIES 391; FAT 11.1g (sat 6.3g, mono 2.9g, poly 1g); PROTEIN 27.7g; CARB 49.5g; FIBER 4.4g; CHOL 33mg; IRON 4.2mg; SODIUM 886mg; CALC 476mg

Halibut en Papillote with Potatoes, Green Beans, and Sweet Onions

8   thin (¼-inch) slices lemon
4   fresh bay leaves (optional)
4   (6-ounce) halibut fillets
¾   teaspoon salt, divided
½   teaspoon freshly ground black pepper, divided
2   tablespoons extra-virgin olive oil, divided
12   ounces small new potatoes, quartered
6   ounces fresh green beans, trimmed
2   tablespoons white wine vinegar
1   tablespoon fresh lemon juice
1   teaspoon Dijon mustard
1   garlic clove, minced
1   cup thinly sliced Vidalia or other sweet onion

1. Preheat oven to 450°.
2. Cut 4 (15 x 24–inch) pieces of parchment paper and fold in half, like a book. Draw a large heart half on each piece with the fold being the center of the heart. Cut out heart, and lay it open.
3. Lay 2 slices of lemon in center of 1 side of each piece of parchment, and top with 1 bay leaf, if desired, and 1 halibut fillet. Sprinkle fillets evenly with ½ teaspoon salt and ¼ teaspoon pepper. Drizzle each fillet with ¾ teaspoon olive oil.

Fold other side of heart on top. Starting at top of the heart, fold up both edges of parchment, overlapping the folds as you move along. Twist end tip to secure tightly.
4. Place parchment packets on an ungreased baking sheet. Bake at 450° for 12 minutes. Remove from oven; let rest 5 minutes.
5. Cook potatoes in boiling water 8 minutes or until potatoes are almost tender. Add green beans to pan; cook 4 minutes or until crisp-tender. Drain well; keep potatoes and green beans warm.
6. Working with one packet at a time, carefully open fish packets and pour liquid from packets into a large bowl. Add remaining 1 tablespoon olive oil, vinegar, juice, mustard, garlic, remaining ¼ teaspoon salt, and remaining ¼ teaspoon pepper; stir well with a whisk. Add potatoes, beans, and onion to oil mixture; toss well to coat. Divide vegetable mixture evenly among 4 plates, and top each serving with 1 fillet. Yield: 4 servings.

CALORIES 335; FAT 11.1g (sat 1.6g, mono 6.3g, poly 2.3g); PROTEIN 38.2g; CARB 20.2g; FIBER 3.5g; CHOL 54mg; IRON 2.6mg; SODIUM 573mg; CALC 114mg

Green Beans

Green beans (also called snap beans) are a legume with an edible pod and range in size from svelte haricots verts to large wax beans. They are a year-round grocery store standby, but May to October is their prime time. Heirloom varieties of the legumes are available at many farmers' markets.

To select: Snap beans should snap when you bend them, and you should choose a darker green bean with a more slender appearance, which is always preferable. Try to avoid green beans that are spotty.

To store: When wrapped tightly in plastic wrap, green beans should last for about 10 days in the refrigerator.

To cook: Green beans are versatile—braise, boil, steam, or stir-fry them, depending on the dish.

The salmon and the main ingredients of the relish are prepared on the grill, infusing both with a bit of smokiness.

Grilled Salmon with Roasted Corn Relish

4   Anaheim chiles
Cooking spray
2   ears shucked corn
1   cup diced tomato
¼   cup chopped fresh cilantro
6   tablespoons fresh lime juice
1   teaspoon salt, divided
½   teaspoon freshly ground black pepper, divided
1   teaspoon ground cumin
4   (6-ounce) skinless salmon fillets

1. Prepare grill.
2. Place chiles on grill rack coated with cooking spray; grill 5 minutes on each side or until blackened. Place chiles in a heavy-duty zip-top plastic bag; seal. Let stand 5 minutes. Peel chiles; cut in half lengthwise. Discard seeds and membranes. Cut chiles into ¼-inch strips.
3. Place corn on grill rack coated with cooking spray; grill 10 minutes or until lightly browned, turning occasionally. Cool slightly. Cut kernels from cobs.
4. Combine chiles, corn, tomato, cilantro, and juice; toss gently. Add ½ teaspoon salt and ¼ teaspoon black pepper.
5. Combine remaining ½ teaspoon salt, remaining ¼ teaspoon black pepper, and cumin, stirring well. Rub spice mixture evenly over both sides of salmon. Place salmon on grill rack coated with cooking spray; grill 4 minutes on each side or until fish flakes easily when tested with a fork or until desired degree of doneness. Serve with relish. **Yield:** 4 servings (serving size: 1 fillet and ¾ cup relish).

CALORIES 304; FAT 11.3g (sat 2.6g, mono 4.8g, poly 2.9g); PROTEIN 33.9g; CARB 18.1g; FIBER 2.7g; CHOL 80mg; IRON 1.7mg; SODIUM 671mg; CALC 39mg

Grilled Shrimp Kebabs with Summer Fruit Salsa

Salsa:
½   cup chopped ripe plum (about 1)
½   cup diced apricots (about 2)
½   cup diced nectarine (about 1)
2   tablespoons thinly sliced fresh mint
2   tablespoons diced red onion
1   tablespoon minced seeded serrano chile
1   teaspoon grated lime rind
3   tablespoons fresh lime juice
1   tablespoon honey
¼   teaspoon salt
⅛   teaspoon ground red pepper
12   sweet cherries, pitted and halved
1   green onion, finely chopped
Kebabs:
2   tablespoons butter, melted
2   teaspoons fresh lemon juice
¼   teaspoon salt
1   garlic clove, minced
24   jumbo shrimp, peeled and deveined (about 2 pounds)
Cooking spray
6   lime wedges
Mint sprigs (optional)

1. To prepare salsa, combine first 13 ingredients in a medium bowl; stir well. Cover and chill 1 hour.
2. Prepare grill.
3. To prepare shrimp, place butter, 2 teaspoons juice, ¼ teaspoon salt, garlic, and shrimp in a large bowl; toss to coat. Thread 4 shrimp onto each of 6 (12-inch) skewers. Place kebabs on a grill rack coated with cooking spray; grill 3 minutes on each side or until shrimp are done. Serve with salsa and lime wedges. Garnish with mint sprigs, if desired. **Yield:** 6 servings (serving size: 1 kebab, ⅓ cup salsa, and 1 lime wedge).

CALORIES 242; FAT 6.8g (sat 2.9g, mono 1.5g, poly 1.3g); PROTEIN 31.6g; CARB 13.4g; FIBER 1.5g; CHOL 240mg; IRON 4.1mg; SODIUM 449mg; CALC 94mg

Grilled Shrimp Kebabs with
Summer Fruit Salsa

The sweetness of peaches and bell peppers contrasts with the cumin-rubbed steak, pungent red onion, and parsley-garlic sauce.

Grilled Sirloin Kebabs with Peaches and Peppers

Kebabs:
1 ½ tablespoons ground cumin
1 ½ tablespoons cracked black pepper
2 ¾ teaspoons kosher salt
2 pounds boneless sirloin steak, cut into 48 (1-inch) pieces
4 peaches, each cut into 8 wedges
2 red onions, each cut into 8 wedges
2 large red bell peppers, each cut into 16 (1-inch) pieces
Cooking spray
Sauce:
½ cup chopped fresh parsley
¼ cup red wine vinegar
1 teaspoon olive oil
¼ teaspoon kosher salt
¼ teaspoon cracked black pepper
3 garlic cloves, minced

1. Prepare grill.
2. To prepare kebabs, combine first 7 ingredients in a large bowl; toss well. Thread 3 steak pieces, 2 peach wedges, 1 onion wedge, and 2 bell pepper pieces alternately onto each of 16 (12-inch) skewers. Place kebabs on grill rack coated with cooking spray; grill 6 minutes or until tender, turning occasionally. Place kebabs on a platter; cover loosely with foil. Let stand 5 minutes.
3. To prepare sauce, combine parsley and remaining ingredients, stirring with a whisk. Spoon over kebabs. **Yield:** 8 servings (serving size: 2 kebabs).

CALORIES 217; FAT 7.2g (sat 2.4g, mono 3g, poly 0.4g); PROTEIN 25.5g; CARB 12.4g; FIBER 3.2g; CHOL 69mg; IRON 3.8mg; SODIUM 768mg; CALC 38mg

1. When storing a bunch of fresh herbs, wrap the stems in a damp paper towel, and store them in a zip-top plastic bag. Wash herbs just before using; pat them dry with a paper towel.

2. Don't worry about stemming cilantro, dill, or parsley; their stems are tender and can be chopped and used with the leaves. Simply place the bunch on a cutting board, and chop with a sharp knife.

howto:

Use, Store, and Prep Fresh Herbs

The flavor of fresh herbs is generally much better than that of dried because most herbs (excluding rosemary, thyme, and dill) lose significant flavor when dried. However, using fresh isn't always practical, so it's important to keep quality dried herbs on hand, especially when it comes to convenience and last-minute meal preparation. Because fresh herbs are not as strong or concentrated as their dried counterparts, substitute one part dried herbs to three parts fresh. This translates into 1 teaspoon dried for 1 tablespoon fresh. The exception is rosemary; use equal amounts of fresh and dried.

3. Strip rosemary and thyme leaves from their tough, inedible stems by holding the top of a stem in one hand, and then pulling in the opposite direction of the way the leaves grow.

4. The stems of mint, oregano, tarragon, and sage are also unusable, but the leaves are large enough that they can be easily pinched off one at a time.

Grill the meat first, and then coat it in the mustard and herb mixture for bright, fresh flavors. Spread the chopped fresh herbs on a sheet of plastic wrap so you can evenly coat the beef with minimal mess. Serve the tenderloin with grilled polenta and a simple salad.

Beef Tenderloin with Mustard and Herbs

1   (2½-pound) beef tenderloin, trimmed
Cooking spray
1   teaspoon salt
1   teaspoon freshly ground black pepper
⅓   cup finely chopped fresh parsley
2   tablespoons chopped fresh thyme

1½   tablespoons finely chopped fresh rosemary
3   tablespoons Dijon mustard

1. Prepare grill.
2. Lightly coat beef with cooking spray; sprinkle evenly with salt and pepper. Place beef on grill rack coated with cooking spray. Reduce heat to medium. Grill 30 minutes or until a thermometer registers 145° or until desired degree of doneness, turning to brown on all sides. Let beef stand 10 minutes.
3. Sprinkle parsley, thyme, and rosemary in an even layer on an 18 x 15–inch sheet of plastic wrap. Brush mustard evenly over beef. Place beef in herb mixture on plastic wrap; roll beef over herbs, pressing gently. Slice beef. **Yield:** 10 servings (serving size: 3 ounces).

CALORIES 191; FAT 9.4g (sat 3.7g, mono 3.9g, poly 0.4g); PROTEIN 23.4g; CARB 1.4g; FIBER 0.2g; CHOL 71mg; IRON 1.7mg; SODIUM 393mg; CALC 23mg

choiceingredient

Honey

Moist, spreadable, and abundant, honey adds more than sweetness to your cooking—it adds a rich, unique flavor to foods. And although honey has no nutritional advantages over sugar, it does add moistness to baked goods. It also spreads more easily than sugar as a glaze on fish and meats, and dissolves in liquids like vinaigrettes.

Because honey is produced in so many places and in such different strengths and flavors, it's important to choose the best blend. Orange blossom, clover blossom, sage blossom, and buckwheat are some of the most common types. The general rule states the lighter the color, the milder the flavor. We usually use mild-flavored honeys, such as alfalfa and clover. If you wish, you can use a stronger variety, such as buckwheat. Like corn syrup, honey adds moisture to cakes and cookies. Unlike corn syrup, which is fairly neutral, honey imparts a distinctive flavor.

The natural sugar in the honey helps the chops caramelize on the grill.

Cumin, Honey, and Mint Marinated Lamb Chops

¼   cup chopped fresh mint
1   tablespoon balsamic vinegar
2   teaspoons ground cumin
1   teaspoon dry mustard
2   teaspoons honey
½   teaspoon salt
½   teaspoon freshly ground black pepper
8   (4-ounce) lamb loin chops, about 1 inch thick, trimmed
Cooking spray

1. Combine first 7 ingredients in a small bowl, stirring well. Place lamb in a single layer in a shallow dish; rub spice mixture evenly over both sides of lamb. Cover and refrigerate 4 hours.
2. Prepare grill.
3. Place lamb on a grill rack coated with cooking spray. Grill 4 minutes on each side or until desired degree of doneness. Serve immediately. **Yield:** 4 servings (serving size: 2 chops).

CALORIES 223; FAT 12.3g (sat 5.5g, mono 4.7g, poly 0.5g); PROTEIN 22.4g; CARB 4.4g; FIBER 0.6g; CHOL 72mg; IRON 2.6mg; SODIUM 353mg; CALC 27mg

Meat is a natural on the summertime grill, and here we've used pork. While the grill is hot, add halved peaches (plums would be a good substitute) drizzled with balsamic vinegar. Grilling caramelizes the fruit's sugar, deepens its flavor, and softens its texture to make a delicious sidekick for the pork. Enjoy this dish on the deck or patio with a glass of chilled riesling, and you have the ingredients for a fine solstice supper.

Grilled Peaches and Pork

4   (4-ounce) boneless center-cut pork loin chops
¼   cup balsamic vinegar, divided
2   tablespoons fresh lime juice
3   teaspoons chopped fresh thyme
½   teaspoon salt
½   teaspoon freshly ground black pepper
4   large peaches, peeled, halved, and pitted (about 12 ounces)
Cooking spray
6   cups trimmed arugula
1   teaspoon turbinado sugar or granulated sugar

1. Place each piece of pork between 2 sheets of heavy-duty plastic wrap, and pound each piece to ¼-inch thickness using a meat mallet or a rolling pin.

2. Combine 2 tablespoons vinegar, juice, thyme, salt, and pepper in a small bowl. Reserve 1 tablespoon juice mixture. Pour remaining juice mixture into a large zip-top plastic bag. Add pork; seal and marinate in refrigerator 1 hour, turning occasionally.

3. Preheat grill to medium heat.

4. Place peaches, cut sides up, on a plate; drizzle with remaining 2 tablespoons vinegar.

5. Place pork on grill rack coated with cooking spray, and grill 3 minutes on each side or until pork is done. Set aside.

6. Place peaches, cut sides down, on grill rack; grill 4 minutes or until soft and slightly browned. Turn and cook 2 minutes or until heated through. Cut each peach half into 4 slices. Slice pieces of pork into 1-inch-thick strips.

7. Drizzle trimmed arugula with reserved 1 tablespoon juice mixture, tossing to coat. Place 1½ cups arugula on each of 4 plates. Top with grilled pork strips and peach slices; sprinkle evenly with turbinado sugar. **Yield:** 4 servings (serving size: 3 ounces pork, 8 peach slices, 1½ cups arugula, and ¼ teaspoon sugar).

CALORIES 216; FAT 7g (sat 2.4g, mono 3g, poly 0.6g); PROTEIN 25.5g; CARB 12.7g; FIBER 0.6g; CHOL 65mg; IRON 1.5mg; SODIUM 234mg; CALC 84mg

Grill the plums after cooking the pork tenderloins; it intensifies their natural sweetness.

Peppered Pork Tenderloin with Blue Cheese Plums

2 tablespoons chopped fresh rosemary
2 teaspoons fennel seeds
2 teaspoons coriander seeds
1 teaspoon kosher salt
1 teaspoon freshly ground black pepper
2 (1-pound) pork tenderloins, trimmed
2 ½ teaspoons olive oil, divided
Cooking spray
8 plums, halved and pitted
¾ cup (3 ounces) crumbled blue cheese
Rosemary sprigs (optional)

1. Place first 3 ingredients in a spice or coffee grinder; process until finely ground. Combine spice mixture, salt, and pepper in a small bowl. Rub pork with 1 teaspoon oil. Sprinkle spice mixture evenly over pork; wrap with plastic wrap. Refrigerate 2 hours.

2. Prepare grill.

3. Place pork on grill rack coated with cooking spray; grill 16 minutes or until a thermometer inserted in thickest portion registers 155°, turning once. Let stand 10 minutes; slice pork crosswise into ¼-inch-thick slices.

4. Place plum halves in a shallow dish. Drizzle with remaining 1½ teaspoons olive oil, and toss gently to coat. Place plums, cut sides down, on grill rack coated with cooking spray. Grill 3 minutes or until golden. Serve with blue cheese and pork. Garnish with rosemary sprigs, if desired. **Yield:** 8 servings (serving size: 3 ounces pork, 2 plum halves, and 1½ tablespoons blue cheese).

CALORIES 222; FAT 8.5g (sat 3.5g, mono 3.5g, poly 0.6g); PROTEIN 25.5g; CARB 10.6g; FIBER 1.6g; CHOL 71mg; IRON 1.6mg; SODIUM 429mg; CALC 73mg

Peaches

The state fruit of Georgia, peaches are in season from May to late September.

To select: Look for fruit that is firm; with a taut, unblemished skin; and no signs of bruising or wrinkles. If you smell peaches when you walk up to the stand, you know they are ripe.

To store: Ripen peaches at room temperature. If ripe, put them in the refrigerator; they'll keep for a few days.

To prepare: From cobblers to turnovers and ice cream to soup, peaches are a delight. You'll also find they are great in sauces and chutneys.

To cook: Vitamin A-rich peaches work with sweet and savory dishes. Cook with sugar (1 pound fruit per 2 cups sugar) on the stove until thickened for a delicious jam. Try sautéing, grilling, or roasting them to serve with duck, chicken, or pork or as a simple dessert.

Health benefits: Studies show that adequate vitamin C intake may help maintain a strong immune system. Peaches fill the bill. In addition, they are fat free.

This dish features the down-home flavors of corn bread, smoked ham, and peaches. The dressy presentation lends itself to a memorable summer dinner. You can also try this versatile salsa with grilled pork tenderloin or duck breast.

Corn Bread Shortcake with Ham and Fresh Peach Salsa

Salsa:

3   cups diced peeled peaches
¼   cup dried cranberries, chopped
¼   cup fresh orange juice
3   tablespoons minced shallots
2   tablespoons chopped fresh cilantro
1   tablespoon brown sugar
1   tablespoon fresh lime juice
¼   teaspoon ground cumin
⅛   teaspoon ground red pepper

Shortcake:

2.25 ounces all-purpose flour (about ½ cup)
1¼   cups cornmeal
2   tablespoons granulated sugar
1½   teaspoons baking powder
½   teaspoon salt
1¼   cups low-fat buttermilk
2   tablespoons canola oil
1   large egg
Cooking spray

Remaining Ingredients:

9   (1½-ounce) slices 33%-less-sodium smoked ham
Cilantro sprigs (optional)

1. To prepare salsa, combine first 9 ingredients in a bowl, and toss gently. Cover and chill 1 hour.
2. Preheat oven to 425°.
3. To prepare shortcake, lightly spoon flour into a dry measuring cup; level with a knife. Combine flour and next 4 ingredients, stirring well with a whisk. Make a well in center of mixture. Combine buttermilk, oil, and egg in a bowl; add to flour mixture. Stir just until moist. Spoon batter into an 8-inch square baking pan coated with cooking spray. Bake at 425° for 20 minutes or until a wooden pick inserted in center comes out clean. Cool in pan 5 minutes on a wire rack. Turn shortcake out onto a cutting board or work surface; cut into 9 equal pieces.
4. Heat a large nonstick skillet over medium-high heat. Coat pan with cooking spray. Add ham to pan, and sauté 1 minute on each side or until lightly browned. Remove from heat; keep warm.
5. Cut shortcake pieces in half horizontally. Place 1 bottom half on each of 9 plates; top each serving with 1 tablespoon salsa, 1 ham slice, and top half of shortcake. Top each serving with 2 tablespoons salsa. Garnish with cilantro sprigs, if desired.
Yield: 9 servings.

CALORIES 264; FAT 7.8g (sat 1.8g, mono 3.8g, poly 1.6g); PROTEIN 12g; CARB 37.3g; FIBER 2.7g; CHOL 51mg; IRON 1.4mg; SODIUM 679mg; CALC 98mg

Marinated Grilled Chicken Breast with Watermelon-Jalapeño Salsa

1 tablespoon chopped fresh oregano
1 tablespoon extra-virgin olive oil
1 teaspoon chili powder
¾ teaspoon ground cumin
½ teaspoon salt
3 garlic cloves, minced
4 (6-ounce) skinless, boneless chicken breast halves
Cooking spray
2 cups (½-inch) cubed seeded watermelon
1 cup (½-inch) cubed peeled ripe mango
¼ cup finely chopped red onion
2 tablespoons chopped fresh cilantro
2 tablespoons finely chopped seeded jalapeño pepper (about 1 small)

1 tablespoon fresh lime juice
½ teaspoon sugar
¼ teaspoon salt

1. Combine first 6 ingredients in a large zip-top plastic bag. Add chicken to bag; seal. Marinate in refrigerator up to 4 hours, turning bag occasionally.
2. Prepare grill.
3. Place chicken on a grill rack coated with cooking spray. Grill 5 minutes on each side or until done. Combine watermelon and remaining ingredients. Serve watermelon mixture with chicken. **Yield:** 4 servings (serving size: 1 chicken breast half and 1 cup salsa).

CALORIES 304; FAT 8.3g (sat 1.8g, mono 4.1g, poly 1.4g); PROTEIN 40.7g; CARB 15.9g; FIBER 1.5g; CHOL 108mg; IRON 1.8mg; SODIUM 540mg; CALC 44mg

Grilled Chicken Thighs with Roasted Grape Tomatoes

Chicken:

1	tablespoon grated lemon rind
2	tablespoons fresh lemon juice
1	teaspoon olive oil
2	garlic cloves, minced
8	skinless, boneless chicken thighs (about 1½ pounds)
½	teaspoon salt
¼	teaspoon freshly ground black pepper

Cooking spray

Tomatoes:

2	cups grape tomatoes
2	teaspoons olive oil
2	tablespoons chopped fresh parsley
1	teaspoon grated lemon rind
1	tablespoon fresh lemon juice
1	tablespoon capers
⅛	teaspoon salt
⅛	teaspoon freshly ground black pepper

1. Prepare grill.

2. To prepare chicken, combine first 4 ingredients in a large zip-top plastic bag. Add chicken to bag; seal. Marinate in refrigerator 15 minutes, turning bag occasionally.

3. Remove chicken from bag; discard marinade. Sprinkle chicken evenly with ½ teaspoon salt and ¼ teaspoon pepper. Place chicken on grill rack coated with cooking spray; grill 5 minutes on each side or until done.

4. Preheat oven to 425°.

5. To prepare tomatoes, combine tomatoes and 2 teaspoons oil in an 8-inch square baking dish; toss gently. Bake at 425° for 18 minutes or until tomatoes are tender. Combine tomato mixture, parsley, and remaining ingredients, stirring gently. Serve with chicken. **Yield:** 4 servings (serving size: 2 chicken thighs and ¼ cup tomato mixture).

CALORIES 194; FAT 7.8g (sat 1.7g, mono 3.4g, poly 1.6g); PROTEIN 25.9g; CARB 4.5g; FIBER 1.1g; CHOL 106mg; IRON 1.9mg; SODIUM 329mg; CALC 23mg

WINENOTE

Chicken is a flexible partner for wine, but the capers, lemon, and parsley in this dish call for a varietal that can handle the briny, tart, and herbal qualities of these ingredients: **sauvignon blanc.**

choiceingredient

Zucchini

Summer is the perfect time to savor just-harvested zucchini. With its slightly curved cylinder-like shape, this green summer squash is perfect for blending with other ingredients or in simple preparations highlighting the taste of fresh herbs. Because zucchini has a high water content, it doesn't require much cooking; raw, it adds nice texture to a salad of greens or a crudités plate. Like its yellow summer squash counterpart, zucchini is also a good source of vitamins A and C, and fiber.

If you have your own garden, you probably know you'll have an abundance of zucchini from early to late summer. Its peak season is June through late August, but you may see zucchini in markets in some regions year-round. Whether you're gathering them from the backyard or from supermarket produce bins, choose small zucchini with bright-colored, blemish-free skins. Refrigerate in plastic bags for no more than five days.

The mild acids in yogurt make it a great base for a tenderizing marinade.

Spiced Chicken Kebabs

Kebabs:

¾ cup plain low-fat yogurt
1 tablespoon grated peeled fresh ginger
2 teaspoons ground coriander
2 teaspoons paprika
1 teaspoon ground cumin
¼ teaspoon ground cardamom
¼ teaspoon ground turmeric
¼ teaspoon saffron threads, crushed
⅛ teaspoon ground cinnamon
⅛ teaspoon ground cloves
3 garlic cloves, minced
2 pounds skinless, boneless chicken thighs, cut into 1-inch chunks
1 medium red onion, cut into 1-inch chunks (about 8 ounces)
1 large red bell pepper, cut into 1-inch chunks (about 8 ounces)
1 medium zucchini, cut into 1-inch chunks (about 8 ounces)
Cooking spray
½ teaspoon salt
½ teaspoon freshly ground black pepper

Raita:

½ cup plain low-fat yogurt
⅓ cup diced seeded tomato
¼ cup cucumber, peeled, seeded, grated, and squeezed dry
¼ cup reduced-fat sour cream
1 tablespoon minced seeded jalapeño pepper
1½ teaspoons chopped fresh cilantro
¼ teaspoon ground cumin
¼ teaspoon salt

1. To prepare kebabs, combine first 12 ingredients in a large zip-top plastic bag; seal and marinate in refrigerator overnight, turning bag occasionally.

2. Prepare grill.

3. Remove chicken from bag; discard marinade. Thread chicken, onion, bell pepper, and zucchini alternately on each of 8 (12-inch) wooden skewers. Coat kebabs with cooking spray, and sprinkle with ½ teaspoon salt and black pepper. Place kebabs on grill rack coated with cooking spray. Grill 25 minutes or until chicken is done, turning occasionally. Remove from grill; keep warm.

4. To prepare raita, combine ½ cup yogurt and remaining ingredients in a small bowl. Serve with kebabs. **Yield:** 8 servings (serving size: 1 kebab and about 2 tablespoons raita).

CALORIES 189; FAT 6g (sat 2g, mono 1.7g, poly 1.3g); PROTEIN 24.9g; CARB 8.5g; FIBER 1.7g; CHOL 99mg; IRON 1.7mg; SODIUM 344mg; CALC 81mg

Prepare the slaw and dressing one day ahead, and store separately in the refrigerator.

Thai Summer Slaw

Slaw:
- 3 cups thinly sliced napa (Chinese) cabbage
- ½ cup (⅛-inch) julienne-cut yellow squash
- ½ cup (⅛-inch) julienne-cut zucchini
- ½ cup (⅛-inch) julienne-cut red bell pepper
- ½ cup (⅛-inch) julienne-cut yellow bell pepper
- ½ cup (⅛-inch) julienne-cut seeded peeled cucumber
- ½ cup shredded carrot
- ½ cup chopped fresh cilantro
- ¼ cup thinly sliced green onions
- ¼ cup grated radishes
- 1 minced seeded jalapeño pepper

Dressing:
- 3 tablespoons fresh lime juice
- 1 tablespoon fish sauce
- 1 tablespoon water
- 1½ teaspoons sugar
- ½ teaspoon chile paste with garlic (such as sambal oelek)

1. To prepare slaw, combine first 11 ingredients in a large bowl.

2. To prepare dressing, combine juice and remaining ingredients in a small bowl; stir with a whisk until sugar dissolves. Drizzle over slaw; toss well to coat. Serve immediately. **Yield:** 10 servings (serving size: about ½ cup).

CALORIES 20; FAT 0.1g (sat 0g, mono 0g, poly 0.1g); PROTEIN 0.9g; CARB 4.6g; FIBER 1.1g; CHOL 0mg; IRON 0.2mg; SODIUM 156mg; CALC 28mg

Serve stir-fried chicken breast and brown rice or buckwheat noodles to complement this nutrient-rich salad.

Asian Snap Pea Salad with Sesame-Orange Dressing

Dressing:
- 1 large orange
- 1 tablespoon rice vinegar
- 2 teaspoons low-sodium soy sauce
- 1½ teaspoons dark sesame oil
- 1 teaspoon brown sugar
- 1 teaspoon hot chile sauce (such as Sriracha)

Salad:
- 2 teaspoons canola oil
- 1½ cups thinly sliced red bell pepper
- ¾ cup thinly sliced carrot
- 12 ounces sugar snap peas, trimmed
- ½ teaspoon kosher salt
- ½ cup diagonally cut green onions
- 1 (6-ounce) package fresh baby spinach
- 1 teaspoon sesame seeds, toasted

1. To prepare dressing, grate 1 teaspoon rind; squeeze ⅓ cup juice from orange over a bowl. Set rind aside. Combine juice, vinegar, and next 4 ingredients in a small bowl; stir with a whisk.

2. To prepare salad, heat 2 teaspoons canola oil in a large nonstick skillet over medium-high heat. Add bell pepper and carrot to pan; sauté 1 minute, stirring occasionally. Add reserved orange rind, sugar snap peas, and salt to pan; sauté 2 minutes, stirring occasionally. Transfer pea mixture to a large bowl, and cool 5 minutes. Stir in green onions and spinach. Pour dressing over salad; toss gently to coat. Sprinkle with sesame seeds. Serve immediately. **Yield:** 6 servings (serving size: 1⅓ cups).

CALORIES 98; FAT 3.1g (sat 0.3g, mono 1.5g, poly 1.1g); PROTEIN 3g; CARB 15.7g; FIBER 4.5g; CHOL 0mg; IRON 2.1mg; SODIUM 318mg; CALC 83mg

Haricots verts are tender, young French green beans. If not labeled as such in your market, look for slim, petite green beans. Crème fraîche adds a nutty flavor and rich texture to the dressing; look for it near the gourmet cheeses in your supermarket. Substitute whole sour cream, if you prefer.

Haricots Verts and Grape Tomato Salad with Crème Fraîche Dressing

1 pound haricots verts, trimmed
¼ cup finely chopped fresh basil
2 tablespoons minced shallots
2 tablespoons fresh lemon juice
2 tablespoons crème fraîche
1 tablespoon honey
½ teaspoon salt
1 pint grape or cherry tomatoes, halved
1 tablespoon pine nuts, toasted

1. Cook haricots verts in boiling water 2 minutes or until crisp-tender. Drain and rinse with cold water; drain.

2. Combine basil and next 5 ingredients in a large bowl, stirring with a whisk. Add haricots verts and tomatoes; toss gently to coat. Place salad mixture on each of 6 plates; sprinkle with nuts. **Yield:** 6 servings (serving size: about ¾ cup salad and ½ teaspoon nuts).

CALORIES 74; FAT 2.8g (sat 1.1g, mono 0.8g, poly 0.6g); PROTEIN 1.7g; CARB 11.4g; FIBER 3.5g; CHOL 7mg; IRON 0.7mg; SODIUM 203mg; CALC 47mg

Chickpeas, black-eyed peas, or lady peas could be used in place of the pink-eyed peas in this refreshing summertime salad.

Fresh Pea Salad with Radishes, Tomatoes, and Mint

1½ cups fresh pink-eyed peas
3 tablespoons fresh lemon juice
1 tablespoon rice wine vinegar
1 tablespoon olive oil
2 cups grape or cherry tomatoes, halved
1 cup thinly sliced radishes (about 8)
¼ cup chopped fresh mint
¼ teaspoon salt
¼ teaspoon freshly ground black pepper
Mint sprigs (optional)

1. Sort and wash peas; place in a small saucepan. Cover with water to 2 inches above peas; bring to a boil. Cover, reduce heat, and simmer 20 minutes or until tender. Drain.
2. Combine juice, vinegar, and oil in a small bowl; stir well with a whisk.
3. Combine peas, tomatoes, and remaining ingredients in a medium bowl. Drizzle juice mixture over salad, tossing to coat. Cover and chill. Garnish with mint sprigs, if desired. **Yield:** 6 servings (serving size: ⅔ cup).

CALORIES 217; FAT 5.4g (sat 0.7g, mono 2.4g, poly 1.6g); PROTEIN 10.2g; CARB 34g; FIBER 9.6g; CHOL 0mg; IRON 3.5mg; SODIUM 145mg; CALC 65mg

Prepare Fresh Peas and Beans

Legumes such as field peas and fresh beans add earthy flavor, protein, and fiber to your plate. Most varieties, such as black-eyed, crowder, and lady peas, are available fresh throughout the summer, which makes it the right time to freeze them for year-round enjoyment.

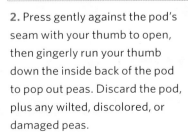

1. Snap off each pod's end, and remove the vein or string that runs along the length of the pod. Don't tug—just pull gently. (The veins from many supermarket peas will already have been removed for you.)

2. Press gently against the pod's seam with your thumb to open, then gingerly run your thumb down the inside back of the pod to pop out peas. Discard the pod, plus any wilted, discolored, or damaged peas.

3. To freeze, fill a heavy-duty zip-top plastic bag with the peas, and place in the freezer without rinsing. (Water frozen inside the bag could make the peas mushy when defrosted.) Use within three months for the best taste.

For the prettiest presentation, choose purple, orange, green, and red heirloom tomatoes. Cilantro lends peppery flavor and a subtle green hue to the dressing. Vary the taste of the dressing by using basil and lemon rind.

Heirloom Tomato and Avocado Stack

Dressing:

⅓ cup low-fat buttermilk

¼ cup chopped fresh cilantro

2 tablespoons reduced-fat sour cream

1 tablespoon reduced-fat mayonnaise

½ teaspoon grated lime rind

¼ teaspoon minced fresh garlic

¼ teaspoon salt

⅛ teaspoon ground cumin

Dash of ground red pepper

Salad:

4 medium heirloom tomatoes (about 2 pounds)

¼ teaspoon salt

¼ cup very thinly vertically sliced red onion

1 cup diced peeled avocado (about 1 small)

Coarsely ground black pepper (optional)

1. To prepare dressing, place first 9 ingredients in a small food processor or blender; process 30 seconds or until pureed, scraping sides of bowl occasionally. Cover and chill.

2. To prepare salad, slice each tomato crosswise into 4 equal slices (about ½ inch thick). Place 1 tomato slice on each of 4 salad plates; sprinkle slices evenly with ¼ teaspoon salt. Top each serving with a few onion pieces and about 1 tablespoon avocado. Repeat layers 3 times, ending with avocado. Drizzle 2 tablespoons dressing over each serving; sprinkle with black pepper, if desired. **Yield:** 4 servings.

CALORIES 115; FAT 7.6g (sat 1.8g, mono 4g, poly 0.9g); PROTEIN 3g; CARB 11.1g; FIBER 3.5g; CHOL 4mg; IRON 0.9mg; SODIUM 366mg; CALC 53mg

choiceingredient

Heirloom Tomatoes

Heirloom is a term used to describe any tomato plant that's openly pollinated (by wind and bees) and has been cultivated for more than 50 years. Seeds from the best plants are saved at the end of the growing season for future use. They come in many shapes and sizes—from the two-pound beefsteak to cherry tomatoes as tiny as currants. Because they ripen on the vine and are not stored under refrigeration, heirlooms are more likely than hybrids to have succulent flesh. But they vary in texture, running the gamut from firm and barely seedy to soft and moist. Some, like the little yellow pear tomato, seem at once juicy and firm. The colors of heirloom tomatoes vary from classic ketchup red to orange, gold, taxi yellow, nearly white, pink to purplish-black, and even green, when ripe. Several varieties are multicolored; Mr. Stripey, for example, is a pretty yellow-orange with pinkish red and green stripes.

A cornichon is the French version of a gherkin. You'll find these small, tart pickles in gourmet grocery stores; otherwise, gherkins will work just fine. Or, if you have capers on hand, you may substitute 1 tablespoon drained capers for the pickles. Make up to two hours ahead.

Potato Salad with Herbs and Grilled Summer Squash

Salad:

2   pounds small red potatoes

¾   pound yellow squash, cut lengthwise into
       ½-inch slices

Cooking spray

¼   teaspoon kosher salt

⅛   teaspoon freshly ground black pepper

Dressing:

⅓   cup chopped fresh chives

3   tablespoons chopped fresh parsley

2   tablespoons chopped fresh basil

1   tablespoon chopped fresh tarragon

¼   teaspoon grated lemon rind

3   tablespoons fresh lemon juice

2   tablespoons water

2   tablespoons extra-virgin olive oil

2   tablespoons finely chopped cornichons

¼   teaspoon kosher salt

⅛   teaspoon freshly ground black pepper

1. Preheat grill to medium-high heat.

2. To prepare salad, place potatoes in a large saucepan; cover with water. Bring to a boil. Reduce heat, and simmer 18 minutes or until tender. Drain; cut potatoes into quarters, and place in a large bowl. Set aside.

3. Lightly coat squash with cooking spray. Sprinkle evenly with ¼ teaspoon salt and ⅛ teaspoon pepper. Place squash on grill rack; grill 2 minutes on each side or until browned and tender. Remove squash from heat, and add to potatoes.

4. To prepare dressing, combine chives and remaining ingredients in a small bowl; stir with a whisk. Pour dressing over potato mixture, tossing gently to combine. Serve salad warm or chilled.

Yield: 6 servings (serving size: 1 cup).

CALORIES 160; FAT 5g (sat 0.8g, mono 3.4g, poly 0.8g); PROTEIN 3.8g; CARB 27g; FIBER 3.4g; CHOL 0mg; IRON 1.5mg; SODIUM 206mg; CALC 33mg

Summer Squash

Unlike winter squashes, such as butternut or acorn, summer squash has edible skin and seeds. The most common summer varieties are yellow squash (also called crookneck), pattypan squash, and zucchini.

To select: Whether you're gathering them from the backyard or from the supermarket produce bins, choose small, firm squashes with bright-colored, blemish-free skins.

To store: Refrigerate in plastic bags up to five days before cooking.

To prepare: Summer squash is great for blending with other ingredients or in simple preparations highlighting fresh herbs. Delicate yellow squash is perfect in chilled soups.

To cook: Whether they have a backyard plot or a few planters on a balcony or fire escape, cooks with home gardens can savor the seasonal taste of just-harvested summer squash. Because it has high water content, summer squash doesn't require much cooking; raw, it adds nice texture to a salad of simple greens or a crudité plate.

Health benefits: Summer squash is a good source of vitamins A and C, as well as fiber.

Here's a light, fresh, and colorful salad that combines two summer favorites: green beans and tomatoes. Use assorted colors of cherry tomatoes for even more color. This is hands-down one of the quintessential summer side dishes.

Green Bean and Cherry Tomato Salad

1¼   pounds fresh green beans, trimmed
1¼   pounds cherry tomatoes, quartered
1   teaspoon chopped fresh oregano
1   tablespoon minced shallots
2   tablespoons red wine vinegar
2½   teaspoons extra-virgin olive oil
½   teaspoon salt
¼   teaspoon freshly ground black pepper

1. Cook beans in boiling water 7 minutes or until tender. Drain. Place beans, tomatoes, and oregano in a large bowl; toss gently to combine.
2. Combine shallots and vinegar, stirring with a whisk. Let vinegar mixture stand 10 minutes. Add oil, salt, and pepper to vinegar mixture, stirring with a whisk until well blended. Pour vinaigrette over bean mixture; toss well. **Yield:** 8 servings (serving size: 1 cup).

CALORIES 51; FAT 1.7g (sat 0.2g, mono 1.1g, poly 0.3g); PROTEIN 1.9g; CARB 8.7g; FIBER 3.2g;
CHOL 0mg; IRON 1.1mg; SODIUM 158mg; CALC 32mg

Be sure to use true baby carrots with tops. So-called baby carrots sold in bags are often whittled-down mature vegetables; their texture will be too tough for this recipe.

Steamed Carrots with Garlic-Ginger Butter

2   garlic cloves
1   pound baby carrots with tops, peeled
1   tablespoon butter
1   teaspoon minced peeled fresh ginger
1   tablespoon chopped fresh cilantro
½   teaspoon grated lime rind
1   tablespoon fresh lime juice
¼   teaspoon salt

1. Mince garlic; let stand 10 minutes.
2. Steam carrots, covered, 10 minutes or until tender.
3. Heat butter in large nonstick skillet over medium heat. Add garlic and ginger to pan; cook 1 minute, stirring constantly. Remove from heat; stir in carrots, cilantro, and remaining ingredients. **Yield:** 4 servings.

CALORIES 69; FAT 3g (sat 1.8g, mono 0.8g, poly 0.2g); PROTEIN 0.9g; CARB 10.3g; FIBER 3.4g; CHOL 8mg; IRON 1.1mg; SODIUM 257mg; CALC 41mg

The combination of sweet corn and smoky bacon gives this uncomplicated dish sublime flavor. It's a delicious way to put fresh end-of-summer corn to use.

Creamed Corn with Bacon and Leeks

6   ears shucked corn
2   cups 1% low-fat milk
1   tablespoon cornstarch
1   teaspoon sugar
½   teaspoon salt
¼   teaspoon freshly ground black pepper
4   slices bacon
1   cup chopped leek

1. Cut kernels from ears of corn to measure 3 cups. Using dull side of a knife blade, scrape milk and remaining pulp from cobs into a bowl. Place 1½ cups kernels, low-fat milk, cornstarch, sugar, salt, and pepper in a food processor; process until smooth, scraping sides.

2. Cook bacon in a large cast-iron skillet over medium heat until crisp, turning once. Remove bacon from pan, reserving 1 teaspoon drippings in pan; crumble bacon. Add leek to pan, and cook 2 minutes or until tender, stirring constantly. Add pureed corn mixture, remaining 1½ cups corn kernels, and corn milk mixture to pan; bring to a boil. Reduce heat, and simmer 3 minutes or until slightly thick, stirring constantly. Sprinkle with crumbled bacon just before serving. **Yield:** 6 servings (serving size: ⅔ cup).

CALORIES 151; FAT 4.6g (sat 1.7g, mono 1.9g, poly 0.8g); PROTEIN 7g; CARB 23.1g; FIBER 2.4g; CHOL 9mg; IRON 0.8mg; SODIUM 325mg; CALC 111mg

Shuck Corn and Remove Kernels

Look for ears of corn in their husks when buying fresh corn. The husk helps retain the corn's natural moisture, making it taste fresher. Select green husks that don't appear dry. Pull back an edge of the husk to check that the kernels are plump, tight, and a vivid color. They should not appear dull, wrinkled, or dry.

1. Hold corn with tip facing down; pull husk and silks up toward your body. This helps remove more silks. Use a damp paper towel to remove remaining silks by twisting it back and forth over the corn.

2. Cut about ½ inch from the tip to create a flat base on which to stand the cob while removing kernels.

3. Stand corn upright in a pie plate. Use a sharp knife to slice away kernels in a slow, sawing motion.

Looking for something to add to your next summer grilling menu? Try this colorful veggie side dish. Great with anything from basic grilled flank steak to burgers, this recipe is always a good choice. Use parsley or chives in place of cilantro, if you prefer. Garnish with chives.

Corn and Summer Vegetable Sauté

1	tablespoon canola oil
½	cup chopped green onions (about 4)
1	garlic clove, minced
1	cup sliced fresh okra (about 4 ounces)
1	cup chopped red bell pepper (about 1)
1	finely chopped seeded jalapeño pepper
1	cup fresh corn kernels (about 2 ears)
1	(15-ounce) can black beans, rinsed and drained
⅓	cup minced fresh cilantro
⅛	teaspoon salt
⅛	teaspoon freshly ground black pepper

1. Heat oil in a large nonstick skillet over medium-high heat. Add onions and garlic; sauté 1 minute. Add okra; sauté 3 minutes. Reduce heat to medium.

Corn and Summer
Vegetable Sauté

Add bell pepper and jalapeño; cook 5 minutes. Add corn; cook 5 minutes. Stir in beans; cook 2 minutes. Stir in cilantro; sprinkle with salt and black pepper. **Yield:** 6 servings (serving size: ⅔ cup).

CALORIES 90; FAT 2.7g (sat 0.2g, mono 1.5g, poly 0.9g); PROTEIN 3.7g; CARB 15.9g; FIBER 4.8g; CHOL 0mg; IRON 1.2mg; SODIUM 232mg; CALC 43mg

Sweet Corn and Parmesan Flans

Cooking spray

2½	cups fresh corn kernels (about 5 ears)
1	cup 1% low-fat milk
⅓	cup grated Parmesan cheese
1	teaspoon all-purpose flour
½	teaspoon salt
¼	teaspoon freshly ground black pepper
4	large eggs
18	small tear-drop cherry tomatoes (pear-shaped), halved
2	tablespoons thinly sliced fresh basil

1. Preheat oven to 350°.
2. Heat a large nonstick skillet over medium heat. Coat pan with cooking spray. Add corn, and cook 5 minutes or until tender, stirring occasionally. Remove from heat. Set aside 1 cup corn kernels.
3. Place remaining corn in a food processor; pulse 5 times or until coarsely chopped. Add milk and next 5 ingredients to food processor; pulse 4 times or until combined.
4. Pour about ½ cup corn mixture into each of 6 (6-ounce) ramekins coated with cooking spray. Place ramekins in a 13 x 9–inch baking pan; add hot water to pan to a depth of 1 inch. Bake at 350° for 35 minutes or until the center barely moves when ramekins are touched. Remove ramekins from pan; cool 5 minutes on a wire rack. Invert flans onto each of 6 plates. Garnish each serving with about 2½ tablespoons reserved corn kernels, 6 tomato halves, and 1 teaspoon basil. **Yield:** 6 servings.

CALORIES 152; FAT 5.9g (sat 2.2g, mono 2g, poly 1g); PROTEIN 9.8g; CARB 17g; FIBER 2.4g; CHOL 147mg; IRON 1.2mg; SODIUM 344mg; CALC 125mg

Sweet Corn and Parmesan Flans

Southerners are well acquainted with the joys of okra, especially the crunchy-tender combination that results from deep-frying the pods. But anyone can enjoy this dish, which keeps all the crunch and dispenses with the grease.

Oven-Fried Okra

1½ cups yellow cornmeal
¾ teaspoon kosher salt, divided
½ teaspoon freshly ground black pepper
Dash of ground red pepper
½ cup fat-free buttermilk
1 large egg, lightly beaten
1 pound fresh okra pods, trimmed and cut
    into ¾-inch slices (about 3 cups)
Cooking spray

1. Preheat oven to 450°.

2. Combine cornmeal, ½ teaspoon salt, black pepper, and red pepper in a shallow dish; set aside.

3. Combine buttermilk and egg in a large bowl, stirring with a whisk. Add okra, and toss to coat. Let stand 3 minutes.

4. Dredge okra in cornmeal mixture. Place okra on a jelly-roll pan coated with cooking spray. Lightly coat okra with cooking spray. Bake at 450° for 40 minutes, stirring once. Sprinkle with remaining ¼ teaspoon salt. **Yield:** 8 servings (serving size: about ½ cup).

CALORIES 144; FAT 0.7g (sat 0.2g, mono 0.3g, poly 0.1g); PROTEIN 4.5g; CARB 29.3g; FIBER 2.6g; CHOL 27mg; IRON 1.3mg; SODIUM 204mg; CALC 68mg

choiceingredient

Okra

Available fresh year-round in the South, and elsewhere from May to October, okra has a mild flavor similar to that of green beans and, once cooked, a characteristic viscous texture. Select smaller, more tender okra pods (less than four inches long) that are firm, brightly colored, and free of blemishes. Refrigerate for up to three days in a plastic bag.

Baby Squash

As with their full-grown counterparts, baby summer squash are best enjoyed during their peak season of early to late summer. Baby squash varieties include miniature versions of the popular yellow and zucchini squashes, as well as the more exotic-looking pattypan and scallopini, which resemble flattened, scallop-shaped saucers.

Baby squash are big when it comes to nutritional value. The baby zucchini variety is an excellent source of vitamin C, and its high potassium content may help lower high blood pressure.

Baby squash boast a mildly sweet, nutty flavor and tender flesh. Enjoy them raw in salads or as part of a vegetable tray with your favorite dip. Petite pattypan or scallopini squash are also good in stir-fries, and they fare well on the grill. Or showcase squash alongside other summer vegetables in a quick ratatouille by sautéing squash, onions, garlic, bell peppers, eggplant, and tomatoes, and then simmering the mixture to a thick sauce.

Choose baby squash with shiny, bright-colored skin, avoiding those with spots, bruises, or cracks, and handle gently. Store in a perforated plastic bag in the refrigerator for no more than five days.

Grilling underscores the earthiness of the cumin and coriander, and enhances the nuttiness of pattypan squash. Use white, orange, or yellow squash for the most colorful kebabs.

Indian-Spiced Grilled Baby Squash

1   tablespoon olive oil
1   teaspoon grated peeled fresh ginger
½   teaspoon salt
½   teaspoon ground coriander
¼   teaspoon ground cumin
1   pound baby pattypan squash,
      cut in half crosswise
1   medium red onion, cut
      into 1-inch pieces
Cooking spray
1   tablespoon fresh lemon juice
1   tablespoon thinly sliced fresh
      mint leaves

1. Preheat grill.
2. Combine first 7 ingredients in a large bowl; toss well. Thread squash and onion alternately onto each of 8 (10-inch) skewers. Place skewers on grill rack coated with cooking spray; grill 10 minutes or until tender, turning frequently. Drizzle with juice. Sprinkle with mint. **Yield:** 4 servings (serving size: 2 kebabs).

CALORIES 61; FAT 3.6g (sat 0.5g, mono 2.5g, poly 0.5g); PROTEIN 1.7g;
CARB 6.9g; FIBER 1.8g; CHOL 0mg; IRON 0.6mg; SODIUM 299mg; CALC 26mg

This supereasy side can also be made with zucchini or a colorful combination of zucchini and yellow squash.

Yellow Squash Ribbons with Red Onion and Parmesan

4   medium yellow squash (about 1½ pounds)
1   teaspoon olive oil
1   cup thinly vertically sliced red onion
1   garlic clove, minced
¼   teaspoon salt
¼   to ½ teaspoon crushed red pepper
¼   teaspoon freshly ground black pepper
¼   cup (1 ounce) shaved fresh Parmesan cheese

1. Using a vegetable peeler, shave squash into ribbons to measure 5 cups. Discard seeds and core of squash.

2. Heat oil in a large nonstick skillet over medium heat. Add squash, onion, and garlic; cook 4 minutes or until onion is tender, gently stirring occasionally. Remove from heat. Add salt, red pepper, and black pepper, and toss gently to combine. Sprinkle with cheese. **Yield:** 4 servings (serving size: about ¾ cup).

CALORIES 84; FAT 3.4g (sat 1.4g, mono 1.4g, poly 0.3g); PROTEIN 4.5g; CARB 10.4g; FIBER 3.8g; CHOL 5mg; IRON 1mg; SODIUM 266mg; CALC 128mg

We found a way to get the flavor of a fried tomato without all the oil. To make sure the pan is hot enough to yield a crispy crust, preheat it while you're preparing the green tomatoes.

Unfried Green Tomatoes with Fresh Tomato Gravy

Green Tomatoes:

1.1 ounces all-purpose flour (about ¼ cup)

¼ cup yellow cornmeal

¼ teaspoon salt

¼ teaspoon black pepper

Dash of sugar

16 (½-inch-thick) slices green tomatoes (about 3 green tomatoes)

⅓ cup fat-free milk

Cooking spray

Gravy:

1 tablespoon butter

1 cup chopped mushrooms

½ cup finely chopped onion

2 cups finely chopped peeled red tomato

¼ teaspoon salt

¼ teaspoon black pepper

1. Preheat oven to 400°.

2. To prepare green tomatoes, combine flour and next 4 ingredients in a shallow dish. Dip tomato slices in milk; dredge in flour mixture. Lightly coat both sides of tomato slices with cooking spray.

3. Place a baking sheet in oven; heat at 400° for 5 minutes. Remove from oven; immediately coat with cooking spray.

4. Place tomato slices on preheated baking sheet. Bake at 400° for 25 minutes, turning slices after 15 minutes.

5. To prepare gravy, melt butter in a medium non-stick saucepan over medium heat. Add mushrooms and onion, and cook 4 minutes or until tender, stirring frequently. Add chopped red tomato; bring to a boil, and cook 10 minutes or until liquid almost evaporates. Stir in ¼ teaspoon salt and ¼ teaspoon pepper. Spoon gravy over tomato slices. **Yield:** 4 servings (serving size: 4 tomato slices and about ⅓ cup gravy).

CALORIES 142; FAT 4.2g (sat 1.9g, mono 1g, poly 0.5g); PROTEIN 4.2g; CARB 23.5g; FIBER 3g; CHOL 8mg; IRON 1.7mg; SODIUM 348mg; CALC 41mg

Tomatoes

In-season tomatoes are prized for their gorgeous colors and incomparable taste.

To select: Some of the best-tasting tomatoes are some of the homeliest. And picture-perfect tomatoes can be flavorless. When you buy tomatoes, smell them—a good tomato should smell like a tomato, especially at the stem end.

To store: Place tomatoes at room temperature in a single layer, shoulder side up, and out of direct sunlight. To store ripe tomatoes for any extended period, keep them between 55° and 65°.

To prepare: To seed or not? Basically, you should seed when you don't want too much juice, since seeding causes you to lose most of it. To seed a tomato, core it, and then cut it in half crosswise. Use your thumbs to push the seeds out of the tomato halves.

Health benefits: Lycopene is the disease-fighting antioxidant behind the bold red color of tomatoes. Researchers have found that people with high levels of lycopene in their blood have the lowest levels of cardiovascular disease.

Serve with a grilled burger or chicken. You can prepare this recipe up to two days in advance. The longer the tomatoes marinate, the more flavor they acquire. Remove the seeds from the pepper if you prefer mild heat.

Spiced Marinated Tomatoes

4   cups halved red, yellow, or orange cherry tomatoes
⅓   cup thinly sliced green onions (about 4)
4   garlic cloves, minced
1   jalapeño pepper, thinly sliced
⅓   cup white balsamic vinegar
1   tablespoon light brown sugar
1   tablespoon extra-virgin olive oil
2   teaspoons minced peeled fresh ginger
1   teaspoon ground cumin
½   teaspoon salt
½   teaspoon freshly ground black pepper

1. Combine first 4 ingredients in a large bowl. Combine vinegar and remaining ingredients in a small bowl; stir until blended. Pour vinegar mixture over tomato mixture, tossing to coat. Chill 1 hour. **Yield:** 8 servings (serving size: ½ cup).

CALORIES 58; FAT 2g (sat 0.3g, mono 1.3g, poly 0.3g); PROTEIN 1g; CARB 10.1g; FIBER 1.2g; CHOL 0mg; IRON 0.8mg; SODIUM 159mg; CALC 17mg

This recipe yields lots of cucumber pickles to keep on hand for picnics or snacks. Try them on sandwiches or burgers, as a complement to field peas, or as a snack with whole-grain mustard, Cheddar cheese, and crackers. Thin-skinned pickling cucumbers are essential.

Bread-and-Butter Pickles

5 ½ cups thinly sliced pickling cucumbers
    (about 1½ pounds)
1 ½ tablespoons kosher salt
1   cup thinly sliced onion
1   cup sugar
1   cup white vinegar
½   cup cider vinegar
¼   cup packed brown sugar
1 ½ teaspoons mustard seeds
½   teaspoon celery seeds
⅛   teaspoon turmeric

1. Combine cucumbers and salt in a large bowl; cover and chill 1½ hours. Drain; rinse cucumbers under cold water. Drain, and return cucumbers to bowl. Add onion to bowl.

2. Combine sugar and remaining ingredients in a medium saucepan; bring to a simmer over medium heat, stirring until sugar dissolves. Pour hot vinegar mixture over cucumber mixture; let stand at room temperature 1 hour. Cover and refrigerate 24 hours. Store in an airtight container in refrigerator up to 2 weeks. **Yield:** 16 servings (serving size: about ¼ cup drained pickles).

CALORIES 18; FAT 0.1g (sat 0g, mono 0g, poly 0g); PROTEIN 0.4g; CARB 4.4g; FIBER 0.5g; CHOL 0mg; IRON 0.1mg; SODIUM 168mg; CALC 8mg

The vibrant color and fruity flavor of this easy no-cook sauce are the essence of summer. Try it over ice cream, pound cake, or angel food cake. The optional framboise adds sublime flavor; you can also use a raspberry-flavored liqueur, such as Chambord.

Fresh Raspberry Sauce

4   cups fresh raspberries, divided
¼   cup sugar
1   tablespoon framboise (raspberry brandy; optional)
½   teaspoon fresh lemon juice

1. Place 2 cups raspberries and sugar in a food processor; process until pureed. Press mixture through a fine sieve over a medium bowl; discard solids. Stir in remaining 2 cups raspberries, framboise, if desired, and lemon juice. Cover and chill. **Yield:** 2 cups (serving size: ¼ cup).

CALORIES 61; FAT 0.4g (sat 0g, mono 0g, poly 0.2g); PROTEIN 0.7g; CARB 13.6g; FIBER 1g; CHOL 0mg; IRON 0.4mg; SODIUM 1mg; CALC 15mg

Raspberries

Intensely flavored berries, raspberries are composed of many connecting sections of fruit, each with its own seed, surrounding a central core. There are three main varieties of raspberries: black, golden, and red, with red being the most common. These berries are usually available from May through November.

Choose brightly colored, plump berries without hulls. Like blackberries, if the hulls are still attached, the berries are not mature and will be tart. Store raspberries in the refrigerator in a moisture-proof container for two to three days. Because they are fragile, store them in a single layer if possible.

Fresh berries need very little embellishment. They're excellent in jam, baked goods, and sauces. Antioxidant-packed raspberries contain some of the highest antioxidant levels of foods measured by the U.S. Department of Agriculture.

Serve this no-cook condiment with grilled chicken, pork, or fish. Or use as a topping for grilled bread or a dip for toasted tortilla wedges.

Nectarine and Radish Salsa

2 ¼ cups (¼-inch) diced nectarines
1 ½ cups radishes, halved lengthwise and thinly sliced
½ cup chopped cucumber
¼ cup finely chopped red onion
1 tablespoon fresh lime juice
2 teaspoons chopped fresh cilantro
1 ½ teaspoons sugar
¼ teaspoon salt

1. Combine all ingredients in a medium bowl; toss well. Let salsa mixture stand 30 minutes. **Yield:** 4 cups (serving size: ⅓ cup).

CALORIES 18; FAT 0.1g (sat 0g, mono 0g, poly 0.1g); PROTEIN 0.5g; CARB 4.3g; FIBER 0.8g; CHOL 0mg; IRON 0.1mg; SODIUM 55mg; CALC 7mg

Nectarine and Radish Salsa

Fresh Blueberry Sauce

1 cup water
¾ cup sugar
1 cup fresh blueberries
1 teaspoon butter
1 teaspoon fresh lemon juice
½ teaspoon vanilla extract
⅛ teaspoon ground nutmeg

1. Combine 1 cup water and sugar in a small saucepan over medium-high heat, and bring to a boil. Cook 5 minutes or until sugar dissolves, stirring constantly. Add blueberries and remaining ingredients to pan, and return to a boil. Reduce heat to medium; cook 4 minutes or until berries pop, stirring occasionally. Remove from heat. **Yield:** 12 servings (serving size: about 3 tablespoons).

CALORIES 59; FAT 0.4g (sat 0.2g, mono 0.1g, poly 0g); PROTEIN 0.1g; CARB 14.3g; FIBER 0.3g; CHOL 1mg; IRON 0mg; SODIUM 2mg; CALC 1mg

Pair this sweet and slightly hot condiment with grilled chicken or pork, or curry dishes. It can also perk up a turkey or ham sandwich. Store in the refrigerator for up to one week.

Peach Chutney

5   cups chopped peeled peaches
     (about 1¾ pounds)
1½ cups finely chopped red onion
½   cup packed brown sugar
½   cup white wine vinegar
3   tablespoons minced peeled
     fresh ginger
½   teaspoon salt
1   minced seeded jalapeño pepper
½   cup chopped fresh cilantro
2   tablespoons fresh lime juice

1. Combine first 6 ingredients in a saucepan; bring to a boil. Cover, reduce heat, and simmer 45 minutes. Stir in jalapeño. Simmer, uncovered, 5 minutes. Remove from heat; stir in cilantro and juice. Cool to room temperature. **Yield:** 4 cups (serving size: ¼ cup).

CALORIES 57; FAT 0.1g (sat 0g, mono 0g, poly 0.1g); PROTEIN 0.6g; CARB 14.4g; FIBER 1.5g; CHOL 0mg; IRON 0.4mg; SODIUM 78mg; CALC 14mg

This sauce is great with any grilled meat and as a spread with low-fat mayonnaise on sandwiches. Store it, covered, in the refrigerator for up to one week. A good rule for selecting apricots: If they smell sweet, they probably taste terrific. For spicier chutney, leave the seeds in the serrano chile.

Fresh Apricot Chutney

3 ½ cups cubed pitted apricots (about 1¼ pounds)
½ cup packed light brown sugar
½ cup chopped red onion
⅓ cup cider vinegar
¼ cup golden raisins
2 tablespoons honey
1 tablespoon minced seeded serrano chile (1 small)
½ teaspoon salt
½ teaspoon mustard seeds
½ teaspoon ground coriander
½ teaspoon ground cumin
½ teaspoon freshly ground black pepper

1. Combine all ingredients in a medium saucepan over medium-high heat; bring to a simmer, stirring constantly. Reduce heat, and simmer 15 minutes or until thick, stirring occasionally. Serve warm or at room temperature. **Yield:** 2 cups (serving size: 2 tablespoons).

CALORIES 63; FAT 0.2g (sat 0g, mono 0.1g, poly 0g); PROTEIN 0.7g; CARB 15.6g; FIBER 1g;
CHOL 0mg; IRON 0.4mg; SODIUM 78mg; CALC 15mg

Apricots

Apricots are among the first fruits of summer. With delicate flavor and creamy texture, they're a quintessential treat to usher in the season.

A relative of the peach, apricots were first grown in China more than 4,000 years ago. Today, California produces 90 percent of the United States' crop. Smaller Chinese apricots are one of the most common types available, but you might find other varieties like Riland, Tilton, and Royal in specialty stores and farmers' markets. Many aficionados favor Blenheim apricots, a yellow and green-skinned variety with especially sweet, succulent flesh.

Select apricots that are plump, reasonably firm, and evenly colored, but don't expect perfection. Often the fruit ripens unevenly, with the side that faces the sun as soft as jam and the other still hard. Baking apricots in a crisp or tart or using them in preserves or chutney can help even out texture and flavor. You can store apricots in a plastic bag in the refrigerator for up to five days.

This recipe received our Test Kitchens' highest rating. The sauce is delicious served over ice cream, as well. For a pretty presentation, cut each cake slice in half. Place the two halves on a plate, and top them with compote.

Lemon Pound Cake with Cherry Compote

Cake:

Cooking spray

13 ⅔ ounces all-purpose flour (about 3 cups plus 2 tablespoons), divided

2 teaspoons baking powder

½ teaspoon baking soda

½ teaspoon salt

2 cups granulated sugar

¾ cup butter, softened

2 large eggs

1 cup low-fat buttermilk

1 tablespoon grated fresh lemon rind

3 tablespoons fresh lemon juice

1 teaspoon chopped fresh mint

1 tablespoon powdered sugar

Compote:

4 cups pitted sweet cherries (about 1½ pounds)

¼ cup granulated sugar

2 tablespoons water

2 teaspoons cornstarch

¼ teaspoon almond extract

1. Preheat oven to 350°.

2. To prepare cake, coat a 10-inch tube pan with cooking spray; dust with 2 tablespoons flour.

3. Lightly spoon remaining 3 cups flour into dry measuring cups; level with a knife. Combine 3 cups flour, baking powder, baking soda, and salt in a bowl, stirring well with a whisk. Combine 2 cups granulated sugar and butter in a large bowl; beat with a mixer at medium speed until light and fluffy. Add eggs, 1 at a time, beating well after each addition. Add flour mixture to sugar mixture alternately with buttermilk, beating at low speed, beginning and ending with flour mixture. Add rind, juice, and mint; beat just until blended.

4. Spoon batter into prepared pan; sharply tap pan once on counter to remove air bubbles. Bake at 350° for 45 minutes or until a wooden pick inserted in center comes out clean. Cool in pan 10 minutes on a wire rack; remove from pan. Cool completely on a wire rack. Sift powdered sugar over top of cake. Cut cake into 16 slices.

5. To prepare compote, combine cherries, ¼ cup granulated sugar, 2 tablespoons water, and cornstarch in a medium saucepan; bring to a boil. Cook 1 minute, stirring constantly. Remove from heat; stir in extract. Cool. Serve with cake. **Yield:** 16 servings (serving size: 1 slice cake and ¼ cup compote).

CALORIES 319; FAT 9.9g (sat 5.8g, mono 2.6g, poly 0.6g); PROTEIN 4.4g; CARB 54.8g; FIBER 1.6g; CHOL 50mg; IRON 1.5mg; SODIUM 260mg; CALC 68mg

Make the cake ahead, and freeze it for up to two weeks. Thaw in the refrigerator, and bring to room temperature before glazing. Follow the directions for applying the glaze in two steps to allow it to permeate the cake more thoroughly. A fresh basil sprig is a lovely garnish.

Pound Cake with Lemon-Basil Glaze

Cake:

10   tablespoons butter, softened and divided
1¾   cups plus 2 tablespoons granulated sugar, divided
10   ounces all-purpose flour (about 2¼ cups)
1   teaspoon baking powder
¼   teaspoon baking soda
¼   teaspoon salt
2   teaspoons grated lemon rind
2   teaspoons vanilla extract
3   large eggs

½   cup low-fat buttermilk
2   tablespoons fresh lemon juice
3   large egg whites

Glaze:

¼   cup half-and-half
3   tablespoons chopped fresh basil
1½   cups powdered sugar, sifted
2   tablespoons fresh lemon juice
Dash of salt
Basil leaves (optional)

1. Preheat oven to 325°.

2. To prepare cake, coat a 12-cup Bundt pan with 1 tablespoon butter, and dust with 2 tablespoons granulated sugar.

3. Lightly spoon flour into dry measuring cups, and level with a knife. Combine flour and next 3 ingredients in a bowl, stirring well with a whisk. Combine 1½ cups granulated sugar and remaining 9 tablespoons butter in a large bowl; beat with a mixer at medium-high speed until light and fluffy. Beat in rind and extract. Add eggs, 1 at a time, beating well after each addition. Combine buttermilk and 2 tablespoons juice. Add flour mixture and buttermilk mixture alternately to sugar mixture, beginning and ending with flour mixture.

4. Place egg whites in a large bowl; beat with a mixer at high speed until soft peaks form, using clean, dry beaters. Add remaining ¼ cup granulated sugar, 1 tablespoon at a time, beating until stiff peaks form. Gently fold one-third of egg white mixture into batter; fold in remaining egg white mixture. Spoon batter into prepared pan. Bake at 325° for 55 minutes or until a wooden pick inserted in center comes out clean. Cool cake in pan on a wire rack 10 minutes. Remove cake from pan; cool completely on wire rack.

5. To prepare glaze, combine half-and-half and basil in a small microwave-safe bowl; microwave at HIGH 45 seconds. Let stand 5 minutes. Strain mixture through a sieve over a bowl; discard basil. Combine half-and-half, powdered sugar, 2 tablespoons juice, and dash of salt; stir with a whisk until smooth. Drizzle half of glaze over cake; let stand 5 minutes or until set. Repeat procedure with remaining glaze. Garnish with basil leaves, if desired. **Yield:** 16 servings (serving size: 1 slice).

CALORIES 284; FAT 8.9g (sat 5.3g, mono 2.4g, poly 0.5g); PROTEIN 4.2g; CARB 47.3g; FIBER 0.5g; CHOL 61mg; IRON 1mg; SODIUM 173mg; CALC 42mg

Basil

There are more than 60 types of basil, all members of the mint family. Basil is available year-round in supermarkets, but summer is the herb's best season. Much like tomatoes, basil is far superior when it is grown and picked in season. Basil enlivens dishes from classic pesto to contemporary sorbets. We suggest using it with abandon!

To select: Look for basil that isn't wilted and doesn't have dark spots. And if you're growing your own, be sure to harvest it on a sunny day, as the sun will bring out the essential oils that won't be present otherwise.

To store: Place stems in a glass of water up to a week. Just be sure to change the water every few days.

To cook: Match the variety of basil to the dish you are preparing. Lemon basil is great in gelatos and sorbets, while Thai basil holds up well to the strong flavors of spicy foods. Purple opal's complexity shines in salads, baked goods, and beverages. And don't forget the sweet Italian basil, the most common variety of basil, known for its licorice-clove flavor. It's an ideal match with fresh tomatoes and Italian dishes.

Sweet, juicy, peak-season berries make this dish shine. For convenience, make the berry mixture, whipped cream, and shortcakes in advance, then assemble just before serving. Prepare the berry mixture and whipped cream earlier in the day, and refrigerate; bring the berry mixture to room temperature or warm slightly in a pan before serving. Make the shortcakes as time permits, freeze them, then defrost at room temperature when ready to serve.

Gingered Blueberry Shortcake

- 4 cups fresh blueberries
- 3 tablespoons granulated sugar
- 1 tablespoon fresh lime juice
- 9 ounces all-purpose flour (about 2 cups)
- 1 tablespoon baking powder
- ½ teaspoon salt
- 6 tablespoons chilled butter, cut into small pieces
- 3 tablespoons minced crystallized ginger
- ¾ cup 2% reduced-fat milk
- 1 large egg white
- 1 tablespoon water
- 1 tablespoon turbinado sugar or granulated sugar
- ⅓ cup heavy whipping cream
- 2 tablespoons powdered sugar

1. Preheat oven to 400°.

2. Combine first 3 ingredients in a medium saucepan over medium-low heat; cook 3 minutes or until berries begin to pop, stirring frequently. Set aside.

3. Weigh or lightly spoon flour into dry measuring cups; level with a knife. Place flour, baking powder, and salt in a food processor; pulse 3 times to combine. Add butter and ginger to processor; pulse until mixture resembles coarse meal. Place mixture in a large bowl; add milk, stirring just until moist. Turn mixture out onto a lightly floured surface. Press mixture into a 7-inch circle; cut into 8 wedges. Place wedges 1 inch apart on a baking sheet. Combine egg white and 1 tablespoon water in a small bowl. Lightly brush tops of wedges with egg white mixture; sprinkle evenly with turbinado sugar. Bake at 400° for 20 minutes or until golden brown. Cool on a wire rack.

4. Place cream in a medium bowl; beat with a mixer at medium speed until soft peaks form. Add powdered sugar, beating until stiff peaks form. Split shortcakes in half horizontally; spoon ⅓ cup berry mixture over each bottom half. Top each with 1½ tablespoons whipped cream; cover with shortcake tops. **Yield:** 8 servings (serving size: 1 shortcake).

CALORIES 319; FAT 12.8g (sat 8g, mono 3.4g, poly 0.6g); PROTEIN 5.4g; CARB 47g; FIBER 2.6g; CHOL 38mg; IRON 2.2mg; SODIUM 415mg; CALC 149mg

choiceingredient

Blueberries

Of all the popular summer fruits, blueberries have an advantage, nutritionally speaking. They've earned the distinction of one of the most potent source of antioxidants, which help counteract heart disease, cancers, and other types of illnesses. Blueberries are also full of fiber and high in vitamin C. To pick the best of the crop, look for powder-blue berries that are firm and uniform in size. Store them in a single layer, if possible, in a moisture-proof container for up to five days, and don't wash until you're ready to use them.

Most of our recipes call for fresh or frozen wild blueberries, however you can also substitute an equal amount of fresh grocery-store berries. If using frozen wild blueberries, you can often toss them in without thawing. But in baked recipes, frozen berries will often discolor the batter, and fresh will not. The taste in this application is pretty much the same.

Frozen blueberries work well in many recipes, but sometimes only fresh will do. When eating with cold cereal, tossing into fruit salad, or incorporating in pies, use fresh blueberries, whose texture and moisture content are ideal.

Streusel-Topped Key Lime Squares

¼ cup butter, softened

¼ cup granulated sugar

1 teaspoon grated lime rind

⅛ teaspoon salt

⅛ teaspoon lemon extract

4.5 ounces all-purpose flour (about 1 cup)

Cooking spray

⅔ cup granulated sugar

3 tablespoons all-purpose flour

¾ teaspoon baking powder

⅛ teaspoon salt

½ cup fresh Key lime juice

3 large eggs

1 tablespoon powdered sugar

1. Preheat oven to 350°.

2. Place first 5 ingredients in a medium bowl; beat with a mixer at medium speed until creamy (about 2 minutes). Lightly spoon 1 cup flour into a dry measuring cup; level with a knife. Gradually add 1 cup flour to butter mixture, beating at low speed until mixture resembles coarse meal. Gently press two-thirds of mixture (about 1⅓ cups) into bottom of an 8-inch square baking pan coated with cooking spray; set remaining ⅔ cup flour mixture aside. Bake at 350° for 12 minutes or until just beginning to brown.

3. Combine ⅔ cup sugar, 3 tablespoons flour, baking powder, and ⅛ teaspoon salt in a medium bowl, stirring with a whisk. Add lime juice and eggs, stirring with a whisk until smooth. Pour mixture over crust. Bake at 350° for 12 minutes. Remove pan from oven (do not turn oven off); sprinkle remaining ⅔ cup flour mixture evenly over egg mixture. Bake an additional 8 to 10 minutes or until set. Remove from oven; cool in pan on a wire rack. Sprinkle evenly with powdered sugar. **Yield:** 16 servings (serving size: 1 square).

CALORIES 121; FAT 3.9g (sat 1.7g, mono 1.5g, poly 0.3g); PROTEIN 2.2g; CARB 19.9g; FIBER 0.3g; CHOL 47mg; IRON 0.6mg; SODIUM 93mg; CALC 21mg

These parfaits come together in a few minutes if you purchase orange sections from the refrigerated part of the produce section.

Blueberry-Orange Parfaits

1½ tablespoons Demerara sugar or turbinado sugar
½   teaspoon grated orange rind
2   (7-ounce) containers reduced-fat plain Greek-style yogurt
2   cups fresh blueberries
2   cups orange sections (about 2 large)
¼   cup wheat germ

1. Combine first 3 ingredients in a small bowl, stirring until blended. Spoon ¼ cup blueberries into each of 4 tall glasses. Spoon about 2½ table-spoons yogurt mixture over blueberries in each glass. Add ¼ cup orange to each serving. Repeat layers with remaining blueberries, yogurt mixture, and orange. Sprinkle 1 tablespoon wheat germ over each serving; serve immediately. **Yield:** 4 servings (serving size: 1 parfait).

CALORIES 186; FAT 3g (sat 1.6g, mono 0.1g, poly 0.5g); PROTEIN 11.8g; CARB 31.9g; FIBER 4.2g; CHOL 5mg; IRON 1mg; SODIUM 34mg; CALC 125mg

Late-Harvest Riesling
Sorbet with Berries

The late-harvest version of the wine has a higher sugar content than standard riesling. Fresh lime juice offsets the sweetness in our refreshing dessert. Use a combination of any fresh berries you have on hand, including strawberries.

Late-Harvest Riesling Sorbet with Berries

Sorbet:

1⅔ cups late-harvest riesling
½ cup water
½ cup sugar
¼ cup fresh lime juice

Berries:

1 cup fresh blackberries
1 cup fresh blueberries
½ cup fresh raspberries
2 tablespoons sugar
3 tablespoons late-harvest riesling
½ teaspoon grated lime rind

1. To prepare sorbet, combine first 4 ingredients in a small saucepan over medium heat; cook 3 minutes or until sugar dissolves, stirring occasionally. Increase heat to medium-high; bring to a boil. Cook 30 seconds. Pour mixture into a bowl; cool. Cover and chill 1 hour.

2. Pour mixture into the freezer can of an ice-cream freezer; freeze according to manufacturer's instructions. Spoon sorbet into a freezer-safe container; cover and freeze 2 hours or until firm.

3. To prepare berries, combine blackberries and remaining ingredients; toss gently. Cover and chill. Serve sorbet topped with berries. **Yield:** 6 servings (serving size: about ⅔ cup sorbet and about ⅓ cup berries).

CALORIES 125; FAT 0.3g (sat 0g, mono 0g, poly 0.1g); PROTEIN 0.8g; CARB 30.7g; FIBER 2.5g; CHOL 0mg; IRON 0.6mg; SODIUM 6mg; CALC 18mg

Lemonade Iced Tea Sorbet

Full-flavored English Breakfast tea is usually made from a blend that includes black tea leaves. But consider substituting your favorite tea to make this refreshing sorbet.

Lemonade Iced Tea Sorbet

2 cups boiling water
4 regular-sized English Breakfast tea bags
¾ cup sugar
¾ cup fresh lemon juice (about 4 lemons)
1 cup ice water
Mint sprigs (optional)

1. Combine 2 cups boiling water and tea bags in a large bowl; steep 5 minutes. Discard tea bags. Add sugar to tea mixture, stirring until sugar dissolves. Cool completely. Stir in juice and 1 cup ice water; chill 1 hour.

2. Pour tea mixture into the freezer can of an ice-cream freezer; freeze according to manufacturer's instructions. Spoon sorbet into a freezer-safe container. Cover and freeze 1 hour or until firm. Garnish with mint sprigs, if desired. **Yield:** 8 servings (serving size: ½ cup).

CALORIES 78; FAT 0g; PROTEIN 0.1g; CARB 20.7g; FIBER 0.1g; CHOL 0mg; IRON 0mg; SODIUM 0mg; CALC 2mg

Make Great Ice Cream

1. The most important piece of equipment is an ice-cream maker. You've got a couple of options: an old-fashioned bucket churn or a countertop freezer. Traditional bucket-style freezers require rock salt and ice, but tabletop models rely strictly on a freezer bowl filled with a coolant.

2. Heat the milk, and combine the egg yolks and sugar separately. Sugar may cause the milk to curdle if heated, and the egg yolks may coagulate if exposed to extremely high temperatures. Gradually add half the hot milk to slowly heat the egg mixture.

3. It's important to completely cool the ice-cream mixture before freezing it. Accomplish this quickly by placing the pan in a large ice-filled metal bowl.

4. Use coarse rock salt because it will not slip easily between the ice cubes or drain through the cracks of the bucket.

5. Ripen the ice cream by transferring it to a freezer-safe container. Let it stand in the freezer at least one hour or until firm.

6. Let the ice cream stand at room temperature for about five minutes to soften slightly after it ripens. If it's still frozen solid, heat the scoop under hot running water, pat it dry, and scoop.

Ripe peaches at peak season are key to this creamy, refreshing ice cream. It's best eaten the same day it's prepared.

Peach Ice Cream

3 cups sliced peeled ripe peaches (about 1½ pounds)
1 cup half-and-half
½ cup sugar
½ cup whole milk
1 teaspoon vanilla extract

1. Place peaches in a blender or food processor, and process until finely chopped. Combine peaches and remaining ingredients in a large bowl. Pour peach mixture into the freezer can of an ice-cream freezer; freeze according to manufacturer's instructions. Spoon ice cream into a freezer-safe container; cover and freeze 2 hours or until firm. **Yield:** 8 servings (serving size: ½ cup).

CALORIES 125; FAT 4g (sat 2.5g, mono 1.2g, poly 0.2g); PROTEIN 1.8g; CARB 21.3g; FIBER 1.2g; CHOL 13mg; IRON 0.1mg; SODIUM 20mg; CALC 53mg

Berries

Berries add sweet tartness to muffins, smoothies, milk shakes, and jams. They're at their peak from late May through August, but freezing them allows you to enjoy them year-round.

To select: Pick plump, juicy berries with a shine (blackberries), luster (raspberries), or bloom (blueberries) that have no trace of mold or discoloration. Look for firm, uniformly sized berries with deep color and no hulls or stems. Hulls and stems are a sure sign berries were picked too soon.

To store: If eating berries within 24 hours of picking, store them at room temperature; otherwise, keep them refrigerated in a moisture-proof container up to three days.

To prepare: Wash berries just before using them.

To use: Fresh berries need little embellishment. They're excellent in jam, baked goods, and sauces.

Health benefits: Antioxidant-packed berries, such as blueberries, blackberries, and raspberries, contain some of the highest antioxidant levels of foods measured by the U.S. Department of Agriculture.

You may make this heavenly shake kid-friendly by omitting the brandy. The recipe is equally delicious with or without the alcohol.

Brandied Berry Milk Shake

2   cups vanilla low-fat ice cream
½   cup blackberries
½   cup blueberries
½   cup sliced strawberries
½   cup 1% low-fat milk
¼   cup brandy
Fresh mixed berries (optional)

1. Place all ingredients in a blender; process until smooth. Garnish with fresh mixed berries, if desired. Yield: 4 servings (serving size: 1 cup).

CALORIES 182; FAT 3.7g (sat 2.1g, mono 1g, poly 0.3g); PROTEIN 4.7g; CARB 24.3g;
FIBER 1.9g; CHOL 19mg; IRON 0.4mg; SODIUM 65mg; CALC 153mg

Roasted Nectarines with Buttermilk Custard

Sauce:

⅛   teaspoon salt

4   large egg yolks

⅓   cup sugar

1   cup 1% low-fat milk

2   tablespoons low-fat buttermilk

¼   teaspoon vanilla extract

Nectarines:

6   medium nectarines, halved and pitted
    (about 2 pounds)

Cooking spray

1   tablespoon sugar

Verbena sprigs (optional)

1. To prepare sauce, combine salt and egg yolks in a medium bowl. Gradually add ⅓ cup sugar, beating 2 minutes with a mixer at medium-high speed.
2. Heat 1% low-fat milk over medium heat in a small, heavy saucepan to 180° or until tiny bubbles form around edge (do not boil). Gradually add hot milk to sugar mixture, stirring constantly. Return milk mixture to pan; cook over medium-low heat 5 minutes or until slightly thick and mixture coats the back of a spoon, stirring constantly (do not boil). Remove from heat. Stir in buttermilk and vanilla. Place pan in a large ice-filled bowl until mixture cools completely, stirring occasionally. Spoon mixture into a bowl. Cover and chill.
3. Preheat oven to 400°.
4. To prepare nectarines, place nectarines, cut sides up, in a 9 x 13–inch baking dish coated with cooking spray. Sprinkle nectarines evenly with 1 tablespoon sugar. Bake at 400° for 25 minutes or until nectarines are soft and lightly browned. Serve with chilled sauce. Garnish with verbena sprigs, if desired. **Yield:** 6 servings (serving size: 2 nectarine halves and ¼ cup sauce).

CALORIES 176; FAT 3.4g (sat 1.4g, mono 1.4g, poly 0.5g); PROTEIN 4.3g; CARB 32.8g; FIBER 1g; CHOL 138mg; IRON 0.7mg; SODIUM 80mg; CALC 70mg

choiceingredient

Nectarines

Nectarines are part of the plum family, thought to hail from Persia. Technically, they're a type of peach but with smooth skin and a tangier taste. There are more than 150 types of nectarines, including the ever-popular yellow HoneyKist. Nectarines' peak season is in July and August, though you can find them well into September in some areas.

When shopping for nectarines, especially at farmers' markets, the prettiest fruits aren't always the best. Some nectarines are like heirloom tomatoes—some of the ugliest ones are the best tasting. In general, choose aromatic nectarines that yield slightly when touched.

Refrigeration is never a good idea for stone fruit such as nectarines. It can really affect the taste. Simply storing nectarines on the counter in a shady spot is the best option.

Since nectarines are interchangeable with peaches, the recipe possibilities are endless. However, nectarines shine best when grilled and when used in pies and other baked goods.

Seared Figs and White Peaches
with Balsamic Reduction

Ripe figs and peaches have naturally high levels of sugar, which means they'll caramelize beautifully without additional sugar or copious amounts of fat. Toasted whole black peppercorns add an interesting savory finish.

Seared Figs and White Peaches with Balsamic Reduction

1   teaspoon black peppercorns
2   teaspoons butter, divided
2   teaspoons chopped fresh thyme, divided
4   firm ripe white peaches (about 1¾ pounds), halved and pitted
8   firm ripe Black Mission figs, halved lengthwise (about 1 pound)
⅓   cup balsamic vinegar
⅓   cup crème fraîche
⅛   teaspoon salt

1. Cook peppercorns in a small skillet over medium heat 6 minutes or until fragrant and toasted. Cool. Place peppercorns in a heavy-duty zip-top plastic bag; seal. Crush peppercorns with a meat mallet or rolling pin; set aside.
2. Melt 1 teaspoon butter in a large skillet over medium-high heat; stir in 1 teaspoon thyme. Add peaches, cut sides down, to pan. Cook 2 minutes or until browned. Remove from pan. Place 1 peach half, cut side up, on each of 8 plates. Melt remaining 1 teaspoon butter in pan; stir in remaining 1 teaspoon thyme. Add figs, cut sides down, to pan; cook 2 minutes or until browned. Place 2 fig halves on each plate.
3. Add vinegar to pan; cook over medium-low heat until reduced to 3 tablespoons (about 3 minutes). Cool slightly. Spoon about 2 teaspoons crème fraîche into center of each peach half; drizzle about 1 teaspoon vinegar mixture over each serving. Sprinkle each serving with about ⅛ teaspoon pepper. Sprinkle evenly with salt. **Yield:** 8 servings.

CALORIES 133; FAT 4.8g (sat 2.8g, mono 0.4g, poly 0.2g); PROTEIN 1.6g; CARB 22.4g; FIBER 3.2g; CHOL 12mg; IRON 0.6mg; SODIUM 50mg; CALC 32mg

Peaches with Cava and Lemon Verbena

You can find lemon verbena plants at your local nursery. Some farmers' markets and specialty stores also sell fresh sprigs. If you can't find it, cook strips of lemon rind with the wine, and add ½ teaspoon grated lemon rind before serving.

Peaches with Cava and Lemon Verbena

10   (3-inch) lemon verbena leaves
1   (750-milliliter) bottle Cava or other sparkling wine
½   cup sugar
6   cups sliced peaches (about 2 pounds)
½   teaspoon minced lemon verbena leaves

1. Combine whole verbena leaves and wine in a large saucepan; bring to a boil over medium heat. Cook until reduced to 1 cup (about 15 minutes). Remove and discard whole leaves. Add sugar, stirring until dissolved. Add peaches; bring to a boil. Remove from heat. Cover and chill. Stir in minced verbena leaves just before serving. **Yield:** 5 servings (serving size: 1 cup).

CALORIES 157; FAT 0.5g (sat 0g, mono 0.1g, poly 0.1g); PROTEIN 1.9g; CARB 39.5g; FIBER 2.7g; CHOL 0mg; IRON 1.1mg; SODIUM 11mg; CALC 23mg

choiceingredient

Plums

A plum's skin is tart and a little rough, yet its flesh is sweet, soft, and juicy. When you cook plums, something magical happens. The sweetness of the flesh, tartness of the skin, and spectrum of colors come together in harmony.

Deciding which plum to buy, however, can be daunting. You never know which of the more than 250 varieties might turn up in the produce section on any given summer day. Relax. Fact is, all plums taste about the same: sweet flesh inside tart skins. The choices are not so much about flavor as appearance or seasonal availability. A green or black plum may be best for presentation, and a red Santa Rosa may be ready for market before a green Kelsey, but other than that, a plum's pretty much a plum.

Ripe plums yield slightly to the touch; but don't squeeze them. Let the fruit sit in your palm. It should give a little. If you buy firmer fruit, though, don't put it in the refrigerator or the kitchen window—put it in a paper bag in a dark place for a day or two. Although the plums might taste sweeter, it's actually a trick on the palate. The sugar level remains the same after picking, but the acidity falls, so it only seems sweeter.

Choose tart plums for a less-sweet galette, or very ripe plums for a sugary result. The jam is a tasty glaze for the galette; serve leftovers spread on toast for breakfast.

Plum Galette

4.5 ounces all-purpose flour (about 1 cup)
3 ½ tablespoons chilled butter, cut into small pieces
¼ teaspoon salt
3 tablespoons ice water
1 tablespoon cornmeal
4 medium ripe red plums, each cut into 8 wedges
1 tablespoon cornstarch
¼ cup Plum Jam
1 tablespoon Plum Jam
1 tablespoon sugar

1. Lightly spoon flour into a dry measuring cup; level with a knife. Place flour, butter, and salt in a food processor; process until mixture resembles coarse meal. With processor on, slowly add ice water through food chute, processing just until combined (do not form a ball). Press mixture gently into a 4-inch circle on plastic wrap. Cover and chill 30 minutes.
2. Preheat oven to 425°.
3. Line a baking sheet with parchment paper; sprinkle paper with cornmeal. Unwrap dough; roll dough into a 9-inch circle on a lightly floured surface. Place dough on baking sheet. Combine plums and cornstarch in a large bowl, tossing to coat. Add ¼ cup Plum Jam; toss well to coat. Arrange plum mixture on top of dough, leaving a 1½-inch border. Fold edges of dough over plum mixture. Bake at 425° for 20 minutes.
4. Remove galette from oven (do not turn oven off). Brush crust with 1 tablespoon Plum Jam; sprinkle galette with sugar. Bake at 425° for 20 minutes or until crust is golden brown. Cool in pan on a wire rack 10 minutes before serving. **Yield:** 6 servings (serving size: 1 wedge).

(Totals include Plum Jam) CALORIES 208; FAT 7.3g (sat 3.4g, mono 2.8g, poly 0.3g); PROTEIN 2.8g; CARB 33.8g; FIBER 1.6g; CHOL 18mg; IRON 1mg; SODIUM 146mg; CALC 5mg

Plum Jam

4 ½ cups chopped ripe red plums (about 8 medium)
1   cup sugar
1   cup water

1. Combine plums, sugar, and water in a large saucepan; bring to a boil. Cover, reduce heat, and simmer 10 minutes. Uncover and simmer 50 minutes or until mixture begins to thicken, skimming foam from surface of mixture occasionally. Cool; pour into an airtight container. (Mixture will thicken as it cools.) Cover and chill. Yield: 2 cups (serving size: 2 tablespoons).

Note: Refrigerate jam in an airtight container for up to three weeks.

CALORIES 68; FAT 0.3g (sat 0g, mono 0.1g, poly 0.1g); PROTEIN 0.3g; CARB 17.2g; FIBER 0.5g; CHOL 0mg; IRON 0mg; SODIUM 0mg; CALC 0mg

Tarte tatin is an impressive-looking dessert, and is a tasty way to showcase nectarines. Using a stainless-steel skillet makes it easier to see when the sugar has caramelized, but you can use a nonstick pan. The tart is great served warm with low-fat vanilla ice cream.

Nectarine Tarte Tatin

7   medium nectarines
½   cup sugar
2   tablespoons water
1½ teaspoons fresh lemon juice
2   teaspoons butter
¾   teaspoon vanilla extract
½   (15-ounce) package refrigerated pie dough
    (such as Pillsbury)

1. Preheat oven to 425°.
2. Cut 1 nectarine in half. Quarter one nectarine half and remaining 6 nectarines.
3. Combine sugar, water, and juice in an ovenproof 12-inch stainless-steel skillet. Cook 2 minutes or until sugar is golden (do not stir). Remove from heat; stir in butter and vanilla. Let stand 3 minutes.
4. Place nectarine half, cut side down, in center of sugar mixture; arrange nectarine quarters, cut side down, around center. Return pan to medium heat. Cook 10 minutes or until sugar mixture is bubbly (do not stir). Remove from heat; let stand 3 minutes.
5. Roll pie dough into a 12-inch circle on a lightly floured surface. Place dough over nectarine mixture, fitting dough between nectarines and skillet.
6. Bake at 425° for 15 minutes or until lightly browned. Remove from oven, and cool 10 minutes. Carefully invert tart onto a serving plate. Cut into wedges. **Yield:** 10 servings (serving size: 1 wedge).

CALORIES 183; FAT 6.6g (sat 2.9g, mono 2.7g, poly 0.8g); PROTEIN 1.8g; CARB 30.4g; FIBER 1.6g; CHOL 6mg; IRON 0.3mg; SODIUM 84mg; CALC 6mg

Fresh cherries are crisp and explode with rich, sweet flavor. The secret to having a cobbler with a juicy filling and a flaky, crisp crust is an easy, old-fashioned method. Bake the crust separately, and then gently slide it onto the hot, baked cherries. The contrast between the luscious cherries and the sugar-dusted crust is as easy to savor as cherry season itself.

Fresh Cherry Cobbler

½ (15-ounce) package
  refrigerated pie dough
  (such as Pillsbury)
Cooking spray
1 large egg white, lightly
  beaten
1 tablespoon sugar
4 cups pitted fresh cherries
  (about 1¾ pounds)
1 cup sugar
3 tablespoons uncooked
  quick-cooking tapioca
1 tablespoon fresh lemon juice
⅛ teaspoon salt
2 tablespoons chilled butter,
  cut into small pieces

1. Preheat oven to 375°.
2. Cut dough into 8 (9 x 1–inch) strips. Arrange dough strips in a lattice design on a baking sheet coated with cooking spray. Brush dough with egg white, and sprinkle evenly with 1 tablespoon sugar. Bake at 375° for 15 minutes or until crust is golden brown. Cool on pan, on a wire rack, 10 minutes. Carefully lift crust using 2 spatulas; cool completely on wire rack.
3. Combine cherries, 1 cup sugar, tapioca, juice, and salt. Let stand 15 minutes. Spoon cherry mixture into an 8-inch baking dish coated with cooking spray. Top with butter. Bake at 375° for 40 minutes or until hot and bubbly. Place crust on top of cherry mixture. **Yield:** 8 servings.

CALORIES 312; FAT 10.4g (sat 4.9g, mono 1g, poly 0.3g); PROTEIN 2.3g; CARB 54g; FIBER 1.7g; CHOL 13mg; IRON 0.3mg; SODIUM 171mg; CALC 12mg

Cherries

Cherries are considered a stone fruit or drupe, which means their outer flesh surrounds a hard center seed; they are a relative of apricots, peaches, and plums.

Cherries mature early June through August. They can be whitish-yellow to bright red to nearly black in color, and they range in size from half an inch to more than an inch across. They come in two species: sweet cherries, such as Bing, Royal Ann, and Rainier; and sour cherries (also called tart or pie cherries), like Montmorency. You'll also find dried cherries in most supermarkets, but check the label—many brands contain added sugars.

Cherries are usually sold with stems attached, as this makes them last longer. Stems should be green and snap back when bent. Choose large, plump cherries with smooth, shiny skins and no discolored, wrinkled, or mushy spots.

Keep whole cherries, unwashed, in a breathable plastic bag in the refrigerator. Wash before serving, and eat them as soon as possible, as they can soften and deteriorate quickly.

Remove stems and pits before using. (This can be most easily done with a cherry pitter.) Be aware that cherry juice can stain fabrics and countertops, so prep them near your sink. Sweet cherries are delicious on their own as a snack, but both varieties can be used in salads, preserves, pies, and ice creams, and they'll add a burst of flavor to savory foods like pork, lamb, and chicken.

Use a fine mesh strainer to sift two tablespoons powdered sugar judiciously over the phyllo as you make the layers. Just a bit of sugar along with the cooking spray helps them adhere to one another. Don't worry if they're loosely stacked; the crisp texture provides a nice contrast to the sautéed grapes and creamy cheese.

Sautéed Grape Napoleons with Port Reduction

9   (14 x 9-inch) sheets frozen phyllo dough, thawed
Cooking spray
2   tablespoons plus 2 teaspoons powdered sugar, divided
¾   cup tawny port
1   tablespoon honey
¼   teaspoon salt, divided
2   teaspoons butter
2   cups seedless green grapes
1   cup seedless red grapes
2   teaspoons granulated sugar

2   teaspoons fresh lemon juice
1   ounce goat cheese, softened
1   (3-ounce) package ⅓-less-fat cream cheese, softened
2   tablespoons chopped walnuts, toasted

1. Preheat oven to 350°.

2. Place 1 phyllo sheet on a large cutting board or work surface (cover remaining dough to keep from drying). Lightly coat dough with cooking spray. Place 2 tablespoons powdered sugar in a small sieve; dust phyllo lightly with powdered sugar. Repeat procedure with 2 phyllo sheets, cooking spray, and powdered sugar, ending with powdered sugar; press layers gently to adhere. Cut phyllo stack lengthwise into 3 (3 x 14–inch) rectangles. Cut each rectangle crosswise into 4 (3 x 3½–inch) rectangles to form 12 rectangles. Carefully stack 1 rectangle on top of another to form 6 stacks; press layers gently. Place stacks on a baking sheet lined with parchment paper. Repeat procedure with remaining phyllo, cooking spray, and powdered sugar to form 18 stacks.

3. Cover phyllo stacks with parchment paper; place another baking sheet on parchment. Bake at 350° for 10 minutes or until stacks are golden and crisp. Carefully remove top baking sheet and parchment. Cool phyllo stacks completely on baking sheet.

4. Bring port to a boil in a small saucepan over medium-high heat. Cook 10 minutes or until reduced to 1½ tablespoons. Remove from heat; stir in honey and ⅛ teaspoon salt.

5. Melt butter in a nonstick skillet over medium-high heat. Add remaining ⅛ teaspoon salt, grapes, granulated sugar, and juice. Sauté 10 minutes or until grapes are tender, stirring occasionally. Remove from heat, and cool to room temperature.

6. Combine cheeses in a small bowl, stirring well.

7. Place 1 phyllo stack on each of 6 plates, and top with 1 teaspoon cheese mixture and 1 tablespoon grape mixture. Repeat layers once, ending with phyllo stack. Drizzle 1 teaspoon port mixture onto each plate. Sprinkle each serving with 1 teaspoon walnuts, and dust evenly with remaining 2 teaspoons powdered sugar. **Yield:** 6 servings (serving size: 1 napoleon).

CALORIES 297; FAT 8.6g (sat 4.1g, mono 1.7g, poly 1.5g); PROTEIN 4.9g; CARB 43g; FIBER 1.4g; CHOL 16mg; IRON 1.2mg; SODIUM 339mg; CALC 39mg

choiceingredient

Grapes

This member of the berry family can be just as versatile as its cousins. Deborah Madison, author of *Local Flavors: Cooking and Eating from America's Farmers' Markets,* combines halved grapes with a bit of crème fraîche, walnuts, and cinnamon or nutmeg for an easy fruit salad. Grapes can also appear in a sorbet or pie—Madison bakes one with Concord grapes every summer. They're also nice in salads (including chicken salad) and salsas. And, of course, they're delicious in jam.

When it comes to selection, "go for grapes with character," Madison advises. The most flavorful ones have seeds. Muscat grapes deliver sweet, musky flavor. Thompson seedless, found in many grocery stores, are best when allowed to ripen until they're yellow-green. You can use red and green seedless grapes interchangeably in recipes.

Look for grapes that are plump, richly colored, and fully attached to their stems. Grapes will keep unwashed in a plastic bag in the refrigerator for up to a week, but they're best eaten sooner. Be sure to rinse grapes thoroughly before eating or using them in a recipe, as dust may cling to the clusters.

autumn

the autumn kitchen

When the air turns cool and the trees blaze with color, it's time to fill up your basket and taste the autumn harvest. Stock up on the finest fresh produce—apples, pears, and pumpkin, sweet potatoes, figs, and butternut squash. With so many items to pick from, you'll never be without a delicious home-cooked meal.

Sweet and savory dishes like Leg of Lamb with Roasted Pear and Pine Nut Relish (recipe on page 254), Pumpkin Mixed Greens Salad with Maple Vinaigrette (recipe on page 269), and Caramelized Fresh Figs with Sweet Cream (recipe on page 305) are the perfect trio for a fancy autumn get-together. If a casual dinner party is more your style, throw together Hot Crab Dip (recipe on page 240) for a tasty appetizer, and pair easy Smashed Potatoes with Goat Cheese and Chives (recipe on page 277) with tender baked chicken breasts for supper. And for the perfect ending to an autumn day: a warming cup of Spiced Cider (recipe on page 237). Serve this after-dinner drink while you catch up with your friends around the fireplace.

If you're really feeling inspired by the season, prepare a traditional Thanksgiving feast that includes a delicious medley of autumn flavors. Serve your bird with Sausage, Apple, and Fennel Corn Bread Dressing (recipe on page 284), Traditional Sweet Potato Casserole (recipe on page 278), and Brussels Sprouts with Honey-Glazed Pearl Onions and Capocollo (recipe on page 273). And instead of standard pumpkin pie, showcase butternut squash in yummy Harvest Pie (recipe on page 295) for a most decadent dessert. There's no better way to celebrate autumn than by enjoying good food with the ones you love.

Autumn's bumper crop of fruits and vegetables offers a range of intense flavors and substantial textures. Groceries and farmers' markets are full of apples, figs, pears, pumpkins, sweet potatoes, and winter squash.

fruits

Apples

Cranberries

Figs

Grapes

Pears

Persimmons

Pomegranates

Quinces

vegetables

Belgian Endive

Bell Peppers

Broccoli

Brussels Sprouts

Cabbage

Cauliflower

Eggplant

Escarole

Fennel

Frisée

Leeks

Mushrooms

Parsnips

Pumpkins

Red Potatoes

Rutabagas

Shallots

Sweet Potatoes

Winter Squash

Yukon Gold Potatoes

herbs

Basil

Bay Leaves

Parsley

Rosemary

Sage

Tarragon

Thyme

autumn
From oatmeal and rice to Cheddar and cinnamon, here are some ideas for staples, seasonings, and other ingredients ideally suited for autumn tailgates, Thanksgiving spreads, and simple suppers for cool nights.

Brown Sugar: Brown sugar is simply white sugar with molasses added to it. Enjoy the deep flavor of the caramel-colored pantry staple at breakfast as a topping for bacon, or in some of your favorite desserts.

Butter: This yummy ingredient certainly comes in handy during the holiday season. Use butter to make fancy sauces, such as hollandaise and béarnaise, or delicious baked goods, like cookies, brownies, and cobblers.

Caramel: Caramel is made by cooking sugar until it melts down to a liquid. This sweet condiment ranges in color from pale golden to dark brown. Use it to add color and flavor to desserts and sauces, especially during the holidays.

Celery: Enjoy this popular green vegetable raw in salads, stuffed as an appetizer, or cooked in soups, stocks, and casseroles. Celery pairs especially well with an array of root vegetables, such as sweet potatoes, butternut squash, and fennel, which are in abundance during autumn.

Cheddar Cheese: Whether it's sprinkled atop a casserole or melted into a dip, Cheddar is the ultimate in versatile cheeses. Use it for breakfast on a skillet dish, in cheese straws as an appetizer, or on a delicious apple pie for dessert.

Chocolate: Whether you use semisweet, dark, or milk chocolate, this sweet ingredient will add rich flavor to any treat—from cookies and pancakes to coffee and smoothies.

Cider Vinegar: The most popular form of vinegar, cider vinegar has a pale, golden brown color with a strong aroma and faint apple flavor. It's an excellent everyday vinegar to use in pickling, salad dressings, and barbecue sauces.

Cinnamon: Although cinnamon may be more familiar in dishes such as sweet rolls, mulled cider, or pumpkin pie, its distinctive notes blend with meats and fish and perk up grains and vegetables in a surprising way.

Cocoa: Cocoa is a brown unsweetened powder made by removing most of the cocoa butter from pure chocolate. When the weather turns cool, use it to make instant cocoa mix. Keep it on hand for a tasty dessert, or give it to friends as a fun gift.

Maple Syrup: Pure maple syrup is made from maple sap that has been boiled down until it's thick and syrupy. While maple syrup is most commonly used as a topping for pancakes and waffles, it can also add depth of flavor to tangy marinades, brines, and vegetables.

Oatmeal: There's nothing like a warm bowl of oatmeal for breakfast to wake you up on a chilly autumn day. Use this wholesome ingredient to add texture to a piecrust; sprinkle it on top of yeast bread dough; or use it in a coating for oven-fried chicken.

Rice: With a mild, nutty, adaptable flavor and aroma, rice is simple enough to be eaten plain or paired with a variety of other ingredients. Add leftover rice to soups and salads for a heartier option.

best ways to cook

Baking, sautéing, and roasting are three cooking techniques that are perfect when the leaves begin to fall. Master these skills, and you're ready for autumn.

Baking

Baking is the process of cooking breads, pizza dough, and pastries, cakes, pies, and other desserts in the dry heat of an oven. The heat changes the starch in the food, creating a browned exterior or surface while sealing in moisture. Certain quick breads, such as pancakes, waffles, and crepes, are prepared on a griddle, in a waffle iron, or in a nonstick pan instead of an oven.

Batters and doughs have humble beginnings in the mixing bowl. They start with basic ingredients, such as flour, salt, sugar, and eggs, that are transformed into delicious treats. Of all cooking techniques, baking is one of the most complex; it's scientific and logical, based on following orderly steps and procedures. And while the nuances of baking are numerous, certain techniques and principles are always observed. Success relies not only on the right proportions of ingredients, but also on some essential skills that are easy to learn.

For Good Measure

Measuring flour is the single most important factor in light baking, so we list flour amounts in our ingredient lists by weight and also give an approximate cup measure, just in case you don't have a kitchen scale. Because precision is crucial in lightened baked goods (too much flour will yield a dry product), it's preferable to measure by weight, which is more accurate and ensures the same great results we achieve in our Test Kitchens.

If you use measuring cups, though, be sure to:
• Use dry measuring cups (without spouts).
• Stir the flour in the canister before spooning it out.
• Lightly spoon the flour into the measuring cup without compacting it, and then level off the excess flour with the flat edge of a knife.

If you measure flour in other ways (scooping it out of the canister, for example), you may end up with

more flour than we intend for the recipe. Also, you should not halve, double, or otherwise multiply or divide a recipe; the ratio of wet to dry ingredients can change as the volumes of both increase or decrease, which can result in undesirable outcomes.

Sautéing

Sautéing is a method of cooking food quickly in a small amount of fat over relatively high heat. It's a great technique for tender vegetables and cuts of meat, such as mushrooms, bell peppers, onions, chicken breasts, and beef tenderloin, that will cook rapidly. Food browns as it sautés, adding another level of flavor to its exterior.

Sautéed dishes come together quickly since the ingredients are comparatively tender to begin with, making this cooking method a perfect choice for weeknight cooking when time can be in short supply. And because you use little fat—usually just enough to coat the pan and prevent food from sticking—it's also a healthful way to cook.

The word sauté comes from the French verb *sauter*, which means "to jump," and it describes not only how food reacts when placed in a hot pan but also the method of tossing the food in the pan. The term also refers to cooking tender cuts of meat (such as chicken breasts or filet mignon) in a small amount of fat over moderately high heat without frequent stirring; the meat is flipped over when one side is browned.

Stir-Fry vs. Sauté

Stir-frying and sautéing share some similarities. Both methods cook food quickly in a small amount of fat. But stir-frying requires stirring the food constantly while it cooks over intensely high heat. Sautéing involves only moderately high heat, and the food is not in continuous motion.

Best Bets for Sautéing

Whether it's meat or vegetables, time in the pan is brief so it's important that the food be naturally tender. Cuts such as beef tenderloin, fish fillets, and chicken breasts are good candidates; tougher cuts such as brisket or pork shoulder are better for long cooking over low heat. The same principle holds for produce—asparagus tips will be more successfully sautéed than beets. Many other tender vegetables, including baby artichokes, sugar snap peas, mushrooms, and bell peppers, also lend themselves to this technique. That's not to say that denser, tougher vegetables can't be sautéed—they just may need to be blanched (briefly cooked in boiling water) first to get a head start on cooking.

Toss and Turn

When sautéing tender vegetables and bite-sized pieces of meat, stir frequently (but not constantly) to promote even browning and cooking. Dense vegetables such as cubed potatoes, though, should be stirred once every few minutes so they don't fall apart as they become tender. Portion-sized cuts of meat (chicken breasts, steaks, or pork medallions, for example) should be turned only once so they have enough time to form a nice crust, which will also keep the meat from sticking to the pan.

Don't Overcrowd

It's crucial that only one layer of food cooks in the pan at a time. When sautéing cuts of meat, leave at least a half inch between each piece. Food releases steam when cooking. If that steam doesn't have enough room to escape, it stays in the pan, and the food won't brown because it ends up steaming rather than sautéing. If you've ever tried to sauté a large amount of cubed beef for a stew, you may have experienced this problem. Simply sauté the food in smaller batches.

Roasting

Roasting may be one of the easiest cooking techniques because your oven does most of the work. The food cooks in an uncovered heavy pan where dry, hot air surrounds it and browns it, intensifying the flavors with a minimal amount of added fat. Foods can be simply prepared—meats rubbed with seasonings, vegetables cut up—and then they cook, virtually hands free, making roasting an especially handy technique for busy weeknight meals or hectic holidays.

Roasting involves cooking food in an uncovered pan in the oven. It's a dry cooking technique, as opposed to wet techniques like braising, stewing, or steaming. Hot air surrounds the food, cooking it evenly on all sides. Depending on the food you're preparing, you can roast at low, moderate, or high temperatures.

Best Bets for Roasting

Large cuts of meat work well: ham, whole turkeys and chickens, and tenderloins. Smaller cuts like boneless chicken breasts or fish fillets may dry out in the oven if they're not watched closely. Roasting is also ideal for dense fruits and vegetables, such as apples, nectarines, potatoes, beets, and winter squash, because it concentrates their natural sugars and intensifies their flavor.

Equipment

A roasting pan with a rack is a good investment for your kitchen. It has low sides, allowing more of the oven's heat to make contact with the food. Choose a heavy pan; it will distribute heat evenly and isn't as likely to burn pan drippings. A rack is helpful to suspend food that produces a lot of drippings (whole poultry or fatty roasts, for example) out of the liquid. If you don't have a rack, place a wire cooling rack in the pan. You can also use a broiler pan for roasting, but these pans are shallow, so be careful not to spill hot drippings out of the pan. You'll need kitchen twine to truss (tie) chickens, turkeys, and some roasts so they hold their shape as they cook. Look for food-safe kitchen twine at cookware stores, some hardware stores, and many large supermarkets. Or ask your butcher to include some twine with your purchase. A meat thermometer is essential since the key to perfectly roasted meats is to not overcook them. Choose an instant-read or a remote digital model.

Cloves

Cloves are an ancient spice, used for millennia in China and imported by the Romans from the Moluccas (now part of Indonesia). Today, Zanzibar and Madagascar are important producers.

The dried unopened flower bud of the tropical evergreen clove tree, cloves are shaped like a nail. This dark reddish-brown spice has an intensely sharp, slightly bitter taste and pungent aroma.

Whole cloves are commonly used in pickles of all sorts and spiced teas and mulled beverages, especially during autumn and winter. You'll also typically see hams studded with whole cloves during the holidays; this technique adds both flavor and decorative flair. Ground cloves are well known for their use in baked goods like cookies, gingerbread, and pumpkin pie, but they also make a great addition to pea and bean soups, root vegetables, and fruit compotes.

When cooking with cloves, use them sparingly as they can overpower other flavors. If you use whole cloves to flavor a dish, be sure to remove them before serving. They don't need toasting before use.

Cloves also have some health benefits. Eugenol, the primary oil found in cloves, functions as an anti-inflammatory agent. They're also loaded with antioxidant powers. You can find both whole and ground cloves year-round on the spice aisle at your grocery.

Welcome guests to your home with an inviting warm beverage. Steep the cider a day ahead of time, keep it refrigerated, and then reheat just before serving. For a nonalcoholic version, simply omit the brandy.

Spiced Cider

5 cups apple cider
1 (3-inch) cinnamon stick
1 whole clove
1 (½-inch-thick) slice orange
1 (½-inch-thick) slice lemon
½ cup brandy
12 (3-inch) cinnamon sticks (optional)

1. Combine cider, cinnamon stick, clove, orange slice, and lemon slice in a medium saucepan; bring to a boil. Cover, reduce heat, and simmer 30 minutes. Strain cider mixture through a sieve into a bowl; discard solids. Stir in brandy. Serve warm. Garnish each serving with 2 cinnamon sticks, if desired. **Yield:** 6 servings (serving size: about ⅔ cup).

CALORIES 173; FAT 0g; PROTEIN 0.9g; CARB 29.6g; FIBER 0.1g; CHOL 0mg; IRON 0mg; SODIUM 0mg; CALC 2mg

This is a time-saving concoction for a party. Simply prepare the gingered sugar syrup (step 1), and refrigerate it until you're ready to shake and serve the cocktails.

Gingered Pear and Brandy Cocktail

¼   cup water
3   tablespoons sugar
¼   cup chopped peeled fresh ginger
3   cups pear juice
1   cup cognac
10   lemon rind twists

1. Combine ¼ cup water and sugar in a small saucepan over medium-high heat; cook until sugar dissolves. Remove from heat. Add ginger. Cover and let stand 15 minutes. Strain sugar mixture through a fine sieve. Discard solids. Chill sugar mixture 30 minutes or until ready to use.
2. Fill a large martini shaker half full with ice. Add sugar mixture, juice, and cognac; shake until chilled. Strain ½ cup mixture into each of 10 martini glasses. Garnish each serving with 1 lemon twist. **Yield:** 10 servings.

CALORIES 111; FAT 0g; PROTEIN 0.1g; CARB 15.4g; FIBER 0.5g; CHOL 0mg; IRON 0.4mg; SODIUM 3mg; CALC 5mg

Gingered Pear and
Brandy Cocktail

Orange and
Chipotle-Spiced
Pecan Mix

Prepare a batch of this smoky-sweet mix to have on hand when visitors drop by. Or pack it into handsome jars to give as gifts.

Orange and Chipotle-Spiced Pecan Mix

1   tablespoon grated orange rind
1   tablespoon fresh orange juice
1   large egg white
2   cups pecan halves
1   tablespoon dark brown sugar
1   teaspoon kosher salt
½   teaspoon ground chipotle chile pepper
Cooking spray
½   cup sweetened dried cranberries

1. Preheat oven to 225°.
2. Combine first 3 ingredients in a medium bowl; stir with a whisk. Stir in pecans. Combine sugar, salt, and pepper. Add to pecan mixture; toss well. Spread mixture in a single layer on a jelly-roll pan coated with cooking spray. Bake at 225° for 1 hour, stirring occasionally. Remove from oven; cool completely. Stir in cranberries. **Note:** Store in an airtight container for up to 1 week. **Yield:** 2½ cups (serving size: 2 tablespoons).

CALORIES 91; FAT 7.7g (sat 0.7g, mono 4.6g, poly 2.4g); PROTEIN 1.2g; CARB 4.8g;
FIBER 0.8g; CHOL 0mg; IRON 0.3mg; SODIUM 98mg; CALC 1mg

A hot crab dip is the perfect addition to an autumnal buffet. Serve it warm with melba toast or pita chips.

Hot Crab Dip

1   cup fat-free cottage cheese
½   teaspoon grated lemon rind
2   tablespoons lemon juice
1   tablespoon Dijon mustard
1½ teaspoons Worcestershire sauce
1   teaspoon hot sauce
½   teaspoon salt
⅛   teaspoon freshly ground black pepper
1   garlic clove, minced
1   (8-ounce) block ⅓-less-fat cream cheese,
    softened
2   tablespoons chopped green onions
1   pound lump crabmeat, shell pieces removed
Cooking spray
2   tablespoons grated fresh Parmesan cheese
¼   cup dry breadcrumbs
Chopped green onions (optional)

1. Preheat oven to 375°.
2. Place first 9 ingredients in a food processor; process until smooth.
3. Combine cottage cheese mixture, cream cheese, and onions in a large bowl; gently fold in crab. Place crab mixture in an 11 x 7–inch baking dish coated with cooking spray. Bake at 375° for 30 minutes. Sprinkle with Parmesan and breadcrumbs. Bake at 375° for 15 minutes or until lightly golden. Garnish with chopped green onions, if desired. **Yield:** 20 servings (serving size: about 3 tablespoons).

CALORIES 63; FAT 3.1g (sat 1.8g, mono 0.1g, poly 0g); PROTEIN 6.8g; CARB 1.9g; FIBER 0.1g; CHOL 30mg; IRON 0.3mg; SODIUM 264mg; CALC 29mg

Although this appetizer is delicious with dried figs, fresh figs take it to another level. The Gorgonzola is an ideal combo with the sweet fig jam, but feta or any other soft, pungent cheese will work.

Crostini with Gorgonzola, Caramelized Onions, and Fig Jam

Jam:

1 cup dried Black Mission figs (about 6 ounces)

1 teaspoon lemon juice

2 cups water

2 tablespoons maple syrup

Dash of salt

Onions:

Cooking spray

2 cups vertically sliced yellow onion

1 teaspoon balsamic vinegar

½ teaspoon chopped fresh thyme

¼ teaspoon salt

½ cup water (optional)

Remaining Ingredients:

½ cup (4 ounces) Gorgonzola cheese, softened

24 (1-inch-thick) diagonally cut slices French bread baguette, toasted (about 12 ounces)

1 teaspoon fresh thyme leaves

1. To prepare jam, remove stems from figs. Place figs and juice in a food processor; process until figs are coarsely chopped. Place fig mixture, 2 cups water, syrup, and dash of salt in a medium saucepan; bring to a boil. Reduce heat, and simmer 25 minutes or until thick. Cool completely.

2. To prepare onions, heat a large nonstick skillet over medium heat. Coat pan with cooking spray. Add onion, vinegar, ½ teaspoon thyme, and ¼ teaspoon salt; cover and cook 5 minutes. Uncover and cook 20 minutes or until onion is deep golden brown, stirring occasionally. While onion cooks, add ½ cup water, if desired, ¼ cup at a time, to keep onion from sticking to pan.

3. Spread 1 teaspoon cheese over each baguette slice. Top each slice with about 1 teaspoon onion mixture and 1 teaspoon jam. Sprinkle evenly with thyme leaves. **Yield:** 12 servings (serving size: 2 crostini).

CALORIES 106; FAT 3.4g (sat 1.9g, mono 0.9g, poly 0.3g); PROTEIN 2.9g; CARB 16.3g; FIBER 2.4g; CHOL 8mg; IRON 0.6mg; SODIUM 82mg; CALC 85mg

Pumpkinseed kernels, also known as *pepitas,* are popular in Mexican cuisine. They add a nice crunchy garnish to this soup. Parsley makes a colorful additional garnish.

Pumpkin and Yellow Pepper Soup with Smoked Paprika

1   tablespoon olive oil
3 ½ cups chopped yellow bell pepper (about 2 large)
1 ½ cups chopped carrot (about 2 medium)
1   cup chopped onion (about 1 medium)
½   teaspoon Spanish smoked paprika
2   garlic cloves, chopped
5   cups fat-free, less-sodium chicken broth, divided
¼   teaspoon freshly ground black pepper
1   (15-ounce) can salt-free pumpkin puree
2   tablespoons fresh lemon juice
2   tablespoons unsalted pumpkinseed kernels, toasted
1   tablespoon chopped fresh parsley

1. Heat oil in a Dutch oven over medium-high heat. Add bell pepper, carrot, and onion; cook 10 minutes or until tender, stirring occasionally. Add paprika and garlic; sauté 1 minute. Add 3 cups broth and black pepper; bring to a boil. Cover, reduce heat, and simmer 20 minutes or until the vegetables are tender.

2. Place one-third of vegetable mixture in a blender. Remove center piece of blender lid (to allow steam to escape); secure blender lid on blender. Place a clean towel over opening in blender lid (to avoid spills). Blend until smooth. Pour into a large bowl. Repeat procedure with remaining vegetable mixture.

3. Return pureed vegetable mixture to Dutch oven; stir in remaining 2 cups broth and pumpkin. Cook over low heat 10 minutes or until thoroughly heated, stirring frequently. Remove from heat; stir in juice. Ladle 1 cup soup into each of 7 bowls, and top each serving with about 1 teaspoon pumpkinseeds and about ½ teaspoon parsley. Serve immediately. **Yield:** 7 servings.

CALORIES 88; FAT 2.7g (sat 0.5g, mono 1.6g, poly 0.5g); PROTEIN 3.6g; CARB 14g; FIBER 4.4g; CHOL 0mg; IRON 1.6mg; SODIUM 296mg; CALC 45mg

Spicy fresh ginger complements the sweet roasted winter squash and shallots in this easy recipe. Serve with a grilled cheese sandwich for a simple supper.

Roasted Butternut Squash and Shallot Soup

4   cups (1-inch) cubed peeled butternut squash (about 1½ pounds)
1   tablespoon olive oil
¼   teaspoon salt
4   large shallots, peeled and halved
1   (½-inch) piece peeled fresh ginger, thinly sliced
2½ cups fat-free, less-sodium chicken broth
2   tablespoons (1-inch) slices fresh chives
Cracked black pepper (optional)

1. Preheat oven to 375°.
2. Combine first 5 ingredients in a roasting pan or jelly-roll pan, and toss well. Bake at 375° for 50 minutes or until tender, stirring occasionally. Cool 10 minutes.
3. Place half of squash mixture and half of broth in a blender. Remove center piece of blender lid (to allow steam to escape); secure blender lid on blender. Place a clean towel over opening in blender lid (to avoid splatters). Blend until smooth. Pour into a large saucepan. Repeat procedure with remaining squash mixture and broth. Cook over medium heat 5 minutes or until thoroughly heated. Top with chives and pepper, if desired. **Yield:** 6 servings (serving size: ⅔ cup soup and 1 teaspoon chives).

CALORIES 112; FAT 2.5g (sat 0.4g, mono 1.7g, poly 0.3g); PROTEIN 3.3g; CARB 22.4g; FIBER 3.6g; CHOL 0mg; IRON 1.6mg; SODIUM 266mg; CALC 84mg

Shallots

These petite onions look like large cloves of garlic covered with papery bronze skin. Shallots differ from onions in that many varieties produce a cluster of several bulbs to a plant; they also have finer layers and less water. Because of this low water content, their flavor is more concentrated than that of onions.

You can cook with shallots when you want full onion flavor without the bulk of a full-sized onion. Traditionally, shallots are used to flavor the reduction in some French sauces, including béarnaise, bordelaise, and duxelles. They're also delicious cooked whole—try them caramelized with sugar and a few tablespoons of cognac, port, or sherry, or oven-roasted with rosemary or thyme. Finely chopped shallots are good in salad dressings and as a classic accompaniment to fresh oysters or beef dishes.

Available year-round, shallots should be firm and heavy for their size. Store them in a cool, dry place up to one month. When you're ready to cook with one, peel the shallot by removing a couple of the outer layers along with the peel. You might need an extra one to make up for the discarded layers, but this method is a lot faster than removing only the thin peel.

This easy soup brims with fresh vegetables; canned beans and orzo make it hearty and filling. Use a vegetable peeler to quickly remove the skin from the squash.

Quick Fall Minestrone

1 tablespoon vegetable oil
1 cup chopped onion
2 garlic cloves, minced
6 cups vegetable broth
2 ½ cups (¾-inch) cubed peeled butternut squash
2 ½ cups (¾-inch) cubed peeled baking potato
1 cup (1-inch) cut green beans (about ¼ pound)
½ cup diced carrot
1 teaspoon dried oregano
½ teaspoon freshly ground black pepper
¼ teaspoon salt
4 cups chopped kale
½ cup uncooked orzo (rice-shaped pasta)

1 (16-ounce) can cannellini beans or other white beans, rinsed and drained
½ cup (2 ounces) grated fresh Parmesan cheese

1. Heat oil in a large Dutch oven over medium-high heat. Add onion and garlic; sauté 2½ minutes or until tender. Add broth and next 7 ingredients; bring to a boil. Reduce heat, and simmer 3 minutes. Add kale, orzo, and beans; cook 5 minutes or until orzo is done and vegetables are tender. Sprinkle with cheese. **Yield:** 8 servings (serving size: 1½ cups soup and 1 tablespoon cheese).

CALORIES 212; FAT 5g (sat 1.6g, mono 1g, poly 1.2g); PROTEIN 9.6g; CARB 36g; FIBER 3.9g; CHOL 5mg; IRON 1.9mg; SODIUM 961mg; CALC 164mg

You can assemble the ravioli a day ahead, cover with plastic wrap, and refrigerate. The ravioli will float when they are perfectly cooked. Serve with a chilled chardonnay to round out your meal.

Pumpkin Ravioli with Gorgonzola Sauce

1¼ cups canned pumpkin
2 tablespoons dry breadcrumbs
2 tablespoons grated fresh Parmesan cheese
½ teaspoon salt
½ teaspoon minced fresh sage
¼ teaspoon freshly ground black pepper
⅛ teaspoon ground nutmeg
30 round wonton wrappers
1 tablespoon cornstarch
Cooking spray
1 cup fat-free milk
1 tablespoon all-purpose flour
1½ tablespoons butter
½ cup (2 ounces) crumbled Gorgonzola cheese
3 tablespoons chopped hazelnuts, toasted
Sage sprigs (optional)

1. Spoon pumpkin onto several layers of heavy-duty paper towels, and spread to ½-inch thickness. Cover with additional paper towels; let stand 5 minutes. Scrape into a medium bowl using a rubber spatula. Stir in breadcrumbs, Parmesan, salt, minced sage, pepper, and nutmeg.
2. Working with 1 wonton wrapper at a time (cover remaining wrappers with a damp towel to keep from drying), spoon 2 teaspoons pumpkin mixture into center of wrapper. Brush edges of wrapper with water and fold in half, pressing edges firmly with fingers to form a half-moon. Place on a large baking sheet sprinkled with cornstarch. Repeat procedure with remaining wonton wrappers and pumpkin mixture.
3. Fill a large Dutch oven with water; bring to a simmer. Add half of ravioli to pan (cover remaining ravioli with a damp towel to keep from drying). Cook 4 minutes or until done (do not boil), stirring gently. Remove ravioli with a slotted spoon; lightly coat with cooking spray; keep warm. Repeat with remaining ravioli.
4. Combine milk and flour in a saucepan, stirring with a whisk. Bring to a boil; cook 1 minute or until thick, stirring constantly. Remove from heat. Add butter; stir until butter melts. Gently stir in Gorgonzola.
5. Place 5 ravioli in each of 6 shallow bowls, and drizzle each serving with 3 tablespoons Gorgonzola mixture. Sprinkle each serving with 1½ teaspoons hazelnuts. Garnish with sage sprigs, if desired. Serve immediately. **Yield:** 6 servings.

CALORIES 250; FAT 9.1g (sat 4.5g, mono 2.7g, poly 0.7g); PROTEIN 9.5g; CARB 33g; FIBER 3.1g; CHOL 22mg; IRON 2.4mg; SODIUM 636mg; CALC 162mg

howto:

Roast Garlic

When garlic is roasted, its flavor mellows to slightly sweet and nutty and its texture becomes like a spread that has the consistency of butter. The method below differs slightly from the recipe for Roasted Garlic and Butternut Squash Cassoulet (page 249), but it can be used for other applications calling for roasted garlic.

1. Remove the white papery skin from the garlic head (do not peel or separate cloves). Cut top third off the head; discard.

2. Drizzle 1 teaspoon oil over cut side of garlic; wrap in foil. Bake at 350° until tender.

3. Separate cloves, and squeeze to extract garlic pulp. Discard skins.

To get a head start, roast the garlic, caramelize the onions, and even assemble this robust casserole the day before you plan to serve it. Use leftover roasted garlic to flavor soups, or combine with olive oil as a spread for toasted baguette slices. Pancetta is Italian unsmoked bacon. You can substitute regular smoked bacon, but use less, as the flavor is more assertive.

Roasted Garlic and Butternut Squash Cassoulet

1	whole garlic head
4	ounces pancetta, chopped
2	cups vertically sliced onion
1	tablespoon olive oil
1	tablespoon white wine vinegar
4 ½	cups (½-inch) cubed peeled butternut squash (about 2 pounds)
½	cup organic vegetable broth (such as Swanson Certified Organic)
½	teaspoon dried thyme
¼	teaspoon salt
⅛	teaspoon freshly ground black pepper
4	(16-ounce) cans cannellini or other white beans, rinsed and drained
1	bay leaf
2	(1-ounce) slices white bread
2	tablespoons grated fresh Parmesan cheese
½	teaspoon olive oil
1	tablespoon chopped fresh parsley

1. Preheat oven to 350°.

2. Remove white papery skin from garlic head (do not peel or separate the cloves). Wrap garlic head in foil. Bake at 350° for 1 hour; cool 10 minutes. Separate cloves; squeeze to extract garlic pulp. Set half of garlic pulp aside; reserve remaining garlic pulp for another use. Discard skins.

3. Heat a large Dutch oven over medium-high heat. Add pancetta; sauté 5 minutes or until crisp.

Remove pancetta from pan, reserving drippings in pan. Add onion and 1 tablespoon oil to drippings in pan; sauté 5 minutes. Reduce heat to medium-low; cook 25 minutes or until onion is very tender and browned, stirring frequently. Stir in vinegar.

4. Preheat oven to 375°.

5. Add garlic pulp, pancetta, squash, and next 6 ingredients to onion mixture, stirring well. Place bread in a food processor, and pulse 10 times or until coarse crumbs measure about 1 cup. Combine breadcrumbs, Parmesan cheese, and ½ teaspoon olive oil; sprinkle evenly over squash mixture. Cover and bake at 375° for 50 minutes or until squash is tender. Uncover and bake an additional 15 minutes or until topping is browned. Discard bay leaf, and sprinkle with parsley. **Yield:** 8 servings (serving size: 1¾ cups).

CALORIES 259; FAT 7.7g (sat 2.6g, mono 3.6g, poly 1.4g); PROTEIN 9.5g; CARB 38.8g; FIBER 8g; CHOL 11mg; IRON 3mg; SODIUM 679mg; CALC 131mg

Prepare and refrigerate the béchamel, covered, up to two days ahead. You may also refrigerate the mushroom–sweet potato mixture and the spinach mixture separately for up to two days.

Lasagna with Fall Vegetables, Gruyère, and Sage Béchamel

Béchamel:

3   ounces all-purpose flour (about ⅔ cup)
6   cups fat-free milk
½   cup finely chopped onion
¼   cup chopped fresh sage
2   tablespoons finely chopped shallots
½   teaspoon sea salt
1   bay leaf

Filling:

1   tablespoon olive oil, divided
2 ½ cups finely chopped onion
3   garlic cloves, minced
1   teaspoon sea salt, divided
1   (10-ounce) package fresh spinach
8   cups chopped portobello mushroom caps (about 1½ pounds)
6   cups (½-inch) cubed peeled sweet potato (about 2½ pounds)
Cooking spray
1   cup (4 ounces) shredded Gruyère cheese
¾   cup (3 ounces) grated fresh Parmesan cheese

Noodles:

12   precooked lasagna noodles
2   cups warm water

1. Preheat oven to 450°.
2. To prepare béchamel, lightly spoon flour into dry measuring cups; level with a knife. Place flour in a Dutch oven, and gradually add milk, stirring with a whisk. Add ½ cup onion, sage, shallots, ½ teaspoon salt, and bay leaf. Bring mixture to a boil; cook 1 minute or until thick. Strain béchamel through a sieve over a bowl, and discard solids. Set béchamel aside.

3. To prepare filling, heat 1½ teaspoons olive oil in a large nonstick skillet over medium-high heat. Add 2½ cups onion and garlic; sauté 3 minutes. Add ½ teaspoon salt and spinach; sauté 2 minutes or until spinach wilts. Set aside.
4. Combine 1½ teaspoons oil, ½ teaspoon salt, mushroom, and sweet potato on a jelly-roll pan coated with cooking spray. Bake at 450° for 15 minutes.
5. Combine cheeses; set aside.
6. To prepare noodles, soak noodles in 2 cups warm water in a 13 x 9–inch baking dish 5 minutes. Drain.
7. Spread ¾ cup béchamel in bottom of a 13 x 9–inch baking dish coated with cooking spray. Arrange 3 noodles over béchamel; top with half of mushroom mixture, 1½ cups béchamel, and ⅓ cup cheese mixture. Top with 3 noodles, spinach mixture, 1½ cups béchamel, and ⅓ cup cheese mixture. Top with 3 noodles, remaining mushroom mixture, 1½ cups béchamel, and 3 noodles. Spread remaining béchamel over noodles. Bake at 450° for 20 minutes. Sprinkle with remaining cheese; bake an additional 10 minutes. Let stand 10 minutes before serving.
Yield: 9 servings.

CALORIES 418; FAT 9.5g (sat 4.5g, mono 3.2g, poly 1g); PROTEIN 22.3g; CARB 62.7g; FIBER 6.4g; CHOL 24mg; IRON 3.7mg; SODIUM 703mg; CALC 505mg

The nutty flavor of fontina and the creaminess of mascarpone create a delicious updated version of mac and cheese. If your supermarket doesn't stock mascarpone cheese, substitute full-fat cream cheese. For a dinner party, bake the pasta in individual gratin dishes for 15 minutes.

Fontina and Mascarpone Baked Pasta

1	pound uncooked penne
1.1	ounces all-purpose flour (about ¼ cup)
3	cups fat-free milk
2	cups (8 ounces) shredded fontina cheese
¼	cup (2 ounces) mascarpone cheese
¾	teaspoon salt
¼	teaspoon freshly ground black pepper

Cooking spray

3	(1-ounce) slices white bread
1	tablespoon butter
1	small garlic clove, minced
1½	tablespoons chopped fresh parsley

1. Cook pasta according to package directions, omitting salt and fat. Drain; keep warm.

2. Preheat oven to 350°.

3. Lightly spoon flour into a dry measuring cup; level with a knife. Combine flour and milk in a large saucepan over medium heat, stirring with a whisk. Cook 10 minutes or until thick, stirring constantly with a whisk. Remove from heat; add cheeses, stirring with a whisk until smooth. Stir in salt and black pepper. Add cooked pasta, stirring to coat. Spoon pasta mixture into a 13 x 9–inch baking dish coated with cooking spray.

4. Tear bread into several pieces. Place bread in a food processor; process until fine crumbs measure 1½ cups.

5. Melt butter in a small skillet over medium heat. Add garlic; cook 30 seconds. Remove from heat. Stir in breadcrumbs until well combined. Sprinkle breadcrumb mixture evenly over pasta mixture. Bake at 350° for 25 minutes or until bubbly. Sprinkle with parsley. **Yield:** 8 servings (serving size: 1¼ cups).

CALORIES 423; FAT 14.3g (sat 8.2g, mono 3.7g, poly 0.7g); PROTEIN 19.3g; CARB 54.6g; FIBER 2.1g; CHOL 46mg; IRON 2.4mg; SODIUM 550mg; CALC 298mg

To serve two, use two (four-ounce) beef tenderloin steaks instead of flank steak, reduce the herbs to ½ teaspoon each, and omit the broth. Finish the tenderloin in the oven for 2 minutes instead of 10.

Roasted Flank Steak with Olive Oil–Herb Rub

1   teaspoon chopped fresh thyme
1   teaspoon chopped fresh oregano
1   teaspoon chopped fresh parsley
2   teaspoons olive oil
⅛   teaspoon grated lemon rind
1   garlic clove, minced
½   teaspoon salt
¼   teaspoon freshly ground black pepper
1   (1½-pound) flank steak, trimmed
Cooking spray
¼   cup dry red wine
¼   cup fat-free, less-sodium beef broth
Thyme sprigs (optional)

1. Preheat oven to 400°.

2. Combine first 6 ingredients in a small bowl.

3. Sprinkle salt and pepper over steak. Heat a large ovenproof skillet over medium-high heat. Coat pan with cooking spray. Add steak to pan; cook 1 minute on each side or until browned. Add wine and broth; cook 1 minute. Spread herb mixture over steak; place pan in oven. Bake at 400° for 10 minutes or until desired degree of doneness. Let stand 10 minutes before cutting steak diagonally across grain into thin slices. Serve with pan sauce. Garnish with fresh thyme sprigs, if desired. **Yield:** 6 servings (serving size: 3 ounces steak and about 1 tablespoon sauce).

CALORIES 167; FAT 7g (sat 2.5g, mono 3.3g, poly 0.4g); PROTEIN 23.9g; CARB 0.5g; FIBER 0.1g; CHOL 37mg; IRON 1.6mg; SODIUM 266mg; CALC 21mg

A variety of black, white, pink, and green peppercorns updates the standard *au poivre* coating. The deeply flavored, slightly sweet sauce balances the spice of the pepper. Serve with haricots verts and mashed potatoes.

Mixed Peppercorn Beef Tenderloin with Shallot-Port Reduction

Beef:

1   (2-pound) beef tenderloin, trimmed
1   teaspoon salt
1½   tablespoons cracked mixed peppercorns
Cooking spray

Reduction:

2   cups ruby port or other sweet red wine
1½   cups fat-free, less-sodium beef broth
¼   cup finely chopped shallots
⅛   teaspoon salt
2   sprigs fresh parsley
1   sprig fresh thyme
1½   tablespoons all-purpose flour
3   tablespoons water
1   tablespoon butter
½   teaspoon balsamic vinegar

1. Preheat oven to 450°.

2. To prepare beef, sprinkle beef evenly with 1 teaspoon salt and peppercorns, pressing firmly to adhere. Place beef in a shallow roasting pan coated with cooking spray. Bake at 450° for 33 minutes or until a thermometer registers 135° or until desired degree of doneness. Let stand 10 minutes before slicing.

3. To prepare reduction, combine port and next 5 ingredients in a medium saucepan; bring to a boil. Cook until reduced to 1¼ cups (about 15 minutes). Strain port mixture through a sieve over a bowl; discard solids. Combine flour and 3 tablespoons water. Return port mixture to pan; add flour mixture to pan, stirring with a whisk. Bring to a boil, and cook 1 minute or until thickened, stirring constantly with a whisk. Remove from heat; stir in butter and vinegar. Serve with beef. **Yield:** 8 servings (serving size: about 3 ounces beef and 2 tablespoons reduction).

CALORIES 173; FAT 6.7g (sat 2.9g, mono 2.5g, poly 0.3g); PROTEIN 23.2g; CARB 3.7g; FIBER 0.4g; CHOL 56mg; IRON 1.9mg; SODIUM 477mg; CALC 28mg

Pears

Pears are sweet and spicy, with a subtle, intoxicating perfume. And although a pear is usually thought of as a fruit to be eaten in its natural state, it's actually as versatile as the apple, especially during its peak season.

To select: Test for ripeness by applying light thumb pressure near the pear's stem. If it is ripe, there will be a slight give.

To store: If pears aren't quite ripe, place them on a kitchen counter in a brown paper bag; check daily. It may take three to five days for them to fully ripen. Once ripe, store in the refrigerator for three to five days.

To prepare: If the neck area yields to gentle thumb pressure, the pear is ready to eat or cook in desserts, pancakes, and even meat dishes.

To cook: The best pears for cooking are varieties such as Bosc, Comice, Seckel, and red and green Anjous.

Health benefits: One medium pear provides 6 grams of fiber as well as vitamin A, vitamin C, and potassium.

You can also serve the relish with roast beef, pork, or chicken. Prepare it up to two days in advance, but be sure to stir in the nuts just before serving so they stay crunchy.

Leg of Lamb with Roasted Pear and Pine Nut Relish

Relish:
6   firm ripe Anjou pears, peeled, cored, and quartered
1   medium Rio or other sweet onion, cut into ¼-inch-thick slices
Cooking spray
2   teaspoons grated lemon rind
1   tablespoon fresh lemon juice
1   tablespoon honey
2   teaspoons olive oil
¼   teaspoon salt
¼   teaspoon ground cumin
¼   teaspoon ground coriander
¼   teaspoon black pepper
¼   cup pine nuts, toasted

Lamb:
1   tablespoon grated lemon rind
¼   cup fresh lemon juice
1   tablespoon olive oil
2   teaspoons ground cumin
2   teaspoons ground coriander
½   teaspoon salt
½   teaspoon paprika
½   teaspoon freshly ground black pepper
¼   teaspoon ground red pepper
4   garlic cloves
1   small onion, cut into 8 wedges
1   (5-pound) boneless leg of lamb, trimmed

1. Preheat oven to 400°.

2. To prepare relish, arrange pears in a single layer in a 13 x 9–inch baking dish. Arrange onion slices in a single layer in another 13 x 9–inch baking dish; lightly coat onion slices with cooking spray. Bake pears and onion slices at 400° for 40 minutes or until tender, turning once. Cool; chop.

3. Combine 2 teaspoons rind and next 7 ingredients in a large bowl; add chopped onion and pears, tossing gently to combine. Stir in nuts just before serving.

4. To prepare lamb, place 1 tablespoon lemon rind and next 10 ingredients in a food processor; process until finely chopped. Roll lamb, and secure at 3-inch intervals with twine. Spread onion mixture over lamb; cover and refrigerate 8 hours or overnight.

5. Preheat oven to 450°.

6. Place lamb on rack of a broiler pan coated with cooking spray; place rack in pan. Bake at 450° for 20 minutes. Decrease oven temperature to 300° (do not remove lamb from oven); bake an additional 1 hour or until thermometer registers 145° (medium-rare) to 160° (medium). Let stand 10 minutes before slicing. Serve relish with lamb. **Yield:** 18 servings (serving size: about 3 ounces lamb and about 3 tablespoons relish).

CALORIES 246; FAT 10g (sat 3.2g, mono 4.3g, poly 1.2g); PROTEIN 25.3g; CARB 13.7g; FIBER 2.6g; CHOL 80mg; IRON 2.3mg; SODIUM 165mg; CALC 21mg

They may have four James Beard Awards to their credit, but cookbook authors Cheryl Alters Jamison and Bill Jamison know that not every culinary experiment is a success. In developing this autumn favorite, they started out with a smothered pork chop with butternut squash, but the butternut squash just overwhelmed the pork. However, a walnut-crusted chop seemed to pair well with wild rice into which they tossed their remaining market-basket ingredients. They found that apples, mushrooms, and Swiss chard made a nice contrast to the wild rice's crunchy texture.

Walnut-Crusted Pork Chops with Autumn Vegetable Wild Rice

Pork:

4   (8-ounce) bone-in center-cut pork chops, trimmed

1½ teaspoons Worcestershire sauce

¾   teaspoon kosher salt

½   teaspoon dried sage

¼   teaspoon freshly ground black pepper

⅓   cup walnuts, finely ground

1   slice bacon

¼   cup fat-free, less-sodium chicken broth

Rice:

Cooking spray

1   cup finely chopped onion

½   cup diced carrot

2   teaspoons diced seeded jalapeño pepper

1   garlic clove, minced

1½ cups finely chopped trimmed Swiss chard

1   cup sliced cremini mushrooms

1   cup chopped peeled Granny Smith apple

2   cups cooked wild rice

½   cup fat-free, less-sodium chicken broth

¼   cup chopped fresh flat-leaf parsley

1. To prepare pork, place chops in a shallow dish; drizzle evenly with Worcestershire. Combine salt, sage, and black pepper in a small bowl. Reserve ¾ teaspoon salt mixture. Add walnuts to remaining salt mixture; toss well. Press walnut mixture onto both sides of pork chops. Cover and refrigerate 30 minutes.

2. Cook bacon slice in a large nonstick skillet over medium heat until crisp. Remove bacon from pan; crumble. Add pork chops to drippings in pan; cook 1½ minutes on each side or until lightly browned. Add ¼ cup chicken broth to pan. Cover, reduce heat, and cook 6 minutes or until desired degree of doneness. Remove pork from pan.

3. To prepare rice, heat a large saucepan over medium heat. Coat pan with cooking spray. Add onion and next 3 ingredients to pan; cover and cook 5 minutes or until onion is tender. Stir in reserved ¾ teaspoon salt mixture, chard, mushrooms, and apple. Cover and cook 5 minutes or until carrot is tender. Stir in rice and ½ cup broth. Bring to a simmer; cook, uncovered, 5 minutes or until liquid is absorbed. Stir in bacon. Place 1 cup rice mixture on each of 4 plates; top each serving with 1 pork chop. Drizzle each serving with pan drippings, and sprinkle each with 1 tablespoon parsley. **Yield:** 4 servings.

CALORIES 379; FAT 14.7g (sat 3.5g, mono 4.4g, poly 5.5g); PROTEIN 29.1g; CARB 34.6g; FIBER 5g; CHOL 69mg; IRON 2.6mg; SODIUM 600mg; CALC 65mg

Prepare Pork Tenderloin

Pork's leanest and most versatile cut is the tenderloin. It requires minimal preparation before use in recipes. Just remove the silver skin, which is the thin, shiny membrane that runs along the surface of the meat. Leaving it on can cause the tenderloin to toughen and lose shape during cooking. Use a small, sharp knife, such as a paring knife.

1. Stretching the membrane with one hand so it's tight, use your other hand to slip the tip of the knife underneath the silvery skin.

2. Slowly slice back and forth, angling the sharp edge of the blade up, rather than down, through the meat. Continue until all the silver skin is removed; then discard it.

The smokiness of adobo sauce calls for a robust Grade A Dark or Grade B maple syrup.

Spiced Pork Tenderloin with Maple-Chipotle Sauce

Pork:

½ teaspoon salt

½ teaspoon dried thyme

¼ teaspoon ground nutmeg

¼ teaspoon ground cinnamon

¼ teaspoon freshly ground black pepper

⅛ teaspoon ground allspice

2 (1-pound) pork tenderloins, trimmed

2 teaspoons olive oil

Sauce:

1 (7-ounce) can chipotle chiles, canned in adobo sauce

½ cup maple syrup

3 tablespoons fat-free, less-sodium chicken broth

1½ tablespoons cider vinegar

1. To prepare pork, combine first 6 ingredients; sprinkle evenly over pork. Place in a large zip-top plastic bag; seal and refrigerate 3 hours.

2. Preheat oven to 375°.

3. Remove pork from bag. Place pork in a roasting pan; drizzle with oil. Bake at 375° for 30 minutes or until a thermometer inserted in center of pork registers 155°. Remove pork from pan; cover and let stand 10 minutes.

4. To prepare sauce, remove 2 teaspoons adobo sauce from can of chiles; reserve remaining chiles and sauce for another use. Add 2 teaspoons adobo sauce, syrup, broth, and vinegar to roasting pan, scraping pan to loosen browned bits. Cook over medium heat 5 minutes, stirring constantly. Remove from heat. Place pork in pan, turning to coat. Remove pork from pan, reserving sauce in pan. Cut pork into ½-inch-thick slices. Strain sauce through a fine sieve into a bowl; serve with pork.

Yield: 8 servings (serving size: 3 ounces pork and about 1 tablespoon sauce).

CALORIES 201; FAT 5.1g (sat 1.5g, mono 2.6g, poly 0.6g); PROTEIN 23.9g; CARB 13.8g; FIBER 0.3g; CHOL 74mg; IRON 1.8mg; SODIUM 229mg; CALC 23mg

The apples create a flavorful chunky sauce. Feel free to leave bits of peel on the apples to make this rustic dish even more colorful. Look for bone-in chicken thighs that are already skinned.

Chicken Thighs with Roasted Apples and Garlic

5   cups chopped peeled Braeburn apple (about 1½ pounds)
1   teaspoon chopped fresh sage
¼   teaspoon ground cinnamon
⅛   teaspoon ground nutmeg
4   garlic cloves, chopped
½   teaspoon salt, divided
Cooking spray
8   bone-in chicken thighs (about 2 pounds), skinned
¼   teaspoon black pepper
Chopped fresh parsley (optional)

1. Preheat oven to 475°.

2. Combine first 5 ingredients. Add ¼ teaspoon salt; toss well to coat. Spread apple mixture on a jelly-roll pan coated with cooking spray.
3. Sprinkle chicken with ¼ teaspoon salt and pepper, and arrange on top of apple mixture. Bake at 475° for 25 minutes or until chicken is done and apple is tender. Remove chicken from pan; keep warm.
4. Partially mash apple mixture with a potato masher, and serve with chicken. Sprinkle with parsley, if desired. **Yield:** 4 servings (serving size: 2 thighs and about ⅔ cup apple mixture).

CALORIES 257; FAT 5.7g (sat 1.4g, mono 1.6g, poly 1.4g); PROTEIN 25.9g; CARB 26.6g; FIBER 3.5g; CHOL 107mg; IRON 1.7mg; SODIUM 405mg; CALC 30mg

Apples

There are thousands of varieties of apples, ranging from tender to crisp and sweet to tart. Apples are available year-round, but they're best from September to November.

To select: Look for firm, vibrantly colored apples with no bruises. They should smell fresh, not musty. Skins should be tight and smooth.

To store: Though you may be tempted to display apples in a fruit bowl, resist the urge. Store them in a plastic bag in the refrigerator up to six weeks. Apples emit ethylene, a gas that hastens ripening; the plastic bag will prevent them from accelerating the ripening of other produce in your refrigerator.

To prepare: Granny Smith is our hands-down favorite cooking apple. It remains tart, juicy, and crisp after baking. It's simply a natural for cooking.

To cook: From cobblers and pies to candied apples and applesauce—apples are sure to please.

Health benefits: Apple peel contains pectin, a soluble fiber that helps lower cholesterol and control blood sugar. Apples are also a good source of fiber.

Chef Laurent Tourondel has earned fame by reinterpreting simple American favorites from a French perspective. This recipe was inspired by the French classic *soupe au pistou*, but Tourondel used American autumn ingredients instead. Habanero peppers are fiery hot, so handle them carefully. In this dish, you simply pierce the chile with a fork, and it floats in the broth. Remove it with a slotted spoon before serving. If you prefer milder heat, use the same technique with a jalapeño.

choiceingredient

Walnuts

Walnuts are the fruit of the walnut tree, which grows throughout Asia, Europe, and North America. There are two popular types found in North America: the English walnut and the black walnut. The English walnut is large, round, light brown, and has a shell that cracks easily. It's the more common variety and is sold in the shell or shelled, in halves or whole. Black walnuts are usually sold whole, are hard to find, and have a stronger, more bitter flavor.

Like pecans, walnuts have dark shells that are hard to break, and their meat is double lobed. To toast walnuts, place them on a baking sheet, and bake at 350° for six to eight minutes until lightly browned and fragrant.

Walnuts are the only nuts that contain both monounsaturated fats and omega-3s. Studies show that eating 1½ ounces per day of walnuts as part of a diet low in saturated fat and cholesterol may reduce the risk of heart disease.

Chicken-Barley Soup with Walnut Pesto

Soup:

5   slices bacon, chopped
1½ cups chopped onion
2   tablespoons minced fresh garlic
2   (4-inch) portobello mushroom caps, chopped
1   (3-pound) whole chicken, skinned
1   fresh thyme sprig
4½ quarts cold water
8   ounces Swiss chard
1   cup uncooked pearl barley, rinsed and drained
1   cup (½-inch) cubed peeled butternut squash
½   cup finely chopped carrot
½   cup finely chopped celery
¼   cup finely chopped Granny Smith apple
1   habanero pepper
¾   teaspoon salt
¼   teaspoon freshly ground black pepper

Pesto:

¼   cup walnuts, toasted
¼   cup (1 ounce) grated fresh Parmigiano-Reggiano cheese
2   tablespoons extra-virgin olive oil
1   tablespoon minced fresh garlic
¼   teaspoon salt

1. Cook bacon in a large skillet over medium heat until crisp. Add onion, garlic, and mushrooms to pan; cook 5 minutes, stirring frequently. Set aside.

2. Remove and discard giblets and neck from chicken. Place chicken and thyme in a large Dutch oven over medium heat. Cover with 4½ quarts cold water; bring to a simmer. Skim fat from surface; discard. Remove stems and center ribs from Swiss chard. Coarsely chop stems and ribs; reserve leaves. Add stems, ribs, and next 5 ingredients to pan; bring to a simmer. Pierce habanero with a fork; add to pan. Cook 35 minutes or until chicken is done.

3. Remove chicken from pan; cool slightly. Remove chicken from bones; chop meat. Discard bones, thyme sprig, and habanero. Strain barley mixture through a sieve over a bowl. Reserve 4 cups of broth for another use. Return remaining 6 cups broth to pan; bring to a boil. Cook 10 minutes. Return chicken and barley mixture to pan; bring to a simmer. Add mushroom mixture. Cook 2 minutes or until thoroughly heated. Stir in ¾ teaspoon salt and black pepper.

4. To prepare pesto, cook Swiss chard leaves in boiling water 2 minutes. Drain and rinse under cold water; drain. Place leaves, walnuts, and remaining ingredients in a food processor; process until smooth. Serve with soup. **Yield:** 8 servings (serving size: 1¾ cups soup and 2 tablespoons pesto).

CALORIES 416; FAT 13.7g (sat 3.1g, mono 5.6g, poly 3.7g); PROTEIN 41.8g; CARB 31.7g; FIBER 6.6g; CHOL 117mg; IRON 3.5mg; SODIUM 641mg; CALC 78mg

Roast a Chicken

Few entrées are as welcoming as a succulent roast chicken. Roasting your own bird outweighs the convenience of supermarket rotisserie chicken in flavor and nutrition. You'll be surprised how easy it is to prepare regardless of your cooking experience.

1. Separate the skin from the flesh, and rub the seasoning mixture directly onto the meat.

2. Tie the legs of the chicken together with twine.

3. The bird cooks more evenly when it's elevated atop vegetables or on a rack.

4. Insert the thermometer into the meaty part of the thigh to get an accurate temperature reading. This is the slowest-cooking part of the bird.

5. Remove and discard the skin before serving for a substantial fat savings.

6. Use a sharp knife to remove the legs first. To carve the breast, hold the knife parallel to the chicken breast, and slice thinly.

Be sure the butter is softened so it combines thoroughly with the herbs. Arrange a variety of herbs around the chicken for an easy, yet sophisticated, presentation.

Classic Roast Chicken with Gravy

Chicken:

1   (3¾-pound) whole roasting chicken
1   tablespoon butter, softened
½   teaspoon salt
½   teaspoon dried thyme
½   teaspoon dried oregano
½   teaspoon dried rubbed sage
⅛   teaspoon freshly ground black pepper
2   carrots, peeled and halved
4   celery stalks, halved
1   onion, quartered

Gravy:

½   cup dry white wine
1½   cups fat-free, less-sodium chicken broth
2   tablespoons all-purpose flour
3   tablespoons water
¼   teaspoon salt

1. Preheat oven to 375°.
2. To prepare chicken, remove and discard giblets and neck from chicken; trim excess fat. Starting at neck cavity, loosen skin from breast and drumsticks by inserting fingers, gently pushing between skin and meat.
3. Combine butter and next 5 ingredients in a small bowl. Rub seasoning mixture under loosened skin and over breast and drumsticks. Tie ends of legs together with twine. Lift wing tips up and over back; tuck under chicken. Place carrots, celery, and onion in a single layer in a roasting pan. Place chicken, breast side up, on top of vegetables.
4. Bake at 375° for 40 minutes.
5. Increase oven temperature to 450°, and bake an additional 20 minutes or until a thermometer inserted in meaty part of thigh registers 170°. Using tongs or insulated rubber gloves, remove chicken from pan, tilting slightly to drain juices. Let stand 15 minutes. Remove vegetables from pan with a slotted spoon; reserve.
6. To prepare gravy, place a zip-top plastic bag in a 2-cup glass measure. Pour wine into bag; add drippings from pan. Let stand 2 minutes (fat will rise to top). Seal bag; carefully snip off bottom corner of bag. Drain drippings into measuring cup, stopping before fat layer reaches opening; discard fat.
7. Return vegetables to pan. Add wine mixture and broth to pan; cook 10 minutes over medium heat, scraping pan to loosen browned bits. Remove vegetables from pan using a slotted spoon; discard. Combine flour and water in a small bowl, stirring with a whisk to form a slurry; add slurry and ¼ teaspoon salt to pan, stirring constantly. Simmer 1 minute or until slightly thick.
8. Remove skin from chicken; discard. Carve chicken, and serve with gravy. **Yield:** 4 servings (serving size: 5 ounces meat and about ¼ cup gravy).

CALORIES 287; FAT 12.4g (sat 4.4g, mono 4.3g, poly 2.3g); PROTEIN 37g; CARB 4.4g; FIBER 0.9g; CHOL 114mg; IRON 2.4mg; SODIUM 721mg; CALC 35mg

Sage

Native to the northern Mediterranean coast, sage is used often in the region's cuisine. Sage's long, narrow leaves have a distinctively fuzzy texture and a musty flavor redolent of eucalyptus, cedar, lemon, and mint. There are some other varieties of sage that boast a slightly different flavor: purple, pineapple, peach, and honeydew melon.

A very versatile herb, sage appears in different cuisines around the world. Italians love it with veal; the French add it to cured meats, sausages, and pork dishes; and Americans associate it with turkey and holiday dressings. Because sage leaves are soft and pliable, they easily tuck under the skin of poultry before roasting, making sage a wonderful addition to a Thanksgiving turkey.

Sage is available either fresh or in three dried forms: ground, coarsely crumbled, or rubbed (finely chopped). To store fresh sage leaves, simply wrap them in a damp paper towel, and place them in a plastic bag. Store them in the refrigerator, where they should keep fresh for several days. Keep dried sage in a tightly sealed glass container in a cool, dark, dry place for about six months. Use sage with discretion, as it can overwhelm a dish.

Parmesan-Sage Roast Turkey with Sage Gravy

3	cups chopped onion
1	cup chopped celery
1	cup chopped carrot
10	garlic cloves
	Cooking spray
1	(13-pound) fresh or frozen turkey, thawed
⅓	cup (1½ ounces) grated fresh Parmigiano-Reggiano cheese
5	tablespoons chopped fresh sage, divided
2	tablespoons butter, softened
1	tablespoon minced garlic
1	teaspoon salt, divided
½	teaspoon freshly ground black pepper, divided
1	lemon, halved
2½	cups fat-free, less-sodium chicken broth, divided
⅓	cup chopped shallots
1	cup sherry
1.1	ounces all-purpose flour (about ¼ cup)
¼	cup water

1. Preheat oven to 425°.
2. Combine first 4 ingredients in a shallow roasting pan coated with cooking spray. Remove and discard giblets and neck from turkey. Rinse turkey with cold water; pat dry. Trim excess fat. Starting at neck cavity, loosen skin from breast and drumsticks by inserting fingers, gently pushing between skin and meat. Lift wing tips up and over back; tuck under turkey.
3. Combine cheese, ¼ cup sage, butter, minced garlic, ¾ teaspoon salt, and ¼ teaspoon pepper; rub mixture under loosened skin and over breast and drumsticks. Rub turkey skin with cut sides of lemon halves; squeeze juice into turkey cavity. Place lemon halves in turkey cavity; tie legs together with kitchen string.
4. Place turkey, breast side up, on vegetable mixture in pan. Bake at 425° for 30 minutes; pour 2 cups broth over turkey. Tent turkey breast loosely with foil. Bake an additional 30 minutes.
5. Reduce oven temperature to 325° (do not remove turkey from oven). Bake at 325° for 1½ hours or until a thermometer inserted into meaty part of thigh registers 180°, basting every 30 minutes. Remove turkey from pan. Cover and let stand 30 minutes; discard skin.
6. Place a large zip-top plastic bag inside a 4-cup glass measure. Pour drippings through a sieve into bag; discard solids. Let drippings stand 10 minutes (fat will rise to the top). Seal bag; carefully snip off 1 bottom corner of bag. Drain drippings into a medium bowl, stopping before fat layer reaches opening; discard fat. Add enough of remaining chicken broth to drippings to equal 3 cups.
7. Heat a medium saucepan over medium-high heat. Coat pan with cooking spray. Add shallots; sauté 1 minute. Add sherry; bring to a boil. Cook until reduced to ½ cup (about 5 minutes). Stir in remaining 1 tablespoon sage, and cook 30 seconds. Add reserved drippings mixture; bring to a boil.
8. Lightly spoon flour into a dry measuring cup; level with a knife. Combine flour and water, stirring well with a whisk. Stir flour mixture into drippings mixture; bring to a boil. Cook 2 minutes or until thickened, stirring constantly. Stir in remaining ¼ teaspoon salt and remaining ¼ teaspoon pepper. Serve gravy with turkey. **Yield:** 16 servings (serving size: about 5 ounces turkey meat and about 3 tablespoons gravy).

CALORIES 285; FAT 9.6g (sat 3.5g, mono 2.5g, poly 2.2g); PROTEIN 40.9g; CARB 3.5g; FIBER 0.3g; CHOL 108mg; IRON 2.7mg; SODIUM 339mg; CALC 64mg

WINE NOTE

One of the best wines for roast turkey (and poultry in general) is **pinot noir**. In this case, the seasonings—sage, Parmesan, garlic—underscore that choice. Pinot noir's earthy flavors provide a delicious backdrop for the meatiness of the turkey, the herbal quality of the sage, the salty-nuttiness of the cheese, and the pungency of the garlic. Be forewarned: Great pinot noirs are expensive, but they're worth the splurge.

This slaw is a healthier version of an original family recipe. It is creamy and delicious, and takes about five minutes to make.

—Kelly McWherter, Houston, TX

New-Fashioned Apple and Raisin Slaw

½   cup light sour cream
3   tablespoons reduced-fat mayonnaise
1½ tablespoons white balsamic vinegar
1   teaspoon sugar
½   teaspoon black pepper
¼   teaspoon salt
2   cups unpeeled chopped Rome apple
     (about 1 medium)
1   cup golden raisins

1   (16-ounce) package cabbage-and-carrot
     coleslaw

1. Combine first 6 ingredients in a large bowl, stirring with a whisk. Add chopped apple, 1 cup raisins, and coleslaw, and toss to combine. **Yield:** 8 servings (serving size: 1 cup).

CALORIES 120; FAT 2.2g (sat 1.2g, mono 0.8g, poly 0.2g); PROTEIN 2.3g; CARB 25.3g; FIBER 3.3g; CHOL 0mg; IRON 0.8mg; SODIUM 162mg; CALC 31mg

Small pumpkins, which have succulent, tender flesh, are best for cooking. They may be labeled as "sweet" or "pie" pumpkins. When chopping the pumpkin, be sure to save the seeds for the salad.

Pumpkin Mixed Greens Salad with Maple Vinaigrette

2 tablespoons raw green pumpkinseed kernels
Cooking spray
1 cup (½-inch) cubed peeled pumpkin (about 8 ounces)
½ teaspoon fresh minced thyme
3 tablespoons red wine vinegar
1 tablespoon extra-virgin olive oil
2 teaspoons maple syrup
¼ teaspoon salt
⅛ teaspoon freshly ground black pepper
8 cups mixed salad greens

1. Place pumpkinseeds in a medium nonstick skillet over medium heat. Cook 5 minutes or until toasted, stirring frequently. Remove from pan.
2. Coat pan with cooking spray. Add pumpkin, and cook 8 minutes or until browned and tender. Remove from pan. Add thyme to pumpkin, tossing to combine. Cool.
3. Combine vinegar, oil, syrup, salt, and pepper, stirring with a whisk. Drizzle over salad greens; toss well to coat. Add pumpkin and pumpkin-seeds; toss. **Yield:** 6 servings (serving size: 1½ cups salad).

CALORIES 51; FAT 3.6g (sat 0.6g, mono 2.1g, poly 0.8g); PROTEIN 8.2g; CARB 18.7g; FIBER 7.4g; CHOL 0mg; IRON 0.8mg; SODIUM 398mg; CALC 11mg

Pumpkins

A staple for autumn festivities, the pumpkin makes its way into a multitude of dishes this time of year. Enjoy this versatile squash while it's fresh—the flavor is vastly superior to canned.

To select: Look for pumpkins that are small, about 5 to 8 pounds, with tough skin. They are prized for their concentrated flavor and sweetness.

To store: Store in the refrigerator up to three months, or in a cool, dry place up to one month.

To prepare: If you've ever carved a jack-o'-lantern, you know how to tackle a fresh pumpkin: Use your hand or a spoon to remove the seeds and stringy flesh.

To cook: To go beyond traditional pumpkin dishes, try this: Quarter, steam, and mash the flesh, mixing it with black pepper or brown sugar to serve as a side dish. For a healthful snack, roast the seeds.

Health benefits: One cup of pumpkin contains 2.7 grams of fiber, 564 milligrams of potassium, and 1.4 milligrams of iron. It's also packed with other nutrients, including beta-carotene, vitamin C, calcium, and folate.

a recipe we crave

Chop the nuts and apples the night before, and combine with the rest of the ingredients in the morning. Serve these juicy baked apples over slices of pumpkin bread, warm bowls of oatmeal, or pancakes. Ida Red and McIntosh apples also work well.

Baked Apples

2 cups dried cranberries

1¼ cups coarsely chopped walnuts

1 cup packed brown sugar

1 cup water

2 teaspoons ground cinnamon

6 Gala apples, cored and chopped (about 3 pounds)

1. Combine all ingredients in a large microwave-safe dish. Microwave at HIGH 20 minutes or until apples are soft, stirring occasionally. **Yield:** 6 cups (serving size: ¼ cup).

CALORIES 126; FAT 4.1g (sat 0.4g, mono 0.6g, poly 3g); PROTEIN 1g; CARB 23.7g; FIBER 2.3g; CHOL 0mg; IRON 1mg; SODIUM 4mg; CALC 16mg

No Thanksgiving spread is complete without green beans. Prepare the butter up to a week ahead and refrigerate, or up to three weeks in advance and freeze. Prepare extra butter to serve with bread or baked potatoes.

Green Beans with Toasted Hazelnut–Lemon Butter

1½   tablespoons butter, softened
3   tablespoons finely chopped hazelnuts, toasted
1½   teaspoons grated lemon rind
2¼   teaspoons salt, divided
8   cups water
1½   pounds green beans, trimmed

1. Combine butter, hazelnuts, rind, and ½ teaspoon salt in a small bowl; stir with a fork until well blended.
2. Bring 8 cups water and remaining 1¾ teaspoons salt to a boil in a large saucepan. Add green beans; cook 3 minutes. Drain. Return pan to medium heat. Add beans and butter mixture; cook 3 minutes or until butter mixture melts. Toss gently to coat. **Yield:** 6 servings (serving size: 1⅓ cups).

CALORIES 54; FAT 3.1g (sat 0.8g, mono 1.9g, poly 0.3g); PROTEIN 1.7g; CARB 6.4g; FIBER 3.8g; CHOL 3mg; IRON 0.6mg; SODIUM 400mg; CALC 51mg

Peel away the outer leaves from trimmed fresh Brussels sprouts, reserving the leaves and centers. This technique shortens the cook time and makes a nice presentation.

Brussels Sprouts with Currants and Pine Nuts

1½ pounds Brussels sprouts, trimmed
1 tablespoon pine nuts
1 tablespoon butter
¼ cup finely chopped shallots
2 tablespoons dried currants
1 teaspoon chopped fresh thyme
¼ teaspoon salt
¼ teaspoon freshly ground black pepper
½ cup fat-free, less-sodium chicken broth

1. Separate sprouts into leaves, leaving just the center intact. Set aside.
2. Heat a large nonstick skillet over medium-high heat. Add nuts to pan; cook 2 minutes or until toasted, stirring constantly. Coarsely chop nuts.
3. Melt butter in pan over medium-high heat. Add shallots to pan; sauté 1 minute or until golden, stirring frequently. Stir in Brussels sprouts centers and leaves, currants, thyme, salt, and pepper; toss to combine. Add broth. Cover, reduce heat, and cook 7 minutes. Increase heat to medium-high. Uncover; cook 4 minutes or until liquid evaporates and sprout centers are tender, stirring frequently. Remove from heat; sprinkle with nuts. **Yield:** 6 servings (serving size: about ½ cup).

CALORIES 90; FAT 3.2g (sat 1.4g, mono 0.8g, poly 0.7g); PROTEIN 4.5g; CARB 13.9g; FIBER 4.7g; CHOL 5mg; IRON 1.9mg; SODIUM 173mg; CALC 56mg

Brussels Sprouts

Members of the cabbage family, Brussels sprouts range from 1 to 1½ inches in diameter. Look for small, firm sprouts with compact, bright-green heads—the smaller the head, the sweeter the taste. Avoid soft, wilted, puffy, or dull-colored heads, as well as those with loose or yellowish leaves. Choose sprouts of similar size so they'll cook evenly.

Remove any loose leaves, seal unwashed sprouts in an airtight plastic bag, and place them in the refrigerator. Use them as quickly as possible since their flavor will start to become unpleasantly strong after three or four days. They're available year-round, but the peak growing season is from September to mid-February.

Capocollo is a delicious, tangy Italian-style cured ham. Look for it sliced in the supermarket deli section. If you can't find capocollo, substitute prosciutto.

Brussels Sprouts with Honey-Glazed Pearl Onions and Capocollo

3   quarts water
3   cups pearl onions
5   cups trimmed and quartered Brussels sprouts
    (about 1¾ pounds)
Cooking spray
½   cup (2 ounces) chopped capocollo ham
¼   cup water
½   teaspoon freshly ground black pepper
¼   teaspoon kosher salt
3   tablespoons honey

1. Bring 3 quarts water to a boil in a Dutch oven. Add onions; cook 1 minute. Remove onions with a slotted spoon. Drain and rinse under cold running water; drain. Set aside. Add Brussels sprouts to boiling water; boil 2 minutes or until crisp-tender. Drain. Pinch stem end of each onion; discard peels. 2. Heat a large nonstick skillet over medium-high heat. Coat pan with cooking spray. Add ham; sauté 5 minutes or until lightly browned. Remove from pan. Wipe pan with a paper towel; recoat pan with cooking spray. Add peeled onions; cook over medium heat 5 minutes. Add Brussels sprouts and ¼ cup water; cover and cook 8 minutes or until tender, stirring occasionally. Sprinkle with freshly ground black pepper and kosher salt. Drizzle with honey; stir gently. Top with ham. **Yield:** 10 servings (serving size: ½ cup).

CALORIES 100; FAT 2g (sat 0.9g, mono 0g, poly 0.1g); PROTEIN 3.5g; CARB 19g; FIBER 2.2g; CHOL 4mg; IRON 1mg; SODIUM 171mg; CALC 45mg

Gruyère's nutty, earthy flavor is a nice match for subtle cauliflower, and crisp breadcrumbs add texture. Substitute broccoli for the cauliflower, if you prefer. You can prepare all the elements for the dish a day ahead, if necessary. Refrigerate the sauce, the cauliflower, and the breadcrumb mixture separately, and simply assemble before baking.

Gratin of Cauliflower with Gruyère

1 medium head cauliflower, trimmed and cut into florets (about 2 pounds)

Cooking spray

½ teaspoon kosher salt, divided

2 teaspoons butter

⅓ cup panko (Japanese breadcrumbs)

½ cup (2 ounces) shredded Gruyère cheese, divided

2 tablespoons finely chopped fresh chives

½ cup finely chopped onion

1 garlic clove, minced

3 tablespoons all-purpose flour

2 cups 2% reduced-fat milk

3 tablespoons chopped fresh flat-leaf parsley

¼ teaspoon freshly ground black pepper

1. Preheat oven to 400°.

2. Place cauliflower in a 2-quart broiler-safe baking dish lightly coated with cooking spray; coat cauliflower with cooking spray. Sprinkle with ¼ teaspoon salt; toss. Bake at 400° for 30 minutes or until almost tender. Cool 5 minutes.

3. Preheat broiler.

4. Melt butter in a saucepan over medium heat. Remove from heat. Stir in panko. Stir in ¼ cup cheese and chives.

5. Heat a medium saucepan over medium-high heat. Coat pan with cooking spray. Add onion to pan; sauté 4 minutes or until almost tender, stirring frequently. Add garlic; sauté 1 minute, stirring constantly. Add flour; cook 1 minute, stirring constantly. Gradually add milk, stirring with a whisk; bring to a boil. Cook 3 minutes or until thick, stirring constantly. Remove from heat; stir in remaining ¼ cup cheese, remaining ¼ teaspoon salt, parsley, and pepper. Pour milk mixture over cauliflower mixture; toss. Top evenly with breadcrumb mixture. Broil 3 minutes or until golden brown and thoroughly heated. **Yield:** 6 servings (serving size: ⅔ cup).

CALORIES 161; FAT 6g (sat 3.6g, mono 1.7g, poly 0.3g); PROTEIN 9.7g; CARB 18g; FIBER 3.6g; CHOL 20mg; IRON 1mg; SODIUM 295mg; CALC 233mg

choiceingredient

Cauliflower

This member of the cabbage family has a fairly round head of tightly packed white florets that are partially covered at the stem end with large, waxy, pale green leaves. Besides the white variety, you'll occasionally find a purple or greenish variety.

Choose a sturdy cauliflower that is compact; you want leaves that are crisp and green without signs of yellowing. The size of the head does not affect the quality.

When cooked, cauliflower has a mild cabbage-like flavor and aroma. It can be cooked in a number of ways including boiling, baking, and sautéing; the whole cauliflower head may be cooked in one piece and topped with a sauce.

Wrap fresh cauliflower in plastic wrap, and refrigerate three to five days. Once cooked, it can be refrigerated one to three days. Cauliflower is high in vitamin C and is a fair source of iron.

Make Great Mashed Potatoes

Whipped or smashed, a bowl of mashed potatoes is comfort food at its best. Here are our secrets for super spuds: Cube the potatoes before cooking; they will take less time to cook than whole. After draining, shake the potatoes gently to dry them before mashing. Place the pan over low heat. To prevent lumps, warm the milk and broth before mashing them with the potatoes.

Mashing potatoes
Potato mashers give you a multitude of options. They're your best bet if you like the texture of the skin in your mashed potatoes.

Ricing potatoes
Loved by food purists, potato ricers and food mills make smooth mashed potatoes. These do double duty, peeling and mashing at the same time.

Whipping potatoes
An electric mixer whips potatoes in an instant. But do not use a food processor; it's so powerful it will overmix potatoes and make them gummy.

If you want to make the potatoes ahead, chill them and reheat just before serving, adding extra liquid until they reach the desired consistency. Stir in the chives just before serving. For a nice presentation, sprinkle additional chives over the top.

Smashed Potatoes with Goat Cheese and Chives

3   pounds peeled baking potatoes, cut into 1-inch pieces
1 ¼   teaspoons salt, divided
2   tablespoons butter
¾   cup (6 ounces) goat cheese
¼   teaspoon freshly ground black pepper
1   cup 2% reduced-fat milk
3   tablespoons finely chopped fresh chives

1. Place potatoes in a saucepan, and cover with cold water to 2 inches above potatoes. Add ¼ teaspoon salt, and bring to a boil. Reduce heat, and simmer 15 minutes or until tender; drain. Return potatoes to pan over low heat; add remaining 1 teaspoon salt and butter to pan. Mash potatoes with a potato masher to desired consistency.
2. Add cheese and pepper to potato mixture; stir until cheese melts. Stir in milk, and cook 1 minute or until thoroughly heated, stirring frequently. Remove from heat; stir in chives. **Yield:** 12 servings (serving size: about ⅔ cup).

CALORIES 155; FAT 5.4g (sat 3.5g, mono 1.3g, poly 0.2g); PROTEIN 5.8g; CARB 21.7g; FIBER 1.5g; CHOL 13mg; IRON 1.3mg; SODIUM 283mg; CALC 61mg

Sweet Potatoes

The two most common types of sweet potatoes are pale-skinned and dark-skinned. The pale sweet potato has a thin, light yellow skin and a pale yellow flesh. After it's cooked, it has a dry, crumbly texture, much like that of a white baked potato, and its flavor is not sweet. The darker variety has a thicker skin and a bright orange flesh that's very sweet and moist when cooked.

To select: Look for small to medium-sized tubers with few bruises and smooth skin.

To store: Store sweet potatoes in a cool, dry, dark place. If the temperature is right (about 55° F), you can keep them three to four weeks. Otherwise, you need to use them within a week. Do not refrigerate.

To prepare: Sweet potatoes can be cooked with the skin on or peeled before cooking.

To cook: This versatile vegetable is best for mashing or tossing into soups and stews but can also be boiled, baked, roasted, and sautéed.

Health benefits: One cup has more than six times the recommended amount of beta-carotene. Sweet potatoes are also a good source of fiber, potassium, and vitamins A, C, and E.

a recipe we crave

To prepare this a day ahead, cook the sweet potatoes; combine with brown sugar, butter, salt, and vanilla. Before baking, stir in half the pecans, place in a baking dish, and top with the remaining pecans and marshmallows. If you're toting this dish to a Thanksgiving celebration, assemble the casserole and bake at your host's home while the turkey stands.

Traditional Sweet Potato Casserole

2 ½ pounds sweet potatoes, peeled and cut into 1-inch cubes
¾ cup packed brown sugar
¼ cup butter, softened
1 ½ teaspoons salt
½ teaspoon vanilla extract
½ cup finely chopped pecans, divided
Cooking spray
2 cups miniature marshmallows

1. Preheat oven to 375°.
2. Place sweet potatoes in a Dutch oven, and cover with cold water. Bring to a boil. Reduce heat, and simmer 15 minutes or until very tender. Drain; cool slightly.
3. Place potatoes in a large bowl. Add sugar and next 3 ingredients. Mash sweet potato mixture with a potato masher. Fold in ¼ cup pecans. Scrape potato mixture into an even layer in an 11 x 7–inch baking dish coated with cooking spray. Sprinkle with remaining ¼ cup pecans; top with marshmallows. Bake at 375° for 25 minutes or until golden.
Yield: 16 servings.

CALORIES 186; FAT 5.5g (sat 2g, mono 2.3g, poly 0.9g); PROTEIN 1.6g; CARB 33.1g; FIBER 2.5g; CHOL 8mg; IRON 0.7mg; SODIUM 272mg; CALC 23mg

This versatile side dish showcases the natural sweetness of the vegetables. Serve with roast pork loin, chicken, beef, ham, or duck.

Honey and Herb-Roasted Root Vegetables

1½   cups sliced fennel bulb (about 1 small bulb)
1½   cups (½-inch) cubed peeled butternut squash
1¼   cups (½-inch) cubed red potato
1   cup (½-inch) cubed peeled turnip
1   cup (½-inch-thick) slices parsnip
1   tablespoon olive oil
¾   teaspoon salt
½   teaspoon chopped fresh thyme
¼   teaspoon freshly ground black pepper
6   garlic cloves, peeled
3   large shallots, peeled and halved
Cooking spray
1   tablespoon honey
1½   teaspoons cider vinegar

1. Preheat oven to 450°.
2. Combine first 11 ingredients in a large bowl; toss well. Arrange vegetable mixture in a single layer on a jelly-roll pan coated with cooking spray. Bake at 450° for 25 minutes or until vegetables are browned and tender. Place vegetable mixture in a large bowl. Add honey and cider vinegar to vegetables, and toss well. **Yield:** 4 servings (serving size: about ⅔ cup).

CALORIES 181; FAT 3.8g (sat 0.5g, mono 2.5g, poly 0.5g); PROTEIN 3.6g;
CARB 36.2g; FIBER 6.4g; CHOL 0mg; IRON 1.8mg; SODIUM 496mg; CALC 104mg

Butternut Squash and Leek Gratins

1   (2-pound) butternut squash, halved lengthwise and seeded
Cooking spray
1   teaspoon butter
4   cups finely chopped leek (about 6 large)
1   tablespoon sugar
¾   teaspoon salt
¼   teaspoon freshly ground black pepper
Dash of ground nutmeg
4   large eggs
1   large egg yolk
¼   cup (1 ounce) grated fresh Parmesan cheese

1. Preheat oven to 375°.
2. Place squash halves, cut sides down, on a baking sheet coated with cooking spray. Bake at 375° for 45 minutes. Cool 30 minutes. Scoop out pulp; mash with a potato masher or fork until smooth.
3. Reduce oven temperature to 325°.
4. Heat a large nonstick skillet over medium heat; coat pan with cooking spray. Melt butter in pan. Add leek; cover and cook 20 minutes or until tender, stirring once. Reduce heat to medium-low; uncover and cook 10 minutes or until lightly browned, stirring occasionally. Cool slightly.
5. Combine sugar and next 5 ingredients in a large bowl; stir with a whisk. Add squash and leek; stir until well combined. Divide squash mixture among 6 (6-ounce) ramekins coated with cooking spray. Place ramekins in a 13 x 9–inch baking pan; add hot water to pan to a depth of 1 inch. Cover pan with foil; bake at 325° for 25 minutes. Uncover and cook an additional 15 minutes or until a knife inserted in center comes out clean. Remove from oven, and place ramekins on a baking sheet.
6. Sprinkle 2 teaspoons cheese over each ramekin.
7. Preheat broiler.
8. Broil gratins 2 minutes or until cheese melts and browns. **Yield:** 6 servings (serving size: 1 gratin).

CALORIES 186; FAT 6.4g (sat 2.6g, mono 2.2g, poly 0.8g); PROTEIN 8.6g; CARB 25.9g;
FIBER 3.6g; CHOL 181mg; IRON 2.9mg; SODIUM 437mg; CALC 170mg

Winter Squash

Winter squash are picked in the autumn and stored until spring. Some popular varieties are acorn, butternut, and spaghetti.

To select: The tastiest winter squashes will be solid and heavy, with stems that are full, firm, and have a corky feel. The skin of the squash should be deeply colored with a matte finish. Avoid squash with cracks, soft spots, and moldy areas.

To store: You don't have to refrigerate winter squash; keep it in a paper bag in a cool, dark place (about 50° F) for about a month. Don't store winter squash in plastic bags for more than three days because the plastic traps moisture and causes the squash to rot.

To prepare: Winter squash are almost impossible to overcook. They can be boiled, baked, roasted, simmered, steamed, microwaved, or sautéed.

To cook: If you're microwaving a whole squash, be sure to pierce the rind in several places with a fork so it won't explode.

Health benefits: Most varieties are rich in vitamins A and C. Color is important—the darker the squash, the more beta-carotene and other nutrients it contains.

For a classic stuffing, place the rice mixture in the cavity of the turkey before roasting. Make sure to get an accurate temperature reading on the stuffing as well as the bird—both should reach an internal temperature of 165°. You can also make this to serve alongside a roast or ham.

Wild Rice Stuffing

Cooking spray

1½	cups chopped celery
1	cup chopped onion
1	cup uncooked wild rice
2	garlic cloves, minced
4	cups fat-free, less-sodium chicken broth
1½	tablespoons chopped fresh sage
1	cup uncooked long-grain brown rice
½	cup dried sweet cherries
½	cup chopped dried apricots
½	cup chopped pecans, toasted
½	teaspoon salt
½	teaspoon freshly ground black pepper

1. Heat a Dutch oven over medium-high heat. Coat pan with cooking spray. Add celery, onion, wild rice, and garlic to pan; sauté 3 minutes. Stir in broth and sage; bring to a boil. Cover, reduce heat, and simmer 25 minutes. Stir in brown rice, and bring to a boil. Cover, reduce heat, and cook 30 minutes or until liquid is absorbed. Remove from heat; let stand, covered, 10 minutes. Stir in cherries and remaining ingredients. **Yield:** 12 servings (serving size: ½ cup).

CALORIES 192; FAT 4g (sat 0.4g, mono 2.1g, poly 1.3g); PROTEIN 5.1g; CARB 34.4g; FIBER 3.6g; CHOL 0mg; IRON 1.2mg; SODIUM 243mg; CALC 35mg

Sourdough Stuffing with Pears and Sausage

8 cups (½-inch) cubed sourdough bread (about 12 ounces)
1 pound turkey Italian sausage
Cooking spray
5 cups chopped onion (about 2 pounds)
2 cups chopped celery
1 cup chopped carrot
1 (8-ounce) package presliced mushrooms
2 cups (½-inch) cubed peeled Bartlett pear (about 2 medium)
1½ tablespoons chopped fresh basil
2 teaspoons chopped fresh tarragon
1 teaspoon salt
1½ cups fat-free, less-sodium chicken broth
½ teaspoon freshly ground black pepper

1. Preheat oven to 425°.
2. Arrange bread in a single layer on a baking sheet. Bake at 425° for 9 minutes or until golden. Place in a large bowl.
3. Remove casings from sausage. Heat a large non-stick skillet over medium-high heat. Coat pan with cooking spray. Add sausage, and cook 8 minutes or until browned, stirring to crumble. Add sausage to bread cubes, tossing to combine. Set aside.
4. Return pan to medium-high heat. Add onion, celery, and carrot; sauté 10 minutes or until onion begins to brown. Stir in mushrooms; cook 4 minutes. Stir in pear, basil, tarragon, and salt; cook 4 minutes or until pear begins to soften, stirring occasionally. Add pear mixture to bread mixture, tossing gently to combine. Stir in broth and pepper.
5. Place bread mixture in a 13 x 9–inch baking dish coated with cooking spray; cover with foil. Bake at 425° for 20 minutes. Uncover; bake stuffing an additional 15 minutes or until top of stuffing is crisp. **Yield:** 12 servings (serving size: about ¾ cup).

CALORIES 199; FAT 5.2g (sat 1.6g, mono 1.5g, poly 1g); PROTEIN 10.7g; CARB 28.6g; FIBER 3.4g; CHOL 23mg; IRON 1.8mg; SODIUM 684mg; CALC 54mg

Corn bread dressing is as traditional to Thanksgiving in the South as turkey and pumpkin pie. We've dressed it up with traditional autumn ingredients—apple and fennel. Prepare the corn bread up to two days ahead to get a jump start.

Sausage, Apple, and Fennel Corn Bread Dressing

Corn Bread:

4.5 ounces all-purpose flour (about 1 cup)

¾ cup yellow cornmeal

1 teaspoon baking powder

½ teaspoon salt

1 cup fat-free milk

2 tablespoons canola oil

1 large egg, lightly beaten

Cooking spray

Dressing:

2 teaspoons olive oil

6 ounces lean, low-sodium smoked turkey sausage, finely chopped (about 1 cup)

2 cups finely chopped onion

1 bay leaf

1½ cups diced Granny Smith apple (about 1 large)

½ cup diced celery

½ cup diced fennel bulb

1 teaspoon minced garlic

¼ teaspoon dried rubbed sage

¼ teaspoon poultry seasoning

¼ teaspoon salt

⅛ teaspoon ground red pepper

⅛ teaspoon freshly ground black pepper

1½ cups fat-free, less-sodium chicken broth

2 large eggs, lightly beaten

1. Preheat oven to 425°.

2. To prepare corn bread, lightly spoon flour into a dry measuring cup; level with a knife. Combine flour, cornmeal, baking powder, and ½ teaspoon salt in a large bowl; make a well in center of mixture. Combine milk, canola oil, and 1 egg in a small bowl. Add to flour mixture, stirring just until moist. Spoon batter into an 8-inch square baking pan coated with cooking spray. Bake at 425° for 16 minutes or until a wooden pick inserted in center comes out clean. Cool 5 minutes in pan on a wire rack. Remove from pan; cool completely.

3. Reduce oven temperature to 375°.

4. To prepare dressing, heat olive oil in a large non-stick skillet over medium-high heat. Add sausage; cook 5 minutes or until browned, stirring occasionally. Add onion and bay leaf; cook 8 minutes or until onion starts to brown, stirring occasionally. Add apple, celery, and fennel; cook 5 minutes. Add garlic and next 5 ingredients; cook 1 minute. Remove from heat; discard bay leaf. Cool to room temperature.

5. Crumble corn bread into a large bowl. Add sausage mixture to bowl; toss to combine. Add broth and 2 eggs; toss to combine. Spoon into a 13 x 9–inch baking dish coated with cooking spray. Bake at 375° for 50 minutes or until top is crisp and golden brown. **Yield:** 10 servings (serving size: about ¾ cup).

CALORIES 212; FAT 7.2g (sat 1.3g, mono 3.5g, poly 1.7g); PROTEIN 9.2g; CARB 26.9g; FIBER 1.7g; CHOL 79mg; IRON 1.8mg; SODIUM 458mg; CALC 83mg

Anise

Known for its distinctive flavor, anise is often compared to licorice and tarragon. Two spices give us anise flavor in the kitchen.

The first—sweet anise—is related to dill and caraway and is used in European cakes, biscuits, breads, and the production of aniseed liqueurs, such as Pernod.

The second and more familiar spice is star anise, probably the world's prettiest spice. It's used widely in Asian cookery, is a principal ingredient in Chinese five-spice powder, and is indispensable in Chinese duck, pork, and beef dishes. It makes an unusual but delicious flavoring for poached fruits such as pears and plums.

Buy star anise whole. One or two "stars" usually impart sufficient flavor to infuse an entire dish. To substitute star anise for aniseed in a recipe, reduce the quantity to half or a third of the recipe's recommendation. Anise extract and anise oil are also available.

This spice is also known for treating digestive problems and relieving toothaches. Anise has also been used to fight congestion.

Aniseed and caraway seeds give this braided bread a licorice flavor. Leave either or both of them out, if you prefer.

Whole Wheat Bread with Caraway and Anise

2   tablespoons honey
1   package dry yeast (about 2¼ teaspoons)
1   cup warm water (100° to 110°)
1   teaspoon water
1   large egg
10.5   ounces all-purpose flour (about 2⅓ cups), divided
4.5   ounces whole wheat flour (about 1 cup)
1½   teaspoons kosher salt
1   teaspoon caraway seeds, divided
½   teaspoon aniseed
Cooking spray

1. Dissolve honey and yeast in 1 cup warm water in a large bowl; let stand 5 minutes. Combine 1 teaspoon water and egg, stirring well with a whisk. Place 1 tablespoon egg mixture in a small bowl. Cover and chill. Add remaining egg mixture to yeast mixture.

2. Lightly spoon flours into dry measuring cups; level with a knife. Add 2 cups all-purpose flour, whole wheat flour, salt, ½ teaspoon caraway seeds, and aniseed to yeast mixture; stir to form a soft dough. Turn dough out onto a floured surface. Knead until smooth and elastic (about 10 minutes); add enough of remaining all-purpose flour, 1 tablespoon at a time, to prevent dough from sticking to hands (dough will feel sticky).

3. Place dough in a large bowl coated with cooking spray, turning to coat top. Cover and let rise in a warm place (85°), free from drafts, 45 minutes or until doubled in size. (Gently press two fingers into dough. If indentation remains, dough has risen enough.) Punch dough down; cover and let rest 5 minutes. Divide dough in half. Working with 1 portion at a time, roll each portion into a 12-inch rope on a lightly floured surface. Twist ropes together, and pinch ends to seal. Place dough braid in an 8-inch loaf pan coated with cooking spray. Cover and let rise 30 minutes or until doubled in size.

4. Preheat oven to 375°.

5. Uncover dough. Brush reserved egg mixture over loaf, and sprinkle with remaining ½ teaspoon caraway seeds. Bake at 375° for 30 minutes or until loaf is browned on bottom and sounds hollow when tapped. Remove from pan; cool on a wire rack. **Yield:** 12 servings (serving size: 1 slice).

CALORIES 142; FAT 0.9g (sat 0.2g, mono 0.2g, poly 0.2g); PROTEIN 2.8g; CARB 29.1g; FIBER 2.1g; CHOL 18mg; IRON 1.8mg; SODIUM 243mg; CALC 12mg

a recipe we crave

Prepare these golden muffins up to two days ahead, and enjoy a light breakfast on Thanksgiving morning.

Pumpkin Muffins

10 ounces all-purpose flour (about 2¼ cups)
2 teaspoons pumpkin pie spice
1½ teaspoons baking soda
1 teaspoon ground ginger
¼ teaspoon salt
1 cup golden raisins
1 cup packed brown sugar
1 cup canned pumpkin
⅓ cup buttermilk
⅓ cup canola oil
¼ cup molasses
1 teaspoon vanilla extract
2 large eggs
Cooking spray
2 tablespoons granulated sugar

1. Preheat oven to 400°.

2. Lightly spoon flour into dry measuring cups; level with a knife. Combine flour, pumpkin pie spice, baking soda, ginger, and salt in a medium bowl, stirring well with a whisk. Stir in raisins; make a well in center of mixture. Combine brown sugar, canned pumpkin, buttermilk, canola oil, molasses, vanilla extract, and eggs, stirring well with a whisk. Add sugar mixture to flour mixture; stir just until moist.

3. Spoon batter into 18 muffin cups coated with cooking spray. Sprinkle with granulated sugar. Bake at 400° for 15 minutes or until a wooden pick inserted in center comes out clean. Remove muffins from pans immediately; cool on a wire rack. **Yield:** 18 servings (serving size: 1 muffin).

CALORIES 202; FAT 5.1g (sat 0.8g, mono 2g, poly 1.9g); PROTEIN 2.9g; CARB 37.5g; FIBER 1.2g; CHOL 24mg; IRON 1.7mg; SODIUM 159mg; CALC 35mg

This recipe makes two loaves. Freeze the extra bread, tightly wrapped in plastic wrap, for up to one month. Omit the nuts or substitute chopped walnuts, if you prefer. Check the bread after 50 minutes of baking—you may need to cover the loaves with aluminum foil for the last 10 minutes to prevent overbrowning.

Pecan-Topped Pumpkin Bread

15	ounces all-purpose flour (about 3⅓ cups)
1	tablespoon baking powder
2	teaspoons baking soda
1	teaspoon salt
1	teaspoon ground cinnamon
1	teaspoon ground nutmeg
½	teaspoon ground allspice
2	cups granulated sugar
½	cup egg substitute
½	cup canola oil
½	cup low-fat buttermilk
2	large eggs
⅔	cup water
1	(15-ounce) can pumpkin
	Cooking spray
⅓	cup chopped pecans

1. Preheat oven to 350°.
2. Lightly spoon flour into dry measuring cups; level with a knife. Combine flour and next 6 ingredients in a bowl.
3. Place sugar, egg substitute, oil, buttermilk, and eggs in a large bowl, and beat with a mixer at high speed until well blended. Add ⅔ cup water and pumpkin, beating at low speed until blended. Add flour mixture to pumpkin mixture, beating at low speed just until combined. Spoon batter into 2 (9 x 5–inch) loaf pans coated with cooking spray. Sprinkle pecans evenly over batter. Bake at 350° for 1 hour or until a wooden pick inserted in center comes out clean. Cool 10 minutes in pans on a wire rack; remove from pans. Cool completely on wire rack. **Yield:** 2 loaves; 12 servings per loaf (serving size: 1 slice).

CALORIES 198; FAT 6.6g (sat 0.7g, mono 3.6g, poly 1.9g); PROTEIN 3.4g; CARB 32.3g; FIBER 1.2g; CHOL 18mg; IRON 1.4mg; SODIUM 287mg; CALC 53mg

Use real maple syrup for best results. I also like to use a maple leaf cookie cutter when I make these.

—Tracy Schuhmacher, Penfield, NY

Autumn Maple Cutout Cookies

¼   cup butter
10   ounces all-purpose flour (about 2¼ cups)
½   teaspoon baking powder
½   teaspoon ground cinnamon
¼   teaspoon baking soda
¼   teaspoon salt
⅛   teaspoon ground nutmeg
6   tablespoons granulated sugar
½   cup maple syrup
1   teaspoon maple flavoring
2   large egg whites, divided
⅓   cup chopped walnuts
2   tablespoons turbinado sugar or granulated sugar
Cooking spray

1. Melt butter in a small saucepan over low heat. Cook until milk solids stop crackling and turn amber (about 5 minutes), stirring occasionally. Transfer butter mixture to a small bowl, scraping pan to include milk solids. Cover and cool butter mixture in refrigerator 20 minutes or until soft and congealed but not firm.
2. Lightly spoon flour into dry measuring cups, and level with a knife. Combine flour and next 5 ingredients in a bowl, stirring with a whisk.
3. Combine chilled butter mixture and granulated sugar in a large bowl; beat with a mixer at medium speed until well blended (about 3 minutes). Add syrup, flavoring, and 1 egg white to butter mixture; beat at low speed 2 minutes or until well blended. Add flour mixture to butter mixture; beat on low speed until blended. Divide dough in half. Shape each portion into a ball; wrap in plastic wrap. Chill 1 hour or until firm.
4. Preheat oven to 350°.

5. Place walnuts and turbinado sugar in a food processor; pulse 15 times or until mixture is coarsely ground. Place remaining 1 egg white in another small bowl; stir with a whisk.
6. Working with 1 portion of dough at a time (keep remaining dough chilled until use), roll dough to a ⅛-inch thickness on a floured surface, and cut with a 2½-inch round or decorative cutter. Place 24 cookies, evenly spaced, on a baking sheet coated with cooking spray. Gently brush tops of cookies with egg white; sprinkle evenly with half of walnut mixture. Bake at 350° for 12 minutes or until pale brown. Remove cookies from pan, and cool completely on wire racks. Repeat procedure with remaining dough, egg white, and walnut mixture. **Yield:** 48 cookies (serving size: 2 cookies).

CALORIES 104; FAT 3.1g (sat 1.3g, mono 0.7g, poly 0.9g); PROTEIN 1.8g; CARB 17.7g; FIBER 0.5g; CHOL 5mg; IRON 0.7mg; SODIUM 66mg; CALC 15mg

Maple Syrup

Known as the ideal pancake and waffle topping, maple syrup packs in sweet distinctive flavor with every teaspoon. Pure maple syrup—the best kind—is made from maple sap that has been boiled down until it's thick and syrupy. It adds moisture and a unique taste to cakes, cookies, and frostings, and it makes a perfect addition to marinades, brines, and vegetables. Sugar and honey may be used more commonly to add dimension to savory dishes, but neither contributes the clean, unique flavor and subtle maple bouquet that maple syrup delivers.

Maple syrup comes in different grades, ranging in color from light golden to dark brown, almost like molasses. As with honey, the lighter the syrup, the milder the flavor. Use light syrups for anything from pouring over waffles or pancakes to baking in cookies and cakes. The darker grades—more amber in color—are also suitable for eating and baking. The darkest kind is best used in baking when you want to add intense maple flavor—it works wonderfully in soft ginger cookies and in gingerbread. Some strongly flavored foods go especially well with maple syrup. Its sweetness is ideal for salmon. Brush it on pork, blend it with vegetables, or stir it into soups.

Whatever maple syrup you buy, make sure the label says "pure maple syrup." Syrups labeled "maple-flavored" are usually just corn syrup with artificial maple flavoring. Although maple-flavored syrup is less expensive, you'll get more bang for your buck when you buy the pure kind.

Maple syrup is produced in the early months of the year, so that's a great time to stock up. Always refrigerate maple syrup after opening to ensure freshness. If crystals have started to form in a bottle of maple syrup, don't throw it out! Simply heat the bottle in a pan of hot water over very low heat until the crystals dissolve. If your container is plastic, pour the syrup into a saucepan and melt the crystals over low heat. You can also use the microwave if your container is microwave-safe. Heat at MEDIUM power 10 to 15 seconds.

Golden Delicious apples are ideal for tarts. And that's what we've used for this French-style tart. Use a paring knife to prepare the apples for this simple dessert.

Thin French Apple Tart

½ (15-ounce) package refrigerated pie dough (such as Pillsbury)
¼ cup sugar
½ teaspoon ground cinnamon
2 pounds Golden Delicious apples, peeled, cored, and thinly sliced
2 ½ tablespoons honey
½ teaspoon vanilla extract

1. Preheat oven to 425°.
2. Place dough on a lightly floured surface; roll into a 12-inch circle. Place on a 12-inch pizza pan. Combine sugar and cinnamon. Sprinkle 1 tablespoon sugar mixture over dough. Arrange apple slices spokelike on top of dough, working from outside edge of dough to center. Sprinkle apple slices with remaining sugar mixture. Bake at 425° for 30 minutes.
3. Combine honey and vanilla in a microwave-safe bowl. Microwave at HIGH 40 seconds. Brush honey mixture over warm tart. Serve warm.
Yield: 8 servings (serving size: 1 wedge).

CALORIES 220; FAT 7.3g (sat 2.9g, mono 3.2g, poly 0.9g); PROTEIN 0.6g; CARB 39g; FIBER 1.9g; CHOL 5mg; IRON 0.2mg; SODIUM 100mg; CALC 6mg

howto:

Cut an Apple

Look for vibrantly colored apples that are firm to the touch and free of bruises. Skins should be tight and smooth. Store in a plastic bag in the refrigerator crisper. After slicing, sprinkle the flesh with lemon juice to prevent it from browning.

1. Pierce center of fruit with an apple corer and rotate to remove core. Use a paring knife to slice in half vertically.

2. Place apple halves, cut sides down, on a cutting board. Cut through skin to create apple wedges or thinner slices.

3. Chop wedges into bite-sized pieces with the paring knife.

This traditional pie calls for Cortland apples, but we found that Pacific Rose apples also work well.

Classic Apple Pie

11.25 ounces all-purpose flour (about 2½ cups)
¾ teaspoon salt
6 tablespoons chilled butter, cut into small pieces
2 tablespoons vegetable shortening, cut into small pieces
1 tablespoon fresh lemon juice
¾ cup ice water
2½ cups thinly sliced peeled Braeburn apple (about 1 pound)
2½ cups thinly sliced peeled Cortland apple (about 1 pound)
1 cup sugar
1 ounce all-purpose flour (about ¼ cup)
¼ teaspoon ground cinnamon
⅛ to ¼ teaspoon ground allspice
Cooking spray

1 tablespoon chilled butter, cut into small pieces
½ teaspoon vanilla extract
1 tablespoon whole milk

1. Lightly spoon 2½ cups flour into dry measuring cups; level with a knife. Combine 2½ cups flour and salt in a large bowl; cut in 6 tablespoons butter and vegetable shortening with a pastry blender or 2 knives until mixture resembles coarse meal. Add lemon juice. Sprinkle surface with ice water, 1 tablespoon at a time, and toss with a fork until moist and crumbly. Shape dough into a ball; wrap in plastic wrap. Chill 1 hour.
2. Divide dough into 2 equal portions. Gently press each portion into a 1-inch-thick circle on heavy-duty plastic wrap; cover and freeze 10 minutes.
3. Preheat oven to 350°.
4. Place apples in a large bowl. Combine sugar, ¼ cup flour, cinnamon, and allspice in a small bowl. Sprinkle sugar mixture over apples; toss well to coat.
5. Working with 1 dough portion at a time, roll dough into a 12-inch circle on a lightly floured surface. Fit dough circle into a 9-inch pie plate coated with cooking spray, allowing dough to extend over the edge. Roll remaining dough portion into a 10-inch circle on a lightly floured surface. Spoon apple mixture into prepared pie plate, and dot with 1 tablespoon butter. Drizzle apple mixture with ½ teaspoon vanilla. Top with 10-inch dough circle. Press edges of dough together. Fold edges under, and flute. Brush surface of dough with milk. Cut 3 (1-inch) slits in top of dough to allow steam to escape. Bake at 350° for 1 hour or until apples are tender. **Yield:** 10 servings (serving size: 1 slice).

CALORIES 326; FAT 10.8g (sat 6g, mono 2.8g, poly 1.2g); PROTEIN 3.8g; CARB 54.1g; FIBER 2.3g; CHOL 21mg; IRON 1.7mg; SODIUM 233mg; CALC 14mg

Butternut squash stands in for pumpkin in this pie, which received our Test Kitchens' highest rating. Prepare a day in advance, and store at room temperature.

Harvest Pie

1	large butternut squash, halved and seeded (about 2¼ pounds)

Cooking spray

½	cup fat-free evaporated milk
¾	cup granulated sugar
½	cup egg substitute
1	teaspoon vanilla extract
½	teaspoon ground cinnamon
⅛	teaspoon ground allspice
⅛	teaspoon ground cloves
1	ounce all-purpose flour (about ¼ cup)
¼	cup packed dark brown sugar
2	tablespoons chilled butter, cut into small pieces
3	tablespoons chopped pecans
½	(15-ounce) package refrigerated pie dough (such as Pillsbury)
10	tablespoons fat-free whipped topping (optional)

1. Position oven rack to lowest setting. Preheat oven to 400°.

2. Place squash, cut sides down, on a foil-lined baking sheet coated with cooking spray. Bake at 400° 30 minutes or until squash is tender. Cool slightly, and peel. Mash pulp to measure 2½ cups. Place pulp and milk in a food processor; process until smooth. Add granulated sugar and next 5 ingredients; process until smooth.

3. Increase oven temperature to 425°.

4. Lightly spoon flour into a dry measuring cup; level with a knife. Combine flour and brown sugar in a medium bowl; cut in butter using 2 knives or a pastry blender. Add pecans; toss to combine.

5. Roll dough into a 13-inch circle; fit into a 9-inch deep-dish pie plate coated with cooking spray. Fold edges under; flute. Pour squash mixture into prepared crust. Place pie plate on bottom rack in oven; bake at 425° for 15 minutes. Remove pie from oven.

6. Reduce oven temperature to 350°.

7. Sprinkle flour mixture evenly over filling; shield edges of piecrust with foil. Return pie plate to bottom rack; bake an additional 40 minutes or until center is set. Cool on a wire rack. Garnish each serving with 1 tablespoon whipped topping, if desired. **Yield:** 10 servings (serving size: 1 wedge).

CALORIES 294; FAT 11g (sat 3.9g, mono 4.9g, poly 1.5g); PROTEIN 4.6g; CARB 46.2g; FIBER 3.5g; CHOL 7mg; IRON 1.7mg; SODIUM 200mg; CALC 97mg

Bartlett or Anjou pears work best in this pie. Be sure to purchase firm, slightly under-ripe fruit, since the pears soften and give off juice as they cook.

Pear Pie with Streusel Topping and Caramel Sauce

Pie:

3   ounces all-purpose flour, divided (about ⅔ cup)

½   cup granulated sugar

½   teaspoon ground cinnamon

⅛   teaspoon salt

3   tablespoons fresh lemon juice

6   medium firm pears, peeled, cored, and cut lengthwise into ½-inch-thick wedges

½   (15-ounce) package refrigerated pie dough (such as Pillsbury)

Cooking spray

⅓   cup packed brown sugar

3   tablespoons chilled butter, cut into small pieces

Sauce:

⅓   cup packed brown sugar

3   tablespoons heavy whipping cream

2   tablespoons butter, softened

2   teaspoons water

1. Preheat oven to 375°.

2. To prepare pie, lightly spoon flour into dry measuring cups; level with a knife. Combine 1½ ounces flour, granulated sugar, cinnamon, and salt in a large bowl. Add juice and pears to flour mixture; toss gently to coat. Roll dough into an 11-inch circle; fit dough into a 9-inch pie plate coated with cooking spray. Fold edges under and flute. Arrange pear mixture in an even layer in prepared crust.

3. Combine remaining 1½ ounces flour and ⅓ cup brown sugar in a bowl. Add 3 tablespoons cold butter to brown sugar mixture; cut in with a pastry blender or 2 knives until mixture resembles coarse meal. Sprinkle butter mixture evenly over pears. Bake at 375° for 1 hour or until lightly browned. Let cool on a wire rack 10 minutes.

4. To prepare sauce, combine ⅓ cup brown sugar, cream, and 2 tablespoons softened butter in a small, heavy saucepan over medium-high heat; bring to a boil. Cook 1 minute or until thickened. Remove from heat; stir in 2 teaspoons water. Serve at room temperature or slightly warmed with pie.

Yield: 12 servings (serving size: 1 pie wedge and about 1½ teaspoons sauce).

CALORIES 287; FAT 11g (sat 5.5g, mono 1.7g, poly 0.3g); PROTEIN 1.5g; CARB 47.5g; FIBER 2.8g; CHOL 20mg; IRON 0.7mg; SODIUM 139mg; CALC 24mg

Apple-Cinnamon Coffeecake

Cake:

6.75	ounces all-purpose flour (about 1½ cups)
1	cup granulated sugar
1½	teaspoons baking powder
1½	teaspoons ground cinnamon
½	teaspoon salt
¾	cup 1% low-fat milk
2	tablespoons butter, melted
1	teaspoon vanilla extract
1	large egg, lightly beaten
1	cup diced peeled Granny Smith apple (about 1 apple)

Cooking spray

Streusel:

¼	cup packed brown sugar
2	tablespoons all-purpose flour
½	teaspoon ground cinnamon
2	tablespoons chilled butter, cut into small pieces

1. Preheat oven to 350°.

2. To prepare cake, lightly spoon 1½ cups flour into dry measuring cups; level with a knife. Combine flour and next 4 ingredients in a large bowl, stirring with a whisk. Make a well in center of mixture. Combine milk, melted butter, vanilla, and egg, stirring with a whisk; add to flour mixture, stirring just until moist. Fold in apple. Pour batter into an 8-inch square baking pan coated with cooking spray.

3. To prepare streusel, combine brown sugar, 2 tablespoons flour, and ½ teaspoon cinnamon; cut in butter with a pastry blender or 2 knives until mixture resembles coarse meal. Sprinkle streusel evenly over batter. Bake at 350° for 45 minutes or until a wooden pick inserted in center comes out clean. Cool in pan 10 minutes on a wire rack before serving. Serve warm. **Yield:** 12 servings (serving size: 1 piece).

CALORIES 197; FAT 4.6g (sat 2.7g, mono 1.2g, poly 0.3g); PROTEIN 2.9g; CARB 36.7g; FIBER 0.8g; CHOL 28mg; IRON 1.2mg; SODIUM 202mg; CALC 68mg

choiceingredient

Cinnamon

Cinnamon's dark, reddish brown color and strong, spicy-sweet aroma add complex flavor to both sweet and savory dishes, from sweet rolls and mulled ciders to glazed salmon and beef Bolognese. Moroccans and Persians use the spice with lamb and chicken. And in Indian food, cinnamon is typically paired with cardamom and used in rice pilafs.

Technically, what we Americans buy in the supermarkets, whether ground or in sticks, is not "true" cinnamon, but it's a close cousin, produced by a similar tree. Most of the cinnamon we buy in the United States comes from Indonesia. "True" cinnamon, also called Saigon cinnamon, comes from Vietnam and is considered the best type.

Cinnamon sticks, or quills, have a sweeter, subtler flavor and a longer shelf life than ground. They make excellent stirrers for beverages. You can grind whole cinnamon at home, but use a clean coffee mill for the best result.

Zucchini, carrot, and apple add moisture and flavor, eliminating the need for excess butter and oil. It only takes about 10 minutes to prepare the batter for this simple cake. I love it for breakfast.

—Jennifer Dunklee, Medford, MA

Garden Harvest Cake

4.5   ounces all-purpose flour (about 1 cup)

¾   cup sugar

2   teaspoons ground cinnamon

1   teaspoon baking soda

¼   teaspoon salt

½   cup grated peeled Granny Smith apple (about 1 medium)

½   cup grated carrot (about 1 medium)

½   cup shredded zucchini

¼   cup chopped walnuts, toasted

¼   cup canola oil

¼   cup nonfat buttermilk

2   large eggs

Cooking spray

1. Preheat oven to 350°.

2. Lightly spoon flour into a dry measuring cup; level with a knife. Combine flour and next 4 ingredients in a large bowl, stirring with a whisk. Add grated apple, grated carrot, shredded zucchini, and walnuts to flour mixture; toss well. Combine canola oil, buttermilk, and eggs in a small bowl, stirring with a whisk. Add egg mixture to flour mixture, stirring just until combined. Spoon batter into an 8 x 4–inch loaf pan coated with cooking spray. Bake at 350° for 50 minutes or until a wooden pick inserted in center comes out clean. Cool 10 minutes in pan on a wire rack; remove cake from pan. Cool completely on wire rack before slicing. **Yield:** 9 servings (serving size: 1 slice).

CALORIES 223; FAT 9.7g (sat 1g, mono 4.4g, poly 3.6g); PROTEIN 3.8g; CARB 31.4g; FIBER 1.3g; CHOL 47mg; IRON 1.2mg; SODIUM 233mg; CALC 30mg

If you don't have individual ramekins, use custard cups or a 1½-quart baking dish, which will require an additional 15 to 20 minutes in the oven.

Double-Ginger Pumpkin Flans

Caramel:

Cooking spray

½ cup sugar

¼ cup water

Flan:

⅓ cup sugar

6 large egg yolks

1 cup canned unsweetened pumpkin

1 teaspoon vanilla extract

½ teaspoon ground ginger

½ teaspoon ground cinnamon

1 cup 2% reduced-fat milk

½ cup half-and-half

1 teaspoon grated peeled fresh ginger

1. Preheat oven to 325°.

2. To prepare caramel, lightly coat 6 (6-ounce) ramekins with cooking spray. Combine ½ cup sugar and ¼ cup water in a small, heavy saucepan over medium heat. Cook 4 minutes or until sugar dissolves, stirring occasionally. Increase heat to medium-high. Cook, without stirring, 6 minutes or until mixture turns golden around outside edges. Divide evenly into prepared ramekins. Set aside.

3. To prepare flan, combine ⅓ cup sugar and egg yolks in a medium bowl, stirring well with a whisk. Stir in pumpkin and next 3 ingredients. Combine milk, half-and-half, and fresh ginger. Heat milk mixture over medium-high heat in a heavy saucepan to 180° or until tiny bubbles form around edge (do not boil). Gradually add half of hot milk mixture to egg mixture, stirring constantly with a whisk. Return milk mixture to pan. Reduce heat, and cook to 160°, stirring constantly with a whisk. Remove from heat. Strain through a sieve over a large bowl; discard solids.

4. Divide milk mixture evenly among prepared ramekins. Place cups in a 13 x 9–inch baking pan; add hot water to pan to a depth of 1 inch. Bake at 325° for 50 minutes or until a knife inserted in center comes out clean. Remove cups from pan; cool completely on a wire rack. Chill at least 8 hours.

5. Carefully loosen edges of custards with a knife. Invert ramekins onto plates. Drizzle any remaining caramel over custards. **Yield:** 6 servings (serving size: 1 flan).

CALORIES 224; FAT 7.6g (sat 3.6g, mono 2.9g, poly 0.8g); PROTEIN 5.1g; CARB 34.9g; FIBER 1.3g; CHOL 215mg; IRON 1.2mg; SODIUM 39mg; CALC 106mg

Quince

A quince is a hard, round or pear-shaped fruit that looks and tastes like a cross between an apple and pear. Ancient Roman suitors used to give quinces to their lovers as a sign of commitment; Greeks associated quinces with romance, too. Mythology holds that the quince was a gift from Aphrodite, the goddess of love, and it was a custom in ancient Greece to toss whole quinces into bridal chariots.

Unlike the apples and pears they resemble, quinces are inedible raw. The pale flesh is pithy and very tannic before cooking, so one bite will genuinely leave a bad taste in your mouth. With cooking, quinces develop a slightly grainy texture similar to a firm pear and a lovely rosy amber color. Their complex taste is compatible with flavors like vanilla, nutmeg, cloves, cinnamon, ginger, and lemon.

British cooks traditionally use quinces to make tarts, preserves, and other sweet items. In Middle Eastern countries, this fruit is a popular addition to meat stews, where they add sweetness, astringency, and texture.

Compared to other fruits, quinces are relatively high in pectin, the natural gelling agent that allows jams and jellies to thicken and set. This quality made quinces very popular as a base for preserves in antiquity. In fact, the word *marmelo,* which is Portuguese for quince, evolved over time into the word marmalade.

Because their season is fleeting—from October to December—you should get quinces while you can. Look for them in large supermarkets, farmers' markets, and specialty or ethnic stores. They'll fill an entire room with their enticing scent.

These whole roasted quinces make a beautiful end to an autumn meal. If quinces are smaller than eight ounces each, they will cook more quickly.

Caramelized Quinces

⅓ cup granulated sugar
⅓ cup packed brown sugar
⅛ teaspoon salt
3 tablespoons fresh lemon juice
6 (8-ounce) quinces, peeled
½ cup apple cider
2 tablespoons butter, cut into small pieces
⅓ cup whipping cream
2 tablespoons powdered sugar
Freshly grated nutmeg (optional)

1. Preheat oven to 400°.
2. Combine first 3 ingredients in a medium bowl, stirring well with a whisk. Place juice in another bowl. Working with 1 quince at a time, dip quince in juice, turning to coat; dredge quince in sugar mixture, turning to coat. Place quince, stem side up, in 8-inch square baking dish. Repeat procedure with remaining quinces, juice, and sugar mixture. Sprinkle quinces evenly with remaining sugar mixture. Pour cider in bottom of dish; place 1 teaspoon butter on top of each quince. Bake at 400° for 1 hour and 30 minutes or until quinces are golden brown and liquid is thick, basting every 30 minutes. Place 1 quince on each of 6 plates; drizzle quinces evenly with remaining syrup in pan.
3. Place cream in a medium bowl; beat with a mixer at medium speed until soft peaks form. Add powdered sugar, 1 tablespoon at a time; continue beating until stiff peaks form. Serve quinces warm with whipped cream. Garnish with freshly grated nutmeg, if desired. **Yield:** 6 servings (serving size: 1 quince and 2 tablespoons whipped cream).

CALORIES 267; FAT 8.8g (sat 5.4g, mono 2.4g, poly 0.4g); PROTEIN 0.9g; CARB 50g; FIBER 2.7g; CHOL 28mg; IRON 1.2mg; SODIUM 93mg; CALC 36mg

Figs

The dense texture and subtle, sweet flavor of fresh figs is hard to beat. There are literally hundreds of varieties of figs—ranging in color from dark purple to almost white.

To select: Don't judge by looks alone. A shrunken and wrinkled fig may actually be a better choice than one that looks pristine. Small cracks won't affect the flavor. Also, ripe figs should be heavy for their size.

To store: Figs are extremely perishable; use them soon after purchasing, or store them in the refrigerator in a single layer no more than two or three days.

To prepare: Fresh figs are best when simply prepared to enhance their natural sweetness, much like you might handle peaches or plums in season.

To cook: Desserts are the most common way to use fresh figs; however, they work in all types of recipes, including chutneys, sauces, and salads. They're also a nice companion for braised meats and poultry.

Health benefits: Figs are known for a mild laxative-like effect. They are also a good source of fiber, manganese, potassium, and vitamin B6.

Honey-coated figs caramelize on the grill to star in this simple dessert.

Caramelized Fresh Figs with Sweet Cream

2   teaspoons honey
8   large fresh figs, cut in half lengthwise
Cooking spray
¼   cup crème fraîche
½   teaspoon sugar

1. Prepare grill to high heat.
2. Brush honey on cut sides of

figs. Lightly spray cut sides of figs with cooking spray.
3. Place figs, cut sides down, on grill rack, and grill 3 minutes or until grill marks appear. Remove from grill. Combine crème fraîche and ½ teaspoon sugar; spoon over figs. **Yield:** 4 servings (serving size: 4 fig halves and 1 tablespoon sauce).

CALORIES 159; FAT 5.6g (sat 3.3g, mono 1.7g, poly 0.4g); PROTEIN 1.4g; CARB 28g; FIBER 3.7g; CHOL 14mg; IRON 0.5mg; SODIUM 6mg; CALC 45mg

winter

the winter kitchen

As each year ends, a new season arrives. And with it a supply of fresh ingredients that offer you comfort from the cold. From hardy root vegetables to bright, sweet citrus, winter produce delivers a surprising range of flavors for you to enjoy with family and friends.

Make the most of wintertime's best fruit, and add a splash of color to your dinner table with festive dishes like Classic Cranberry Sauce (recipe on page 363), Pepper-Crusted Beef Tenderloin with Kumquat Marmalade (recipe on page 336), and Orange-Basmati Salad with Pine Nuts and Pomegranate Seeds (recipe on page 360). For a superb holiday trimming that's bursting with flavor, prepare Cranberry, Cherry, and Walnut Chutney (recipe on page 362), and serve it with roast turkey or chicken, pork tenderloin, or ham at any of your holiday get-togethers. If you really want to be bold, mix up Cranberry-Jalapeño Granita (recipe on page 387), which has a flavor combination so surprisingly delicious, your guests will always ask for more.

To really get in the mood for the holidays, invite your neighbors over for a festive dessert party, and enjoy some sweet treats. Light and luscious Lemon Polenta Cake with Winter Fruit Compote (recipe on page 379) is sure to be a crowd-pleaser, and Chocolate-Dipped Almond Meringues (recipe on page 368) pair deliciously with a warm cup of coffee. For the kids, whip up a batch of yummy Brown Sugar Shortbread (recipe on page 370) and pour some rich, creamy hot chocolate to go along. No matter what the occasion, spread joy and cheer this holiday season with any of the recipes we have here for you.

Let the recipes of winter warm you with hardy root vegetables, tangy cranberries, robust greens, and citrus fruits.

fruits

Apples

Blood Oranges

Cranberries

Grapefruit

Kiwifruit

Kumquats

Lemons

Limes

Mandarin Oranges

Navel Oranges

Pears

Persimmons

Pomegranates

Pomelos

Satsuma Oranges

Tangelos

Tangerines

Quinces

vegetables

Baby Turnips

Beets

Belgian Endive

Brussels Sprouts

Celeriac (Celery Root)

Chile Peppers

Cipollini Onions

Dried Beans

Escarole

Fennel

Frisée

Jerusalem Artichokes

Kale

Leeks

Mushrooms

Onions

Parsnips

Potatoes

Rutabagas

Sweet Potatoes

Swiss Chard

Turnips

Watercress

Winter Squash

herbs

Bay Leaves

Chives

Parsley

Peppermint

Rosemary

Sage

Thyme

winter
From festive, fizzy beverages to hearty soups and stews, here are some ideas for staples, seasonings, and other ingredients ideally suited for your holiday table, cold winter nights, and comforting family meals.

Balsamic and Red Wine Vinegars: Without adding fat, vinegars can add depth and brightness to recipes, from salads to desserts. Use to deglaze pan drippings and add a little acidity to balance a sauce, or reduce them to a syrup for drizzling over fruit or vegetables. Or, add them to cooking liquid, and then braise to subdue the bite, or simply use them in a vinaigrette.

Canned and Dried Beans: Beans are versatile, adaptable, and a great source of nonmeat protein. You can do most anything with beans: bake, puree, sauté, simmer in a slow cooker, stew, or stir-fry. They're also incredibly cheap and in season all year long.

Canned Tomatoes: Opt for canned tomatoes when you want their juice. Otherwise, let the season be your guide and use fresh tomatoes whenever possible. The best winter tomatoes are vine-ripened, Roma, and cherry tomatoes.

Cumin: Cumin is often an ingredient in Indian, Middle Eastern, and Asian cuisines, but it is most frequently used in chili and curry powders—all of which are popular in the winter.

Curry: Curries are any number of spicy gravy-based stews of East Indian origin that include curry powder. Curry recipes are usually served with rice and a variety of condiments. Due to their spicy nature, curry dishes are some of our favorite wintertime meals.

Dried Herbs: We almost always prefer to use fresh herbs, but sometimes that's not practical, especially in the winter. Quality dried herbs are an important part of a basic pantry, particularly when it comes to convenience and last-minute meal preparation.

Fat-Free, Low-Sodium Broths: When our recipes call for canned chicken broth, we use fat-free, less-sodium chicken broth. Swanson Natural Goodness is one we use frequently—it's available in both cans and cartons.

Garlic: Garlic is the most pungent of all alliums, and the more it is chopped, the stronger it tastes. For subtle garlic flavor, add whole unpeeled garlic cloves to pot roasts and roasted vegetable dishes.

Gruyère: An assertive, nutty Swiss cheese, Gruyère pairs well with both sweet and savory dishes. The secret to using this high-fat cheese in a healthy diet lies in its concentrated flavor—a little goes a long way.

Olives: One of the world's greatest delicacies makes even the very simplest fare exquisite. Olives are available either pitted or unpitted and may be packed in brine or oil, dried in salt, or stuffed.

Pasta: Winter is the time for comfort food, and pasta is definitely one of those staples. Some of the pastas you'll find in this chapter include farfalle, pappardelle, and egg noodles.

Sausages: In general, sausage is traditionally high in fat; however, there are many lower-fat versions available, as well as vegetarian sausages made of or flavored with vegetable or bean curd. The flavor of sausages can range from mild to hot and spicy, and sausages can be cooked, cured, smoked, dried, or left uncooked and sold fresh.

Sweet Bell Peppers: Sweet bell peppers are packed with flavor and nutrients, and they add unbeatable color and texture to many types of dishes. Braising bell peppers draws out their strong flavor over time.

best ways to cook

Simmering, braising, and slow cooking are all cooking techniques that help to make winter a season of pure comfort. Nothing warms you up better in the cold months than chicken-vegetable soup, pot roast, or chili.

Simmering

Simmering refers to cooking food in liquid (or cooking just the liquid itself) at a temperature slightly below the boiling point—around 180° to 190°. It's gentler but trickier than boiling because it requires careful temperature regulation so that the surface of the liquid shimmers, with a bubble coming up every few seconds.

Simmering cooks food gently and slowly. Delicate foods such as fish are poached at or below a simmer to prevent them from breaking apart. Meats that are simmered remain moist and fork-tender, while boiled meats are often dry and tough because the heat of boiling liquid can cause the proteins in meat to toughen. Stocks are simmered so the fat and proteins released by the meat or bones float to the top where they can be skimmed off. If heated too intensely, the fat and proteins will emulsify into the liquid, making the stock cloudy.

Simmering, which is more versatile than boiling, lends itself to a variety of foods. We use it to cook proteins (fish, poultry, beef, and pork), often in the form of poaching (cooking in enough liquid to cover the food) and braising (cooking in a small amount of liquid). It's also essential when making broth or stock. Boiling works well for tender green vegetables, but tough, fibrous root vegetables (such as potatoes, turnips, and beets) are best when simmered so they cook evenly throughout.

Slow Cooking

Rich pot roast, warming stews, and other hearty fare can also be prepared in an electric slow cooker. It's a convenient option because it cooks dinner while you're away, and by the day's end, you have a home-cooked meal ready and waiting. Just assemble the ingredients in the morning, and turn on the slow cooker.

Use the slow-cooker size specified by the recipe to ensure proper levels of food, thorough cooking, and safe temperatures. If you use a different-sized cooker than specified, make sure it's still between half and two-thirds full for food safety. Be aware though that changes in slow-cooker size can lead to changes in cooking time. If using a larger slow cooker than called for, the cook time may be less; if using a smaller cooker, your dish may need more cook time. Our Test Kitchens professionals have also found that some slow cookers—particularly some newer models—cook hotter than others.

In one instance, liquid imperceptibly evaporated from the cooker, leaving less sauce than when the same dish was prepared in a different model. Because not all slow cookers are created equal, don't rely on the stated cook time for a recipe until you know how your cooker performs.

Braising

Braising uses low, moist heat to transform food—usually meat—into meltingly tender and flavorful dishes. It's an ideal technique for cooking cold-weather filling foods like pot roasts and daubes. Since much of the cooking time is hands-off as the dish simmers, braising is a boon to the busy cook. The results are always satisfying, partly because the process involves layers of flavors—browned bits from the seared meat enrich the cooking liquid, and the sauce becomes a heady, intense blend of meat juices, sweet vegetables, and fragrant herbs that infuse the dish. And you can remove a substantial amount of fat from the dish by skimming the cooking liquid before reducing it or serving the meal.

Holiday Brunch Tonic

This fizzy beverage takes on a festive feel with the scent of rosemary-infused sugar syrup. Garnish with extra rosemary sprigs, if desired. Serve shortly after mixing everything together so the tonic will sparkle.

Holiday Brunch Tonic

1   cup sugar
1   cup water
4   fresh rosemary sprigs
4   cups cranberry juice cocktail, chilled
2   cups fresh orange juice (about 6 oranges), chilled
3   cups club soda, chilled
Rosemary sprigs (optional)

1. Combine sugar and water in a small saucepan; bring to a boil. Reduce heat, and simmer 4 minutes or until sugar dissolves. Add rosemary; simmer 5 minutes. Remove from heat. Pour sugar syrup into a bowl; cover and refrigerate overnight.
2. Uncover sugar syrup; remove and discard rosemary sprigs. Combine sugar syrup, juices, and soda in a large pitcher. Serve immediately over ice. Garnish with rosemary sprigs, if desired. **Yield:** 12 servings (serving size: about ¾ cup).

CALORIES 131; FAT 0.2g (sat 0g, mono 0g, poly 0.1g); PROTEIN 0.3g; CARB 33.1g; FIBER 0.2g; CHOL 0mg; IRON 0.2mg; SODIUM 15mg; CALC 10mg

Champagne-Pomegranate Cocktail

In the tradition of sparkling libations like the Buck's Fizz and Bellini, this cocktail starts with Champagne and fruit juice.

Champagne-Pomegranate Cocktail

4   cups crushed ice
2   cups pomegranate juice
½   cup ginger ale
¼   cup brandy
1   (750-milliliter) bottle Champagne or sparkling wine
Cranberries (optional)

1. Combine first 5 ingredients in a pitcher. Pour about 1 cup of Champagne mixture into each of 8 glasses. Garnish with cranberries, if desired. **Yield:** 8 servings.

CALORIES 125; FAT 0g; PROTEIN 0.3g; CARB 11.7g; FIBER 0g; CHOL 0mg; IRON 0.1mg; SODIUM 9mg; CALC 10mg

Sparkling Cranberry
Tea Cocktails

This is a fine make-ahead recipe for an open house. Combine the ingredients through step one and chill; stir in the ginger ale just before serving. Serve in goblets, highball glasses, or any pretty clear glasses to show off the concoction's yuletide-red hue.

Sparkling Cranberry Tea Cocktails

4   cups water
½   cup sugar
2   family-sized tea bags
2½   cups no-sugar-added cranberry juice
1   cup vodka
¼   cup Grand Marnier (orange-flavored liqueur)
4   cups ginger ale, chilled
Orange rind strips (optional)

1. Combine 4 cups water and sugar in a large saucepan; bring to a boil. Cook until sugar dissolves, stirring occasionally. Pour over tea bags. Cover and let stand 5 minutes; discard tea bags. Cool. Stir in juice, vodka, and Grand Marnier; chill.
2. Gently stir in ginger ale. Serve over ice; garnish with rind, if desired. **Yield:** 12 servings (serving size: 1 cup).

CALORIES 151; FAT 0.1g (sat 0g, mono 0g, poly 0.1g); PROTEIN 0.2g; CARB 23.5g; FIBER 0.1g; CHOL 0mg; IRON 0.3mg; SODIUM 7mg; CALC 7mg

The combination of hot chocolate and espresso is enjoyed in Spain and throughout Europe. This version shows off the chocolate with a hint of orange and isn't as sweet as traditional American-style cocoa drinks.

Barcelona Hot Chocolate

⅔   cup boiling water
2   ounces good-quality dark or bittersweet (60 to 70% cocoa) chocolate, finely chopped
1⅓   cups 1% low-fat milk
1   cup brewed espresso or strong coffee
¼   cup unsweetened cocoa powder
¼   cup packed brown sugar
1   2-inch piece orange rind strip
¼   cup frozen fat-free whipped topping, thawed
Cocoa powder (optional)

1. Combine ⅔ cup boiling water and chopped chocolate in a medium saucepan, stirring until chocolate melts. Add milk and next 4 ingredients; cook over medium-low heat, stirring with a whisk. Heat 5 minutes or until tiny bubbles form around edge of pan, stirring frequently (do not boil). Discard rind. Pour 1 cup mixture into each of 4 mugs. Spoon 1 tablespoon whipped topping over each serving. Dust with cocoa powder, if desired. **Yield:** 4 servings.

CALORIES 177; FAT 5.4g (sat 3.1g, mono 1.7g, poly 0.1g); PROTEIN 4.4g; CARB 32g; FIBER 1.9g; CHOL 3mg; IRON 1.4mg; SODIUM 62mg; CALC 126mg

choiceingredient

Blood Oranges

This appropriately named sweet-tart orange has blood-red flesh. Although some are grown in California, most blood oranges come from Mediterranean countries (Southern Italy in particular) and are often considered to be among the finest dessert oranges in the world. Like regular oranges, blood oranges are rich in antioxidants, including vitamin C, and are also a great source of fiber.

Sporting a thick, red-blushed orange skin with flesh that ranges in color from pink to brilliant red to burgundy, a blood orange's flavor is tart-sweet and slightly berrylike. When selecting blood oranges, pick those that are firm to the touch and heavy for their size. Avoid any fruits with mold or spongy spots.

To keep these ruby gems fresh longer, choose refrigeration over the fruit bowl—they'll only last a couple of days at room temperature, but up to two weeks in the fridge. Blood oranges are best eaten fresh—out-of-hand, or in salads, salsas, or marmalades. The two most popular varieties are the dark-fleshed Moro, which is available from December through March, and the delicately flavored Tarocco, which you can find from January through May.

Any good-quality, fruity red wine works well in this cold sipper; a combination of pinot noir and Beaujolais is particularly good. The vermilion flesh of blood oranges (which come into season in December) is lovely. But if they're not available, substitute navel oranges.

Blood Orange Sangria

2   cups sliced strawberries
2   cups apple juice
⅔   cup Triple Sec (orange-flavored liqueur)
½   cup sugar
4   whole cloves
3   seedless blood oranges, each cut into 16 wedges
2   (750-milliliter) bottles fruity red wine
2   (3-inch) cinnamon sticks
1   lemon, cut into 8 wedges
1   lime, cut into 8 wedges

1. Combine all ingredients in a large pitcher, and stir until sugar dissolves. Cover and chill 8 hours or overnight. Discard cloves and cinnamon sticks. Pour sangria into individual glasses, including fruit. **Yield:** 16 servings (serving size: about 1 cup).

CALORIES 157; FAT 0.1g (sat 0g, mono 0g, poly 0.1g); PROTEIN 0.6g; CARB 20.5g; FIBER 1.2g; CHOL 0mg; IRON 0.6mg; SODIUM 7mg; CALC 23mg

These appetizers look great assembled like canapés; however, for a more informal get-together, you can set the toasts, cheese, and salmon mixture out and invite guests to build their own crostini. Prepare the salmon topping earlier in the day and keep it refrigerated until ready to assemble.

Smoked Salmon Crostini

½   cup chopped fennel bulb
¼   cup chopped green onions
1   tablespoon extra-virgin olive oil
2   teaspoons chopped fresh dill
1   teaspoon grated lemon rind
1½   tablespoons fresh lemon juice
1   teaspoon freshly ground black pepper
¾   pound cold-smoked salmon, cut into thin strips
48   (½-inch-thick) slices French bread baguette, toasted (about 1½ pounds)

½   cup light garlic-and-herbs spreadable cheese (such as Alouette Light)
Dill sprigs (optional)

1. Combine first 8 ingredients; cover and chill at least 1 hour. Spread each toast slice with ½ teaspoon cheese; top each with 1 tablespoon salmon mixture. Garnish with fresh dill sprigs, if desired. Yield: 24 servings (serving size: 2 crostini).

CALORIES 112; FAT 3g (sat 0.9g, mono 1.4g, poly 0.4g); PROTEIN 5.7g; CARB 15.5g; FIBER 1g; CHOL 6mg; IRON 0.9mg; SODIUM 482mg; CALC 28mg

Here's an intriguing version of the standard cheese dip. Be sure to rinse the crawfish after they thaw to remove any fishy taste. Substitute cooked shrimp for the crawfish, if you prefer; if they're large, roughly chop them so they're easier to scoop with the dip.

Cheese Dip with Crawfish

2   teaspoons butter
½   cup chopped onion
3   garlic cloves, minced
1   pound frozen cooked peeled and deveined crawfish tail meat, thawed, rinsed, and drained
1   pound light processed cheese, cubed (such as Velveeta Light)
1   (10-ounce) can diced tomatoes and green chiles, undrained
1   (10-ounce) can diced tomatoes and green chiles, drained
½   cup chopped green onions
5½ ounces baked tortilla chips
Green onion strips (optional)

1. Melt butter in a large saucepan over medium heat. Add onion and garlic; cook 5 minutes or until tender, stirring frequently. Add crawfish, and cook 2 minutes, stirring frequently. Remove mixture from pan; cover and keep warm.
2. Add cheese and tomatoes to pan; cook over medium-low heat 5 minutes or until cheese melts. Stir in crawfish mixture and chopped green onions. Serve with tortilla chips. Garnish with green onion strips, if desired. **Yield:** about 6 cups (serving size: ⅓ cup dip and about 6 chips).

CALORIES 115; FAT 3.7g (sat 2.1g, mono 0.9g, poly 0.4g); PROTEIN 13.7g; CARB 12g; FIBER 1g; CHOL 39mg; IRON 0.7mg; SODIUM 559mg; CALC 166mg

Oven-Roasted Tomatoes with Goat Cheese

a recipe we crave

Oven-Roasted Tomatoes with Goat Cheese

6   medium tomatoes, halved (about 1¼ pounds)
2   tablespoons extra-virgin olive oil, divided
1   tablespoon balsamic vinegar
½   teaspoon kosher salt
¼   teaspoon freshly ground black pepper
2   tablespoons crumbled goat cheese
12   fresh rosemary sprigs

1. Preheat oven to 200°.
2. Place a wire rack over a baking sheet; set aside.
3. Combine tomatoes, 1 tablespoon oil, and vinegar; toss gently. Place tomatoes, cut sides up, on prepared rack. Sprinkle with salt and pepper.
4. Bake at 200° for 6 hours or until tender and slightly syrupy (do not overbake or tomatoes will be tough and chewy). Remove from oven; cool completely. Place ½ teaspoon cheese onto each tomato half. Fold slightly; secure each tomato half with 1 rosemary sprig. Place on a serving platter; drizzle with remaining 1 tablespoon oil. **Yield:** 6 servings (serving size: 2 tomato halves).

CALORIES 88; FAT 6.4g (sat 1.7g, mono 4g, poly 0.6g); PROTEIN 2.4g; CARB 6.5g; FIBER 1.9g; CHOL 4mg; IRON 0.5mg; SODIUM 189mg; CALC 31mg

Prepare Citrus Fruits

The acidic juices and aromatic oils in fresh citrus fruits heighten and balance the flavors of a variety of dishes. These tips will help you make the most of your fruit. Be sure to wash citrus thoroughly under warm water to remove dirt and wax before you begin.

Rind:
Gently run the fruit up and down a Microplane® grater or the fine face of a box grater. For strips, use a vegetable peeler to remove lengths of rind.

Sections:

1. First, cut the top and bottom portions from the fruit to create a stable cutting surface. Next, stand the fruit upright; then use a paring knife to slice downward in a long, slow curve to remove the rind and the white pith.

2. Hold the fruit in your palm, and gently follow the natural sections of the fruit with the knife to cut out wedges.

Juice:
A handheld press releases the most juice while trapping the seeds. Cut the fruit in half, place it cut side down in the press, and lower handle.

Roast the sweet potatoes, section the oranges, and slice the onion ahead. Keep them refrigerated separately until you're ready to toss the salad.

Roasted Sweet Potato and Orange Salad

Salad:

1   tablespoon chopped fresh rosemary
2   teaspoons olive oil
3   garlic cloves, unpeeled and crushed
1½ pounds peeled sweet potato, cut into ¾-inch pieces
3   cups orange sections (about 6 oranges)
½   cup vertically sliced red onion
3   tablespoons pine nuts, toasted
1   (6-ounce) bag prewashed baby spinach

Dressing:

3   tablespoons fresh orange juice
2   tablespoons olive oil
1   tablespoon stone-ground mustard
1   tablespoon rice vinegar
1   tablespoon honey
¼   teaspoon salt
¼   teaspoon freshly ground black pepper
1   garlic clove, minced

1. Preheat oven to 400°.

2. To prepare salad, combine first 4 ingredients, tossing well. Place potato mixture on a jelly-roll pan lined with parchment paper. Bake at 400° for 40 minutes, stirring occasionally. Remove from oven; cool. Discard garlic. Combine potato mixture, orange sections, onion, pine nuts, and spinach in a large bowl.

3. To prepare dressing, combine orange juice and remaining ingredients in a small bowl, stirring well with a whisk. Drizzle dressing over salad; toss gently to coat. **Yield:** 10 servings (serving size: 1 cup).

CALORIES 160; FAT 5.3g (sat 3.2g, mono 1g, poly 0.8g); PROTEIN 2.9g; CARB 27g; FIBER 4.1g; CHOL 0mg; IRON 1.3mg; SODIUM 101mg; CALC 59mg

Beets

Fresh beets are now commonplace on fine-restaurant menus. With hues ranging from yellow to purple, they lend themselves to dramatic presentations.

To select: Small to medium beets with firm, smooth skin and no soft spots, with stems and leaves attached, are best.

To store: Beets' leafy green tops leach nutrients from the root, so immediately trim them to about an inch. Store in plastic bags in the refrigerator up to two weeks; gently wash before use.

To prepare: Because the juice can stain your hands and countertops, wear disposable latex gloves from the drugstore. They're thin enough to allow dexterity while protecting hands from stains.

To cook: Beets hold up well when julienned raw, roasted, baked, or boiled.

Health benefits: One beet contains 20% of the Recommended Daily Allowance (RDA) for folate.

This ultimate starter salad celebrates the produce of the season and makes a knockout-gorgeous addition to the table.

—Timothy Q. Cebula, Birmingham, AL

Winter Salad with Roasted Beets and Citrus Reduction Sauce

4	medium beets (red and golden)

Cooking spray

¾	cup fresh orange juice
½	teaspoon sugar
1	tablespoon minced shallots
2	tablespoons white wine vinegar
¾	teaspoon kosher salt, divided
½	teaspoon black pepper, divided
¼	cup extra-virgin olive oil
4	cups torn Boston lettuce
2	cups trimmed watercress
2	cups torn radicchio
½	cup (2 ounces) crumbled goat cheese

1. Preheat oven to 400°.

2. Leave root and 1-inch stem on beets; scrub with a brush. Place beets on a foil-lined jelly-roll pan coated with cooking spray. Lightly coat beets with cooking spray. Bake at 400° for 1 hour and 10 minutes or until tender. Cool beets slightly. Trim off beet roots and stems; rub off skins. Cut beets into ½-inch-thick wedges.

3. Bring juice and sugar to a boil in a small saucepan; cook 10 minutes or until reduced to 2 tablespoons. Pour into a medium bowl; cool slightly. Add shallots, vinegar, ½ teaspoon salt, and ¼ teaspoon pepper, stirring with a whisk. Gradually add oil, stirring constantly with a whisk.

4. Combine lettuce, watercress, and radicchio. Sprinkle lettuce mixture with remaining ¼ teaspoon salt and ¼ teaspoon pepper; toss gently to combine. Arrange about 1 cup lettuce mixture on each of 8 salad plates. Divide beets evenly among salads. Drizzle about 1 tablespoon dressing over each salad; sprinkle each salad with 1 tablespoon cheese. **Yield:** 8 servings.

CALORIES 127; FAT 9.1g (sat 2.4g, mono 5.4g, poly 0.8g); PROTEIN 3.1g; CARB 8.2g; FIBER 1.7g; CHOL 6mg; IRON 1mg; SODIUM 253mg; CALC 53mg

Roast the beets, toast the walnuts, and prepare the dressing up to three days in advance. Slice the fennel and endive and toss the salad just before serving.

Roasted Beet, Fennel, and Walnut Salad

Salad:
6   beets
1½ teaspoons canola oil
2   (1¼-pound) fennel bulbs with stalks
2   cups sliced Belgian endive (about 2 small heads)
⅓   cup coarsely chopped walnuts, toasted
1   (6-ounce) package fresh spinach (about 8 cups)
½   teaspoon kosher salt
¼   teaspoon freshly ground black pepper
Dressing:
3   tablespoons red wine vinegar
3   tablespoons honey
1   teaspoon grated orange rind
2   tablespoons fresh orange juice
2   tablespoons chopped fresh basil
2   teaspoons extra-virgin olive oil
2   teaspoons Dijon mustard
½   teaspoon kosher salt

1. Preheat oven to 400°.
2. To prepare salad, leave root and 1 inch of stem on beets; scrub with a vegetable brush. Peel and cut beets into ½-inch-thick wedges. Place beets on a jelly-roll pan. Drizzle with canola oil; toss well to coat. Bake at 400° for 45 minutes or until beets are tender, stirring every 20 minutes.
3. Trim tough outer leaves from fennel; mince feathery fronds to measure 2 tablespoons. Remove and discard stalks. Cut fennel bulbs in half length-

wise; discard cores. Cut bulbs into ¼-inch slices. Combine fennel slices, endive, and next 4 ingredients in a large bowl; toss gently.
4. To prepare dressing, combine vinegar and remaining ingredients, stirring well with a whisk. Drizzle dressing mixture over fennel mixture. Add beets to bowl; toss to combine. Sprinkle with chopped fennel fronds. Serve immediately. **Yield:** 12 servings (serving size: about 1 cup).

CALORIES 87; FAT 3.7g (sat 0.4g, mono 1.2g, poly 1.9g); PROTEIN 2.2g; CARB 13.1g; FIBER 3.4g; CHOL 0mg; IRON 1.2mg; SODIUM 232mg; CALC 48mg

seasonalstar

This simple salad is a refreshing start to winter meals at Simpatica Dining Hall in Portland, Oregon. Owner Benjamin Dyer says they try to use fresh, high-quality ingredients that do all the work. Just by applying a small amount of technique, you can make something simple and tasty. Juicy, winter-fresh oranges require little more than a dressing of olive oil, sea salt, and ground black and red peppers.

Orange and Red Onion Salad with Red Pepper

18 (¼-inch-thick) orange slices (about 4 oranges)
½   cup vertically sliced red onion
½   teaspoon sea salt
¼   teaspoon freshly ground black pepper
¼   teaspoon ground red pepper
2   tablespoons extra-virgin olive oil

1. Arrange orange slices in a single layer on a platter. Top evenly with onion. Sprinkle with salt, black pepper, and red pepper. Drizzle with oil. Serve immediately. **Yield:** 6 servings (serving size: 3 orange slices and about 5 onion pieces).

CALORIES 93; FAT 4.9g (sat 0.7g, mono 3.6g, poly 0.5g); PROTEIN 0.8g; CARB 12.7g; FIBER 2.6g; CHOL 0mg; IRON 0.2mg; SODIUM 192mg; CALC 46mg

A tasty mix of rice, black-eyed peas, and pork, hoppin' John is a southern dish often eaten on New Year's Day for good luck. Corn bread is a traditional accompaniment.

Hoppin' John with Mustard Greens

2   cups water
2   tablespoons whole-grain Dijon mustard
1   teaspoon salt
¼   teaspoon dried thyme
2   tablespoons olive oil
3 ½ cups chopped onion
1   cup uncooked long-grain white rice
⅔   cup finely chopped ham
4   garlic cloves, minced
4   cups cooked black-eyed peas
4   cups chopped trimmed mustard greens

1. Combine first 4 ingredients, stirring with a whisk; set aside.

2. Heat oil in a Dutch oven over medium-high heat. Add onion to pan; sauté 6 minutes. Add rice, ham, and garlic; sauté 2 minutes. Stir in water mixture; bring to a boil. Cover, reduce heat, and simmer 15 minutes. Add peas and greens; cover and cook 5 minutes. Stir rice mixture; cover and cook an additional 5 minutes or until greens and rice are tender. **Yield:** 6 servings (serving size: about 1⅓ cups).

CALORIES 389; FAT 7g (sat 1.4g, mono 4.1g, poly 1g); PROTEIN 18.2g; CARB 63.6g; FIBER 11g; CHOL 14mg; IRON 5.1mg; SODIUM 502mg; CALC 109mg

Prepare Dried Beans

1. Since beans are not washed during processing (the key to processing beans is to dehydrate, not hydrate), it's important to rinse beans before soaking. Remove and discard any small rocks, shriveled beans, and dirt. Soak beans using either the overnight soak or the quick-soak methods. For an overnight soak, place the beans in a large bowl. Cover with cool water to 2 inches above beans; cover and let stand 8 hours or overnight, and then drain. To quick-soak beans, place them in a large Dutch oven. Cover with water to 2 inches above the beans; bring the water to a boil, and cook 2 minutes. Remove from heat; cover and let stand 1 hour, and then drain. Soaking dried beans shortens the cooking time and promotes even cooking. In fact, beans can be cooked after only a quick rinse—they'll just take a good bit longer to cook until they're tender (at least 2 to 3 hours, depending on the variety).

2. Place the drained, soaked beans in a large Dutch oven.

3. Cover with water to 2 inches above the beans, and bring to a boil.

4. Partially cover, reduce heat, and simmer until tender (skim the foam from the surface of the cooking liquid as needed). It is important to cook beans at a simmer, not at a boil—boiling may cook beans too rapidly and cause their skins to split.

5. It's important to taste the beans to make sure they're tender; don't just go by the estimated cooking times because older beans and those cooked in hard water will take longer to cook.

Note: Do not add salt or acidic ingredients (such as tomatoes, vinegar, or citrus) to beans until they are tender; cooking in salted water may lengthen the cooking time, and acid can prevent beans from becoming tender.

howto:

Cook Perfect Pasta

If you can boil water, you can make great dishes using this pantry staple.

1. After adding pasta to boiling water, put the lid on the pot, but prop it open slightly with a wooden spoon so the water doesn't boil over.

2. Drain the cooked pasta in a colander; shake well to remove excess water.

3. Rinse the pasta with cold running water if you plan to use it in a salad or fill it, as you would manicotti shells. This removes the light coating of starch that covers the pasta.

This recipe scored high in our Test Kitchens for its rich flavor and ultra-creamy texture. The exotic mushroom blend, a combination of shiitake, cremini, and oyster mushrooms, is sold in eight-ounce packages. If unavailable, you can use all cremini mushrooms.

Farfalle with Creamy Wild Mushroom Sauce

1   pound uncooked farfalle (bow tie pasta)
1   tablespoon butter
12   ounces presliced exotic mushroom blend
½   cup chopped onion
⅓   cup finely chopped shallots
1   tablespoon minced garlic
1½   teaspoons salt, divided
¼   teaspoon freshly ground black pepper
¼   cup dry white wine
⅔   cup whipping cream
½   cup (2 ounces) grated fresh Parmigiano-Reggiano cheese
2   tablespoons chopped fresh parsley
Minced fresh parsley (optional)

1. Cook pasta according to package directions, omitting salt and fat; drain.

2. Melt butter in a large nonstick skillet over medium-high heat. Add mushrooms, onion, shallots, garlic, 1 teaspoon salt, and pepper; cook 12 minutes or until liquid evaporates and mushrooms are tender, stirring occasionally. Add wine; cook 2 minutes or until liquid evaporates, stirring occasionally. Remove from heat.

3. Add cooked pasta, whipping cream, cheese, and 2 tablespoons parsley, tossing gently to coat. Stir in remaining ½ teaspoon salt. Garnish with minced fresh parsley, if desired. Serve immediately. **Yield:** 8 servings (serving size: 1¼ cups).

CALORIES 336; FAT 11.4g (sat 6.9g, mono 3.1g, poly 0.4g); PROTEIN 12.1g; CARB 47.5g; FIBER 2.3g; CHOL 36mg; IRON 2.3mg; SODIUM 577mg; CALC 124mg

Pappardelle with Roasted Winter Squash,
Arugula, and Pine Nuts

Easy and filling, this handsome entrée is a good choice for a weeknight vegetarian dinner.

Pappardelle with Roasted Winter Squash, Arugula, and Pine Nuts

4   cups (1-inch) cubed peeled butternut squash
2   tablespoons balsamic vinegar
2   teaspoons olive oil
½   teaspoon salt, divided
Cooking spray
8   ounces uncooked pappardelle (wide ribbon pasta) or fettuccine
1   tablespoon butter
2   tablespoons pine nuts
1   tablespoon chopped fresh sage
2   garlic cloves, minced
2   cups trimmed arugula
½   cup (2 ounces) grated fresh Asiago cheese
½   teaspoon coarsely ground black pepper

1. Preheat oven to 475°.
2. Combine squash, vinegar, oil, and ¼ teaspoon salt in a large bowl; toss well to coat. Arrange squash mixture in a single layer on a jelly-roll pan coated with cooking spray. Bake at 475° for 25 minutes or until tender and lightly browned, stirring occasionally.
3. While squash bakes, cook pasta according to package directions, omitting salt and fat. Drain in a colander over a bowl, reserving 1 tablespoon cooking liquid.
4. Melt butter in a large nonstick skillet over medium heat. Add pine nuts, sage, and garlic; cook 3 minutes or just until pine nuts begin to brown, stirring occasionally. Place pasta, reserved cooking liquid, pine nut mixture, and squash mixture in a large bowl; toss gently to combine. Add remaining ¼ teaspoon salt, arugula, cheese, and black pepper; toss gently to combine. Serve immediately. **Yield:** 6 servings (serving size: about 2 cups).

CALORIES 270; FAT 8.2g (sat 3.5g, mono 2.9g, poly 1g); PROTEIN 9.8g; CARB 41.6g; FIBER 4.8g; CHOL 14mg; IRON 2.4mg; SODIUM 249mg; CALC 162mg

All parts of the orange—juice, rind, and pulp—flavor the salsa. Substitute brown, basmati, or jasmine rice, if you prefer.

Roasted Tilapia with Orange-Parsley Salsa

3   oranges (about 1 pound)
¼   cup chopped fresh parsley, divided
2   tablespoons extra-virgin olive oil, divided
¾   teaspoon salt, divided
4   (6-ounce) tilapia fillets
½   teaspoon freshly ground black pepper, divided
2   cups hot cooked instant white rice

1. Grate 2 teaspoons orange rind. Peel and section oranges over a bowl, reserving 2 tablespoons juice. Chop sections. Combine rind, chopped orange, 2 tablespoons parsley, 5 teaspoons oil, and ¼ teaspoon salt in a bowl; toss well.
2. Preheat oven to 400°.
3. Sprinkle fish evenly with ¼ teaspoon salt and ¼ teaspoon pepper. Place fish in an ovenproof skillet coated with remaining 1 teaspoon oil. Bake at 400° for 14 minutes or until fish flakes easily when tested with a fork or until desired degree of doneness.
4. Combine 2 tablespoons reserved juice, remaining 2 tablespoons parsley, remaining ¼ teaspoon salt, remaining ¼ teaspoon pepper, and rice. Spoon ½ cup rice onto each of 4 plates, and top each with 1 fillet and ¼ cup salsa. **Yield:** 4 servings.

CALORIES 423; FAT 12.1g (sat 2.6g, mono 6.7g, poly 2.1g); PROTEIN 47.4g; CARB 32.7g; FIBER 3g; CHOL 97mg; IRON 3mg; SODIUM 543mg; CALC 76mg

Pomegranates

Although the membranes of pomegranates are bitter and inedible, the pulp and seeds contribute a juicy, sweet-tart flavor to many winter recipes.

To select: Choose pomegranates that feel heavy, are bright in color, and are free of blemishes.

To store: Refrigerate whole pomegranates up to three months, or freeze seeds in an airtight container up to three months.

To prepare: Pomegranates need seeding and juicing before use; take caution as the juice will stain. Quarter the fruit; remove the seeds, being careful not to break them. Discard the white membrane.

To use: Seeds can be eaten raw or pureed; the juice is great in marinades, desserts, and beverages.

Health benefits: Pomegranates are a good source of potassium, which helps lower blood pressure, and vitamin C, which is an antioxidant that helps prevent cancer, heart disease, and some eye problems.

The jewel-toned salsa features fresh seasonal fruit and serves as a fitting complement to the shrimp, which is heavily seasoned. It also makes a nice accompaniment to grilled chicken breasts.

Blackened Shrimp with Pomegranate-Orange Salsa

Salsa:

2   cups pomegranate seeds
     (about 4 pomegranates)
1   cup finely chopped orange sections
     (about 2 oranges)
⅓   cup chopped green onions
2   tablespoons minced seeded jalapeño pepper
2   tablespoons chopped fresh cilantro
¼   teaspoon salt

Shrimp:

1   tablespoon paprika
2   teaspoons ground cumin
1   teaspoon garlic powder
1   teaspoon dried oregano
¾   teaspoon dried thyme
¾   teaspoon ground red pepper
½   teaspoon salt
½   teaspoon ground allspice
36   large shrimp, peeled and deveined
     (about 1½ pounds)
5   teaspoons olive oil, divided

1. To prepare salsa, combine first 6 ingredients.
2. To prepare shrimp, combine paprika and next 7 ingredients in a large zip-top plastic bag. Add shrimp to bag; seal and shake well to coat. Remove shrimp from bag.
3. Heat 2½ teaspoons oil in a large nonstick skillet over medium-high heat. Add half of shrimp mixture; cook 2 minutes on each side or until done. Remove from pan. Repeat procedure with remaining 2½ teaspoons oil and remaining shrimp mixture. Serve warm with salsa. **Yield:** 12 servings (serving size: 3 shrimp and ¼ cup salsa).

CALORIES 127; FAT 3.2g (sat 0.5g, mono 1.6g, poly 0.7g); PROTEIN 12.4g; CARB 12.6g; FIBER 1.3g; CHOL 86mg; IRON 1.9mg; SODIUM 235mg; CALC 45mg

Add a teaspoon or two of ground dried porcini mushrooms along with the broth and red wine to give the dish an extra layer of mushroom flavor. Meaty, earthy-tasting mushrooms such as porcini or black trumpet are ideal. Serve over hot cooked egg noodles or steamed rice.

Beef Braised with Red Wine and Mushrooms

½   cup dried porcini mushrooms (about ½ ounce)
1   cup boiling water
1 ¼ pounds lean beef stew meat, cut into 1-inch cubes
¾   teaspoon salt, divided
½   teaspoon freshly ground black pepper, divided
2   tablespoons olive oil
1   cup pearl onions (about 16)
6   cups chopped cremini mushrooms (about 1 pound)
1 ½ cups (¼-inch) slices carrot (about 2 large)
1 ½ cups fat-free, less-sodium beef broth
½   cup dry red wine
4   fresh thyme sprigs
3   garlic cloves, crushed
2   bay leaves
1   tablespoon water
2   teaspoons cornstarch

1. Combine porcini mushrooms and 1 cup boiling water in a small bowl; let stand 30 minutes. Drain mushrooms through a sieve into a bowl, reserving liquid. Chop mushrooms; set aside.
2. Sprinkle beef with ¼ teaspoon salt and ¼ teaspoon pepper. Heat oil in a large Dutch oven over medium-high heat. Add half of beef to pan; sauté 5 minutes or until lightly browned on all sides. Remove beef from pan with a slotted spoon; place in a bowl. Repeat procedure with remaining beef.
3. Add onions to pan, and sauté 3 minutes or until lightly browned. Add cremini mushrooms and carrot; sauté 3 minutes or until mushrooms are tender. Add beef, porcini mushrooms, porcini liquid, remaining ½ teaspoon salt, remaining ¼ teaspoon pepper, broth, and next 4 ingredients; bring to a boil. Cover, reduce heat, and simmer 1½ hours or until beef is tender. Uncover and cook 20 minutes, stirring occasionally.
4. Combine 1 tablespoon water and cornstarch in a small bowl. Add cornstarch mixture to pan; bring to a boil. Cook 1 minute or until liquid thickens. Discard thyme sprigs and bay leaves. **Yield:** 4 servings (serving size: 1¼ cups).

CALORIES 307; FAT 10.3g (sat 3.8g, mono 4.3g, poly 0.6g); PROTEIN 33.5g; CARB 19.9g; FIBER 3.5g; CHOL 88mg; IRON 4.8mg; SODIUM 716mg; CALC 47mg

WINE NOTE

Mushrooms and **merlot** are a natural match. The wine's rich flavor and firm tannins make it a perfect choice for flavorful beef, as well.

Thyme and Spice-Rubbed Roast Beef Tenderloin au Jus

1	tablespoon chopped fresh thyme, divided
1¼	teaspoons salt
½	teaspoon freshly ground black pepper
¼	teaspoon ground allspice
1¾	pounds beef tenderloin, trimmed
	Cooking spray
⅓	cup brandy
¼	cup minced shallots
1½	cups fat-free, less-sodium beef broth

1. Combine 2 teaspoons thyme, salt, pepper, and allspice in a small bowl. Rub mixture evenly over all sides of beef. Wrap tightly in plastic wrap, and refrigerate 24 hours.

2. Preheat oven to 400°.

3. Heat a large nonstick skillet over medium-high heat. Coat pan with cooking spray. Add beef to pan, and cook 5 minutes, turning to brown on all sides.

Transfer beef to a roasting rack coated with cooking spray; place rack in roasting pan. Bake at 400° for 26 minutes or until a thermometer registers 135° or desired degree of doneness. Remove from oven, and let stand 10 minutes before slicing. Pour brandy into roasting pan, scraping pan to loosen browned bits; set aside.

4. Heat skillet over medium heat. Coat skillet with cooking spray. Add shallots to skillet; cook 4 minutes or until tender, stirring occasionally. Add brandy mixture, broth, and remaining 1 teaspoon thyme to skillet, scraping pan to loosen browned bits; simmer until reduced to 1 cup (about 4 minutes). Serve with beef. **Yield:** 7 servings (serving size: 3 ounces beef and about 2 tablespoons jus).

CALORIES 170; FAT 6.7g (sat 2.5g, mono 2.6g, poly 0.3g); PROTEIN 18.5g; CARB 1.2g; FIBER 0.2g; CHOL 54mg; IRON 2.5mg; SODIUM 556mg; CALC 9mg

choiceingredient

Kumquats

These bite-sized oblong citrus fruit look like miniature oranges. While the edible rind is tangy-sweet, the inside flesh is very tart.

Because it has such an intense sour orange flavor, you often see kumquats candied, pickled, or preserved. They can also be sliced and served in salads or used as a garnish. Additionally, kumquats are used to thicken sauces while adding a bittersweet note, and they're often prepared as chutneys and marmalades to accompany roast meats and game. Add them in their raw form to garnish holiday platters and grace ornamental fruit bowls.

Fresh kumquats are in season as early as October and as late as June, but they're most plentiful from December through April. Test them with a gentle squeeze, and buy only firm fruit. Because of their thin skin, kumquats don't keep particularly well. Store them at room temperature if you plan on eating them within a few days. Otherwise, store them in a plastic bag in the refrigerator for up to two weeks.

Kumquats, carrot juice, Dijon mustard, and rice vinegar create a piquant accompaniment for peppered beef tenderloin. Try the kumquat marmalade with pork or chicken as well.

Pepper-Crusted Beef Tenderloin with Kumquat Marmalade

1½ cups vertically sliced onion
½   cup halved, seeded, and vertically sliced kumquats
½   cup carrot juice or orange juice
1   tablespoon Dijon mustard
¼   teaspoon salt
2   fresh thyme sprigs
1   bay leaf
2   teaspoons rice vinegar
2   teaspoons olive oil
1½ to 2 tablespoons freshly ground mixed peppercorns or black peppercorns
4   (4-ounce) beef tenderloin steaks, trimmed (about ¾ inch thick)
½   teaspoon salt
Chives (optional)

1. Combine first 7 ingredients in a small saucepan; bring to a boil. Reduce heat; simmer 15 minutes or until liquid almost evaporates, stirring occasionally. Remove from heat. Discard thyme sprigs and bay leaf. Stir in rice vinegar, and cool.

2. Heat oil in a large nonstick skillet over medium-high heat. Place pepper in a shallow dish. Dredge steaks in pepper; sprinkle evenly with ½ teaspoon salt. Add beef to pan; cook 3 minutes on each side or until desired degree of doneness. Serve with marmalade; garnish with chives, if desired. **Yield:** 4 servings (serving size: 1 steak and about ¼ cup marmalade).

CALORIES 211; FAT 6.9g (sat 1.9g, mono 3.3g, poly 0.4g); PROTEIN 23.8g; CARB 17.1g; FIBER 3.4g; CHOL 60mg; IRON 4.1mg; SODIUM 611mg; CALC 62mg

If your slow cooker includes a removable insert, you can brown the brisket and onion mixture a day ahead, place all the ingredients in the insert, and refrigerate. The next morning, place the insert in the slow cooker, and when you arrive home from work, a tasty entrée will await you.

Slow-Cooker Beef Brisket with Beer

1   (3-pound) beef brisket, trimmed
1   teaspoon salt
½   teaspoon freshly ground black pepper
Cooking spray
¼   cup water
2   cups vertically sliced onion (about 1 large)
1½ cups chopped parsnip (about 2)
1   tablespoon balsamic vinegar
1   bay leaf
1   (12-ounce) bottle light beer

1. Rub brisket with salt and pepper. Heat a large heavy skillet over medium-high heat. Coat pan with cooking spray. Add brisket to pan, and cook 10 minutes, browning on all sides. Remove brisket from pan. Add ¼ cup water to pan, stirring to loosen browned bits. Add onion and parsnip; sauté 5 minutes or until vegetables are tender.
2. Place onion mixture, vinegar, bay leaf, and beer in a large electric slow cooker. Place brisket on top of onion mixture. Cover and cook on low 8 hours. Discard bay leaf. Cut brisket diagonally across the grain into thin slices. Serve with sauce. **Yield:** 12 servings (serving size: about 3 ounces brisket and ⅓ cup sauce).

CALORIES 160; FAT 5g (sat 1.9g, mono 2.1g, poly 0.2g); PROTEIN 20.5g; CARB 5.6g; FIBER 1.1g; CHOL 49mg; IRON 1.9mg; SODIUM 232mg; CALC 20mg

Root vegetables add a touch of sweetness to this savory stew. Yankee cooks traditionally add the vegetables partway through the cooking process, which helps keep them from breaking down.

Yankee Pot Roast

1 teaspoon canola oil
2 pounds boneless chuck roast, trimmed
Cooking spray
1 cup chopped yellow onion
4 cups fat-free, less-sodium beef broth
1 tablespoon whole-grain Dijon mustard
1 teaspoon salt
1 teaspoon dried thyme
½ teaspoon freshly ground black pepper
½ teaspoon dried sage
2 bay leaves
2½ cups (1-inch) cubed peeled rutabaga
(about 1 pound)
2½ cups (1-inch) cubed peeled parsnip (about 1 pound)
1½ cups (1-inch-thick) slices carrot (about 8 ounces)
2 cups (1-inch) cubed peeled baking potato
(about 1 pound)
Thyme sprigs (optional)

1. Preheat oven to 300°.

2. Heat oil in a large Dutch oven over medium-high heat. Add beef to pan, browning on all sides (about 8 minutes). Remove from pan. Coat pan with cooking spray. Add onion to pan; sauté 5 minutes or until beginning to brown. Stir in broth, scraping pan to loosen browned bits. Reduce heat; add mustard and next 5 ingredients. Return roast to pan; bring to a simmer.

3. Cover and bake at 300° for 1½ hours. Stir in rutabaga, parsnip, and carrot. Bake, covered, 1 hour. Stir in potato; cover and bake 30 minutes or until roast and vegetables are very tender. Discard bay leaves. Garnish with thyme sprigs, if desired. **Yield:** 8 servings (serving size: 3 ounces meat and about ¾ cup vegetables).

CALORIES 325; FAT 10.2g (sat 3.3g, mono 4.6g, poly 0.7g); PROTEIN 28.7g; CARB 29.3g; FIBER 5.8g; CHOL 79mg; IRON 4.3mg; SODIUM 642mg; CALC 72mg

Serve with classic condiments such as sour cream, chopped green onions, and shredded Cheddar cheese. For a thinner chili, cook covered the whole time. You can prepare it a day ahead and refrigerate, or up to two weeks ahead and freeze (be sure to thaw the chili overnight in the refrigerator). Look for masa harina, the corn flour used to make tortillas, in the Latin foods aisle at the supermarket, or substitute fine-ground cornmeal.

Beef, Black Bean, and Chorizo Chili

2 links Spanish chorizo sausage (about 6½ ounces), thinly sliced
1½ pounds beef stew meat
1½ cups chopped onion
4 garlic cloves, minced
1 (7-ounce) can chipotle chiles in adobo sauce
3 tablespoons tomato paste
2 teaspoons sugar
1 teaspoon salt
2 teaspoons unsweetened cocoa
1 teaspoon ground coriander
1 teaspoon dried oregano
1 teaspoon ground cumin
1 cup dry red wine
¼ cup fresh lime juice
2 (14-ounce) cans less-sodium beef broth
1 (28-ounce) can whole tomatoes, undrained and chopped
2 tablespoons masa harina
2 (15-ounce) cans pinto beans, rinsed and drained
1 (15-ounce) can black beans, rinsed and drained
Chopped green onions (optional)

1. Heat a Dutch oven over medium-high heat. Add chorizo to pan; sauté 3 minutes or until browned. Remove chorizo from pan. Add half of beef to pan; sauté 5 minutes or until browned. Remove beef from pan. Repeat procedure with remaining beef. Add onion and garlic to pan; sauté 3 minutes.

2. Remove 4 chipotle chiles from can, and chop. Reserve remaining chiles and sauce for another use. Add chorizo, beef, chopped chiles, tomato paste, and next 6 ingredients to pan, and cook 1 minute, stirring constantly. Stir in red wine, lime juice, beef broth, and tomatoes; bring to a boil. Reduce heat, and simmer 1 hour, stirring occasionally.
3. Gradually stir in masa harina. Add pinto beans and black beans, and bring to a boil. Cover, reduce heat, and simmer 30 minutes. Garnish with green onions, if desired. **Yield:** 10 servings (serving size: about 1 cup).

CALORIES 325; FAT 11g (sat 3.8g, mono 4.7g, poly 1g); PROTEIN 25g; CARB 31.4g; FIBER 8.4g; CHOL 53mg; IRON 4.7mg; SODIUM 898mg; CALC 104mg

Mint, a favored partner for lamb, fits nicely into the gremolata. Serve these tender shanks with polenta, mashed potatoes, or risotto and broccoli rabe.

Braised Lamb Shanks with Parsley-Mint Gremolata

Lamb:

1   tablespoon minced fresh thyme
1   teaspoon salt
1   teaspoon minced fresh rosemary
½   teaspoon freshly ground black pepper
4   (12-ounce) lamb shanks
1   tablespoon olive oil
2   cups chopped onion (about 1 large)
1   cup chopped carrot (about 2 large)
3   garlic cloves, minced
2   cups dry red wine
¾   cup fat-free, less-sodium chicken broth
¾   cup fat-free, less-sodium beef broth

Gremolata:

¼   cup finely chopped fresh flat-leaf parsley
2   tablespoons finely chopped fresh mint
1   tablespoon grated lemon rind
1   tablespoon minced garlic

1. To prepare lamb, combine first 4 ingredients; set aside 1 teaspoon herb mixture. Rub lamb evenly with remaining herb mixture. Heat oil in a large Dutch oven over medium heat. Add lamb to pan; cook 2 minutes on each side or until browned. Remove lamb from pan; keep warm. Add onion, carrot, and garlic to pan; cook 5 minutes or until lightly browned and tender, stirring occasionally. Add wine and reserved 1 teaspoon herb mixture; bring to a boil. Cook until mixture is reduced to 2 cups (about 6 minutes). Add broths; bring to a boil. Cook until mixture is reduced to 1¾ cups (about 5 minutes). Return lamb to pan; cover, reduce heat, and simmer 2½ hours or until lamb is tender, turning shanks occasionally.

2. To prepare gremolata, combine parsley and remaining ingredients in a small bowl.

3. Remove lamb and vegetables from pan with a slotted spoon; keep warm. Place a large zip-top plastic bag inside an 8-cup glass measure or bowl. Pour broth mixture into bag; let stand 10 minutes (fat will rise to top). Seal bag, and carefully snip off 1 bottom corner of bag. Drain drippings into pan, stopping before fat layer reaches opening; discard fat. Bring broth mixture to a boil; cook until reduced to 2 cups and thickened (about 12 minutes). Spoon sauce over lamb and vegetables; top with gremolata. **Yield:** 4 servings (serving size: 1 lamb shank plus vegetables, about ½ cup sauce, and 2 tablespoons gremolata).

CALORIES 257; FAT 8.5g (sat 2.6g, mono 4.4g, poly 0.7g); PROTEIN 33.2g; CARB 11.1g; FIBER 2.3g; CHOL 100mg; IRON 3.6mg; SODIUM 870mg; CALC 61mg

Turnips

This root vegetable, distinguishable by its white skin and purple-tinged top, is especially delicious during the winter. With their creamy white flesh, young turnips have a mild, crisp, sweet flavor, but as they age, they develop a stronger flavor and coarser texture.

Turnip greens, the leafy top of the vegetable, have a slightly bitter flavor and can be cooked in a variety of ways, including boiling, sautéing, steaming, and stir-frying. Often called winter greens, turnip greens are actually available almost year-round. But in deep winter, they become sweeter. The greens aren't the only good product of this vegetable, however. The roots can be boiled and mashed, or roasted and pureed; they can also be cubed and tossed with butter or used raw in salads.

Store turnips in a plastic bag in the refrigerator for one to two weeks. Wrap the greens, unwashed, in a damp kitchen towel or paper towel, and place them inside a loose plastic bag in the refrigerator for three to five days. If you don't have turnip greens, you can substitute mustard greens, collards, kale, Swiss chard, or spinach.

This hearty dish combines tart apples with smoky bacon, pungent cabbage, and sweet maple syrup. The apples and vegetables cook along with the pork so the flavors are harmonious. Full-flavored, tart apples, such as Granny Smith, Jonagold, Albemarle (Newtown) Pippin, Roxbury Russet, or Winesap, provide the best flavor.

Roast Pork with Apples, Cabbage, and Turnips

Cooking spray
1   (3-pound) boneless pork loin roast, trimmed
2   cups finely chopped onion
1   slice applewood-smoked bacon, chopped
5   cups thinly sliced peeled tart apple
      (about 1½ pounds)
3   cups thinly sliced green cabbage
3   cups (1-inch) cubed peeled turnips
¾   cup dry white wine
2   tablespoons maple syrup
2   tablespoons cider vinegar
1   teaspoon salt
¼   teaspoon freshly ground black pepper

1. Preheat oven to 375°.
2. Heat a large Dutch oven over medium-high heat. Coat pan with cooking spray. Add pork; cook 15 minutes, browning on all sides. Remove pork from pan. Add onion and bacon to pan; sauté 5 minutes or until onion is tender. Return pork to pan. Add apple and remaining ingredients, and bring to a simmer. Place pan in oven. Bake, uncovered, at 375° for 1 hour and 15 minutes or until a thermometer registers 155°, turning pork after 45 minutes. **Yield:** 10 servings (serving size: 3 ounces pork and about ½ cup apple mixture).

CALORIES 262; FAT 9.8g (sat 3.5g, mono 4.3g, poly 0.9g); PROTEIN 25.7g; CARB 17.6g;
FIBER 2.8g; CHOL 70mg; IRON 1.4mg; SODIUM 333mg; CALC 50mg

This easy pan roast is served with a versatile sauce. Leeks, a mild, sweet member of the onion family, are cooked slowly along with the pork until they're very tender. This dish earned its status as a favorite because the time-honored Italian technique and straight-forward flavor are so reliable.

Pan-Roasted Pork Loin with Leeks

4   large leeks (about 2¼ pounds)
½   cup water
1   tablespoon butter, divided
½   teaspoon salt, divided
½   teaspoon black pepper, divided
1   (2-pound) boneless pork loin, trimmed
½   cup dry white wine
Chopped fresh parsley (optional)

1. Remove roots and tough upper leaves from leeks. Cut each leek in half lengthwise. Cut each half crosswise into ½-inch-thick slices (you should have about 6 cups). Soak in cold water to loosen dirt; drain and rinse under running water.
2. Combine leeks, ½ cup water, 1 teaspoon butter, ¼ teaspoon salt, and ¼ teaspoon pepper in a large Dutch oven or deep sauté pan over medium-high heat. Cook 10 minutes or until leeks wilt. Pour leek mixture into a bowl.
3. Heat remaining 2 teaspoons butter in pan over medium-high heat. Add pork to pan. Cook 5 minutes, turning to brown on all sides. Add remaining ¼ teaspoon salt, remaining ¼ teaspoon pepper, and wine to pan; cook 15 seconds, scraping pan to loosen browned bits. Return leek mixture to pan. Cover, reduce heat, and simmer 2 hours or until pork is tender. Remove pork from pan. Increase heat to reduce leek sauce if too watery. Cut pork

into ¼-inch-thick slices. Serve with leek mixture. Garnish with parsley, if desired. **Yield:** 6 servings (serving size: about 3 ounces pork and about 2½ tablespoons leek mixture).

CALORIES 246; FAT 10.7g (sat 4.2g, mono 4.4g, poly 1.1g); PROTEIN 24.8g; CARB 12.1g; FIBER 1g; CHOL 73mg; IRON 2.8mg; SODIUM 306mg; CALC 60mg

Leeks

Although leeks resemble large green onions, they're milder and sweeter. Leeks are usually cooked since they're very fibrous when raw.

To select: Buy leeks with crisp leaves and blemish-free stalks.

To store: Leeks need to be refrigerated. Keep them tightly wrapped up to five days so their flavor doesn't permeate other items.

To prepare: Cut the bulb in half lengthwise, and wash thoroughly, removing any soil or grit. Trim the root and leaf ends, discarding tough and withered leaves.

To cook: Use leeks to add flavor to quiches, risottos, pilafs, soups, and stews. When preparing leeks, be attentive; they overcook easily. They're ready when the base can be pierced with a knife.

Health benefits: Leeks are a good source of fiber, folate, vitamin C, potassium, and calcium.

For safety reasons, a portion of the glaze is kept separate to baste the pork while raw and during cooking; the remainder is served with the cooked roast. The glaze will thicken significantly if made ahead; microwave at HIGH for a few seconds at a time, stirring after each heating, until glaze is thinned.

Pork Tenderloin with Pomegranate Glaze

2   cups pomegranate juice
¼   cup sugar
2   (¾-pound) pork tenderloins, trimmed
½   teaspoon salt
¼   teaspoon freshly ground black pepper
Cooking spray

1. Preheat oven to 450°.
2. Combine juice and sugar in a medium saucepan over medium heat, and bring to a boil. Cook until reduced to ½ cup (about 8 minutes). Pour half of glaze into a small bowl; set aside.
3. Sprinkle pork evenly with salt and pepper. Place pork on rack of a broiler pan coated with cooking spray, and place rack in pan. Brush pork with half of glaze in saucepan. Bake at 450° for 15 minutes or until a thermometer registers 145°. Baste pork with remaining glaze in saucepan, and

cook an additional 5 minutes or until thermometer registers 155°.

4. Remove pork from oven; baste with half of glaze in bowl. Let pork stand 10 minutes. Cut pork across grain into thin slices. Serve pork with glaze. **Yield:** 6 servings (serving size: 3 ounces pork and 2 teaspoons glaze).

CALORIES 215; FAT 3.9g (sat 1.3g, mono 1.8g, poly 0.4g); PROTEIN 24.2g; CARB 20.1g; FIBER 0g; CHOL 74mg; IRON 1.5mg; SODIUM 263mg; CALC 19mg

americanfavorite

The sliced pork cooks faster than a whole tenderloin, and this gingered cranberry sauce not only has wonderful flavor, but it's also quick and easy.

—Linda Drinkard, Vero Beach, FL

Pork Medallions with Gingered Cranberry Sauce

2   teaspoons butter
1   (1-pound) pork tenderloin, trimmed and cut into 1-inch-thick slices
¼   teaspoon salt
¼   teaspoon freshly ground black pepper
1   tablespoon olive oil
½   teaspoon finely minced peeled fresh ginger
1   garlic clove, minced
½   cup port or other sweet red wine
1   cup canned whole-berry cranberry sauce
¼   cup fat-free, less-sodium chicken broth
1½ teaspoons balsamic vinegar

1. Melt butter in a large nonstick skillet over medium-high heat. Sprinkle both sides of pork evenly with salt and pepper. Add pork to pan; cook 2 minutes on each side or until browned. Remove pork from pan, and keep warm.

2. Wipe pan with a paper towel; return pan to heat. Add olive oil to pan. Add ginger and garlic; sauté 30 seconds. Add port, scraping pan to loosen browned bits; cook until reduced to ¼ cup (about 5 minutes). Add cranberry sauce and chicken broth; cook 3 minutes or until slightly thick, stirring occasionally. Stir in balsamic vinegar; return pork to pan. Cook 1 minute, turning to coat pork. **Yield:** 4 servings (serving size: 3 ounces pork and 3 tablespoons sauce).

CALORIES 310; FAT 9.2g (sat 3g, mono 4.7g, poly 0.9g); PROTEIN 24.1g; CARB 28.7g; FIBER 1.1g; CHOL 79mg; IRON 1.5mg; SODIUM 259mg; CALC 10mg

Clean Leafy Greens

Dark leafy greens, such as kale, Swiss chard, and turnip greens, make ideal sides to main dishes. After buying fresh greens, wrap them, unwashed, in damp paper towels, and store in an unsealed plastic bag in the refrigerator for three to five days. When ready to use, follow these steps to clean them and remove the veins.

1. Pull apart the bunch; remove and discard any yellowed or limp leaves.

2. Wash greens in cool water, agitating with your hands. Replace the water two or three times, until there are no traces of dirt or grit. Pat dry with paper towels or use a salad spinner.

3. Place on a cutting board, and cut away tough stems. To remove the hard center vein, fold the leaf in half and tear or cut away.

Chock-full of vegetables, this one-pot ragout—a thick, well-seasoned stew—warms up a chilly winter evening. If you've never had kale, this dish makes the most of its sweet, earthy flavor.

White Bean and Sausage Ragout with Tomatoes, Kale, and Zucchini

1   tablespoon olive oil
½   cup chopped onion
2   (4-ounce) links chicken sausage, cut into (½-inch) slices
1   zucchini, quartered and cut into (½-inch) slices (about 2 cups)
3   garlic cloves, peeled and crushed
6   cups chopped trimmed kale (about ½ pound)
½   cup water
2   (16-ounce) cans cannellini beans or other white beans, rinsed and drained
1   (14.5-ounce) can diced tomatoes, undrained
¼   teaspoon salt
¼   teaspoon freshly ground black pepper

1. Heat oil in a large skillet over medium-high heat. Sauté onion and sausage 4 minutes or until sausage is browned. Add zucchini and garlic; cook 2 minutes. Add kale and remaining ingredients; bring to a boil. Cover, reduce heat, and simmer 10 minutes or until thoroughly heated. Serve immediately. **Yield:** 4 servings (serving size: 1¾ cups).

CALORIES 467; FAT 10.2g (sat 2.3g, mono 4.6g, poly 2.5g); PROTEIN 28.5g; CARB 71.8g; FIBER 15.4g; CHOL 42mg; IRON 8.8mg; SODIUM 764mg; CALC 370mg

Americans of Eastern European heritage add a variety of root vegetables, such as turnips and parsnips, to chicken soup for subtle sweetness and bite. Feel free to omit them and simply add more carrot and leek, if you prefer. Be sure to cook the egg noodles separately so the starch in the noodles doesn't cloud the clear soup broth.

Chicken-Vegetable Soup

1   (6-pound) roasting chicken
8   cups water
2½   cups chopped celery (about 4 stalks)
2   cups thinly sliced leek (about 2 large)
1½   cups (½-inch) cubed parsnip (about 8 ounces)
1½   cups (½-inch) cubed carrot (about 8 ounces)
1½   cups (½-inch) cubed turnip (about 8 ounces)
1   teaspoon kosher salt
½   teaspoon freshly ground black pepper
1   teaspoon chopped fresh dill (optional)
8   ounces egg noodles

1. Remove and discard giblets and neck from chicken. Remove and discard skin from chicken; trim excess fat. Split chicken in half lengthwise; place in a Dutch oven. Cover with 8 cups water; bring to a boil. Cook 10 minutes. Skim fat from surface of broth; discard fat. Add celery and next 4 ingredients to pan, stirring well; bring to a boil. Reduce heat, and simmer 30 minutes or until vegetables are almost tender, stirring occasionally. Remove chicken; let stand 10 minutes. Remove chicken from bones; shred chicken with 2 forks to yield 6 cups meat. Discard bones. Simmer vegetable mixture 10 minutes or until tender. Return shredded chicken to pan. Stir in salt, pepper, and dill, if desired.

2. Cook noodles according to package directions, omitting salt and fat. Place ½ cup noodles in each of 8 bowls; top each serving with 1½ cups chicken mixture. **Yield:** 8 servings.

CALORIES 404; FAT 14.2g (sat 3.6g, mono 4.7g, poly 3.5g); PROTEIN 36.5g; CARB 31.2g; FIBER 3.6g; CHOL 107mg; IRON 3.4mg; SODIUM 392mg; CALC 76mg

In *Cooking Light* magazine's early days, we shied away from indulgent ingredients like puff pastry. Now, though, we understand that these items can fit into a healthful diet. This dish registers at just 30 percent calories from fat—root vegetables help balance the fat from the flaky topping. You can also bake in individual (10-ounce) ramekins or crocks for the same amount of time.

Chicken and Root Vegetable Potpie

3   cups fat-free, less-sodium chicken broth
1½   cups frozen green peas, thawed
1   cup (½-inch) cubed peeled baking potato
1   cup (½-inch) cubed peeled sweet potato
1   cup (½-inch) cubed peeled celeriac (celery root)
1   cup (½-inch-thick) slices parsnip
1   (10-ounce) package frozen pearl onions
1   pound skinless, boneless chicken breasts,
     cut into bite-sized pieces
3   ounces all-purpose flour (about ⅔ cup), divided
1½   cups fat-free milk
¼   cup chopped fresh parsley
2   tablespoons chopped fresh thyme
1½   teaspoons salt
1   teaspoon freshly ground black pepper
Cooking spray
1   sheet frozen puff pastry dough, thawed

1. Preheat oven to 400°.
2. Bring broth to a boil in a large Dutch oven. Add peas and next 5 ingredients; cover, reduce heat, and simmer 6 minutes. Add chicken; cook 5 minutes or until chicken is done. Remove chicken and vegetables with a slotted spoon; place in a large bowl.
3. Increase heat to medium. Lightly spoon flour into a dry measuring cup; level with a knife. Place all but 1 tablespoon flour in a medium bowl; gradually add milk to bowl, stirring with a whisk until well blended. Add milk mixture to broth; cook 5 minutes or until thickened, stirring frequently. Stir in chicken mixture, parsley, thyme, salt, and pepper. Spoon mixture into an 11 x 7–inch baking dish coated with cooking spray.

4. Sprinkle remaining 1 tablespoon flour on a work surface; roll dough into a 13 x 9–inch rectangle. Place dough over chicken mixture, pressing to seal at edges of dish. Cut small slits into dough to allow steam to escape; coat dough lightly with cooking spray. Place dish on a foil-lined baking sheet. Bake at 400° for 16 minutes or until pastry is browned and filling is bubbly. **Yield:** 8 servings.

CALORIES 388; FAT 13g (sat 2g, mono 3g, poly 7.1g); PROTEIN 21.9g; CARB 45.7g; FIBER 4.4g; CHOL 34mg; IRON 3mg; SODIUM 790mg; CALC 115mg

Parsnips

This hardy root vegetable enjoys cool climates—it requires frost to convert its starches to sugars and to develop its sweet, nutty flavor. Although it bears a striking resemblance to a carrot, a parsnip has pale, cream-colored skin.

Look for small to medium-sized parsnips with beige skin. You'll find them year-round, but their peak season is from autumn to spring. They should be blemish-free and firm. Since parsnips are sometimes sold near similar-looking parsley roots, be sure you're purchasing the right item. Parsnips are sold by the root only, while parsley roots are typically sold with their greens attached.

Like other root vegetables, parsnips store well. Wrap unwashed parsnips in a paper towel, place in a plastic zip-top bag, and store in the vegetable crisper drawer of the refrigerator for up to two weeks. Wash the exterior, and peel. Cut off the top and bottom, and slice or julienne, depending on the recipe's directions. Then steam, roast, or sauté for a hearty side dish. To keep them appealingly tasty, add parsnips during the last 30 minutes of cooking when preparing soups and stews.

Winter is the peak season for rutabagas, turnips, and parsnips. Their strong flavors mellow with cooking.

Braised Root Vegetables and Chicken Thighs

1.1	ounces all-purpose flour (about ¼ cup)
8	chicken thighs (about 2 pounds), skinned
5	teaspoons olive oil, divided
2	cups chopped onion
2	cups (¾-inch) cubed peeled rutabaga
2	cups (¾-inch) cubed peeled turnip (about 1 pound)
2	cups (¾-inch) cubed peeled butternut squash
1	cup (¼-inch-thick) slices parsnip
1	garlic clove, minced
½	cup fat-free, less-sodium chicken broth
1	teaspoon chopped fresh or ¼ teaspoon dried thyme
1	teaspoon chopped fresh or ¼ teaspoon dried rubbed sage
½	teaspoon salt
¼	teaspoon black pepper
1	bay leaf

1. Place flour in a shallow dish; dredge chicken in flour.
2. Heat 1 tablespoon oil in a large nonstick skillet over medium-high heat. Add chicken; sauté 5 minutes, turning once. Remove chicken from pan, and keep warm.
3. Heat 2 teaspoons oil in pan. Add onion; sauté 3 minutes. Add rutabaga, turnip, squash, parsnip, and garlic; sauté 3 minutes. Stir in broth and remaining ingredients; nestle chicken into vegetable mixture. Bring to a boil; cover, reduce heat, and simmer 20 minutes or until chicken is done. Uncover and simmer 3 minutes or until thick. Remove bay leaf. **Yield:** 4 servings (serving size: 2 thighs and 1¼ cups vegetable mixture).

CALORIES 355; FAT 11.3g (sat 2.2g, mono 5.8g, poly 2g); PROTEIN 30.2g; CARB 34g; FIBER 7.5g; CHOL 107mg; IRON 3.1mg; SODIUM 522mg; CALC 114mg

The turkey is simple, but truffle oil in the gravy makes the dish holiday-special. Start making the stock for the gravy while the turkey cooks. Garnish the platter with kumquats, roasted garlic, and fresh thyme, sage, and parsley.

Roast Turkey with Truffle Gravy

Turkey:

1   (12-pound) fresh or frozen turkey, thawed
4   fresh thyme sprigs
4   fresh sage leaves
4   garlic cloves
1   medium onion, quartered
2   tablespoons butter, softened
1½ teaspoons kosher salt
¾   teaspoon freshly ground black pepper
1   cup water

Gravy:

Cooking spray
4   cups water
⅔   cup chopped onion
⅓   cup chopped carrot
⅓   cup chopped celery
6   black peppercorns
4   fresh parsley sprigs
2   fresh thyme sprigs
1   bay leaf
½   teaspoon kosher salt
½   teaspoon freshly ground black pepper
3½ tablespoons all-purpose flour
1½ teaspoons truffle oil

1. Preheat oven to 500°.
2. To prepare turkey, remove giblets and neck from turkey; reserve for gravy. Trim excess fat. Stuff body cavity with 4 thyme sprigs, 4 sage leaves, garlic, and onion quarters. Tie legs together with kitchen string.
3. Starting at neck cavity, loosen skin from breast and drumsticks by inserting fingers, gently pushing between skin and meat. Combine butter, 1½ teaspoons salt, and ¾ teaspoon pepper. Rub butter mixture under loosened skin over breast and drumsticks. Lift wing tips up and over back; tuck under turkey. Pour 1 cup water in bottom of a roasting pan. Place roasting rack in pan. Arrange turkey, breast side up, on roasting rack. Bake at 500° for 30 minutes.
4. Reduce oven temperature to 350° (do not remove turkey from oven).
5. Bake turkey at 350° for 1½ hours or until a thermometer inserted into meaty part of thigh registers 165°. (Shield turkey with foil if it browns too quickly.) Remove turkey from oven; let stand 20 minutes. Discard skin before serving. Reserve pan drippings for gravy.
6. To prepare gravy, while turkey roasts, heat a large saucepan over medium-high heat. Coat pan with cooking spray. Add reserved turkey neck and giblets to pan; cook 5 minutes, browning on all sides. Add 4 cups water and next 7 ingredients; bring to a boil. Reduce heat, and simmer until liquid is reduced to about 2½ cups (about 1 hour). Strain through a colander over a bowl. Discard solids. Return mixture to saucepan; stir in ½ teaspoon salt and ½ teaspoon pepper.
7. Place a zip-top plastic bag inside a 2-cup glass measure. Pour turkey pan drippings into bag; let stand 10 minutes (fat will rise to the top). Seal bag; carefully snip off 1 bottom corner of bag. Drain drippings into strained stock in saucepan, stopping before fat layer reaches opening; discard fat. Combine ½ cup stock mixture and flour in a small bowl, stirring with a whisk until smooth. Stir flour mixture into stock; bring to a boil, stirring frequently. Reduce heat, and simmer 3 minutes or until slightly thickened. Remove from heat; add oil, stirring with a whisk. Serve gravy with turkey. **Yield:** 12 servings (serving size: about 6 ounces turkey and about 2½ tablespoons gravy).

CALORIES 383; FAT 9.6g (sat 3.6g, mono 2.7g, poly 2.2g); PROTEIN 67.7g; CARB 1.9g; FIBER 0.1g; CHOL 232mg; IRON 4.7mg; SODIUM 481mg; CALC 48mg

A suitable side for roast chicken or pork, this low-calorie side dish has about 15 percent of the minimum daily recommended amount of fiber.

Braised Kale with Bacon and Cider

2	slices bacon
1¼	cups thinly sliced onion
1	(1-pound) bag chopped kale
⅓	cup apple cider
1	tablespoon apple cider vinegar
1½	cups diced Granny Smith apple (about 10 ounces)
½	teaspoon salt
¼	teaspoon freshly ground black pepper

1. Place a Dutch oven over medium heat. Add bacon; cook 5 minutes or until crisp, stirring occasionally. Remove bacon from pan, reserving 1 teaspoon drippings in pan. Crumble bacon, and set aside.

2. Increase heat to medium-high. Add onion to pan; cook 5 minutes or until tender, stirring occasionally. Add kale, and cook 5 minutes or until wilted, stirring frequently. Add cider and vinegar; cover and cook 10 minutes, stirring occasionally. Add apple, salt, and pepper; cook 5 minutes or until apple is tender, stirring occasionally. Sprinkle with bacon. **Yield:** 6 servings (serving size: ⅔ cup).

CALORIES 75; FAT 2.3g (sat 0.8g, mono 0.9g, poly 0.4g); PROTEIN 2.5g; CARB 12.7g; FIBER 2.1g; CHOL 3mg; IRON 1mg; SODIUM 255mg; CALC 71mg

Kale

Consider using kale as a stand-in for spinach in other dishes.

To select: Look for a deep blue-green color and choose small bunches devoid of any signs of wilting or discoloration.

To store: When bringing fresh greens home from the market, wash them; then pat dry, wrap in damp paper towels, and store them in an unsealed plastic bag in the refrigerator. They'll stay fresh three to five days.

To prepare: To clean kale, pull apart and examine each leaf. Discard any yellowed or limp portions. Wash in cool water, agitating with your hands. Replace the water a few times until there are no traces of dirt. Lay flat to dry on a dish towel.

To cook: Kale's sturdy leaves are excellent sautéed and added to casseroles. Even though a recipe may appear to ask for too much kale, the leaves will wilt to a more manageable portion during cooking.

Health benefits: Kale contains beta-carotene and the antioxidants lutein and zeaxanthin—which are associated with eye health—as well as potassium, vitamin A, vitamin C, fiber, iron, and calcium. Plus, you get 2 grams of protein in a serving.

howto:

Cut and Clean Leeks

Although they resemble large, sturdy green onions, leeks have a mild, slightly sweet onion flavor. Accessing it requires a little prep work. You'll need to thoroughly clean a leek because dirt can become trapped in its many layers.

1. Trim the feathery root portion just above the base. Slice off the fibrous green tops, leaving only the white-to-light-green stalk. Discard greens.

2. Cut leek in half lengthwise. Slice or chop leek as specified in your recipe.

3. Place cut leek in a colander, and submerge in a bowl of water. Agitate the leek so any dirt falls to the bottom. Drain the leek on paper towels.

Cook the vegetables slowly in a flavorful liquid for our interpretation of leeks vinaigrette. The leek halves will slightly overlap in the dish. Pancetta is Italian cured pork. If you can't find it, substitute your favorite cured bacon.

Braised Leeks with Warm Pancetta Dressing

Leeks:

4   leeks, trimmed and halved lengthwise
¼   teaspoon kosher salt
¼   teaspoon freshly ground black pepper
1½   cups fat-free, less-sodium chicken broth
1   large carrot, cut into (3-inch) pieces
1   garlic clove, crushed
1   fresh thyme sprig
Cooking spray

Dressing:

1   teaspoon olive oil
⅓   cup finely chopped pancetta (about 1 ounce)
2   tablespoons finely chopped leek
2   tablespoons light brown sugar
¼   cup red wine vinegar
⅛   teaspoon freshly ground black pepper
Dash of kosher salt
Remaining Ingredient:
Thyme sprigs (optional)

1. Preheat oven to 325°.

2. To prepare leeks, arrange leek halves in an 8-inch baking dish; sprinkle evenly with ¼ teaspoon salt and ¼ teaspoon pepper. Add broth and next 3 ingredients. Cut 1 (8-inch) square of parchment paper; lightly coat with cooking spray. Place parchment over leek mixture, coated side down. Bake at 325° for 50 minutes or until leeks are tender. Let stand 5 minutes; drain cooking liquid through a sieve over a bowl, reserving solids.

3. Place cooking liquid in a small, heavy saucepan; bring to a boil. Cook until reduced to ¼ cup (about 8 minutes). Chop cooked carrot; set aside. Coarsely chop cooked garlic; set aside.

4. To prepare dressing, heat oil in a small skillet over medium-high heat. Add pancetta to pan; sauté 5 minutes or until crisp. Stir in garlic and chopped leek; sauté 2 minutes, stirring occasionally. Sprinkle with brown sugar; sauté 1 minute or until sugar dissolves. Stir in vinegar; simmer 2 minutes. Add cooking liquid, ⅛ teaspoon pepper, and dash of salt; simmer 2 minutes or until slightly thick. Remove from heat. Arrange leek halves in a serving dish, and sprinkle with carrot. Drizzle pancetta mixture over leek halves. Garnish with thyme sprigs, if desired. **Yield:** 4 servings (serving size: 2 leek halves and 2 tablespoons dressing).

CALORIES 133; FAT 3.8g (sat 1.2g, mono 2g, poly 0.6g); PROTEIN 3.6g; CARB 22.2g; FIBER 2.6g; CHOL 5mg; IRON 2.3mg; SODIUM 391mg; CALC 74mg

Pearl onions or boiling onions also work well in this application. After the onions are blanched to make peeling easier, this assertive side dish comes together with very little work.

Sweet and Sour Cipollini Onions

¼ cup raisins
½ cup hot water
2 pounds cipollini onions
1 tablespoon butter
3 tablespoons water
2 tablespoons red wine vinegar
1 tablespoon sugar
¼ teaspoon salt
¼ teaspoon freshly ground black pepper
2 tablespoons pine nuts

1. Place raisins in a bowl; cover with ½ cup hot water. Let stand 30 minutes or until plump. Drain.

2. Trim top and root end of onions. Cook onions in boiling water 2 minutes. Drain. Cool and peel.

3. Melt butter in a large nonstick skillet over medium-high heat. Add onions to pan, stirring well to coat. Stir in 3 tablespoons water, red wine vinegar, sugar, salt, and black pepper. Cover, reduce heat, and cook 40 minutes, stirring every 10 minutes. Add raisins and pine nuts to pan. Increase heat to medium, and cook, uncovered, 10 minutes or until onions are lightly browned and liquid almost evaporates, stirring occasionally. **Yield:** 6 servings (serving size: ½ cup).

CALORIES 116; FAT 3.9g (sat 1.3g, mono 1g, poly 1g); PROTEIN 2.4g; CARB 19.8g; FIBER 3.9g; CHOL 5mg; IRON 0.3mg; SODIUM 113mg; CALC 4mg

These onions have all the rich flavor of French onion soup and are a good accompaniment to roast beef, baked ham, or lamb.

Peppery Baked Onions with Sage and Gruyère

4   medium yellow onions, peeled and halved
Cooking spray
1½   teaspoons olive oil
¾   teaspoon freshly ground black pepper
¼   teaspoon salt
⅔   cup less-sodium beef broth
2   teaspoons low-sodium soy sauce
¼   teaspoon dried rubbed sage
¼   cup (1 ounce) finely shredded Gruyère cheese

1. Preheat oven to 400°.
2. Arrange onions, cut sides up, in a single layer in a shallow 2-quart baking dish coated with cooking spray. Brush tops of onions with oil; sprinkle with pepper and salt. Bake at 400° for 40 minutes. Add broth and soy sauce; bake 1 hour, basting every 15 minutes. Sprinkle sage and cheese evenly over onions. Bake an additional 5 minutes or until cheese melts. **Yield:** 4 servings (serving size: 2 onion halves).

CALORIES 110; FAT 4.1g (sat 1.6g, mono 2g, poly 0.3g); PROTEIN 4.7g; CARB 14.6g; FIBER 3.2g; CHOL 8mg; IRON 0.6mg; SODIUM 271mg; CALC 116mg

Although best served immediately, this dish can be covered and chilled for a couple of hours. Try it with roast chicken. Pomegranate juice stains, so be careful when extracting the seeds.

Orange-Basmati Salad with Pine Nuts and Pomegranate Seeds

2   cups water
1   cup uncooked basmati rice
1   teaspoon salt, divided
¼   cup white wine vinegar
2   teaspoons grated orange rind
¼   cup fresh orange juice
1½ tablespoons extra-virgin olive oil
¼   teaspoon freshly ground black pepper
2   cups orange sections (about 3 oranges)
½   cup pomegranate seeds
¼   cup pine nuts, toasted
3   tablespoons chopped fresh flat-leaf parsley

1. Bring 2 cups water to a boil in a medium sauce-pan over medium-high heat. Add rice and ¾ tea-spoon salt; cover, reduce heat, and simmer 15 minutes or until liquid is absorbed. Remove from heat; fluff rice with a fork. Cool completely.
2. Combine ¼ teaspoon salt, vinegar, and next 4 ingredients, stirring with a whisk. Combine rice, vinegar mixture, orange sections, and remaining ingredients; toss gently to combine. **Yield:** 6 serv-ings (serving size: about ⅔ cup).

CALORIES 225; FAT 6.8g (sat 1.1g, mono 3.7g, poly 1.7g); PROTEIN 4.8g; CARB 38g; FIBER 2.1g; CHOL 0mg; IRON 1.1mg; SODIUM 393mg; CALC 35mg

Seed a Pomegranate

Unlike with most fruits, the seeds are the edible portion of a pomegranate. Since pomegranates will stain, place the fruit in a bowl of ice water large enough to fit the fruit and your hands. Under water, carefully slice off the crown and opposite end so just the seeds are visible, then score the pomegranate lengthwise into 1½-inch-wide wedges. Wear an apron while you follow these steps for seeding a pomegranate.

1. With your thumbs, carefully pry the pomegranate apart beneath the water and turn each section inside out.

2. Begin to separate the seeds from the inner white membrane, taking care not to burst the individual juice sacs. The membrane will float to the top while the seeds sink to the bottom.

3. With a large slotted spoon, skim off the floating membrane. Sort through the seeds beneath the water, discarding any stray pieces of membrane. Drain the pomegranate seeds in a fine mesh strainer.

Cranberries

To select: Cranberries are usually packaged in 12-ounce plastic bags, so you won't be able to choose them individually. Check the see-through plastic to make sure you get bright, intensely colored berries. One 12-ounce bag equals approximately 3 cups of whole berries.

To store: Leave cranberries in the original bag or tightly wrap them in plastic, and place them in the refrigerator up to one month. For increased longevity, put them in the freezer, where they'll stay fresh for up to nine months. Don't wash before storing.

To prepare: Discard any that are soft, shriveled, withered, or discolored, and remove any stems.

To cook: Unlike any other fruits, cranberries need to be cooked to release their full flavor and to absorb that of other ingredients—one of which is sugar. These tart berries work well in pies, cobblers, muffins, chutneys, and relishes. They also complement meat superbly.

Health benefits: Cranberries contain antioxidants, flavonoids, and fiber, and are a good source of vitamins A and C.

Aside from making a stellar accompaniment to roast turkey, this chutney is great for gift giving; pack in a ribbon-tied jelly jar. It also goes well with roast chicken, pork tenderloin, or ham.

Cranberry, Cherry, and Walnut Chutney

1	cup sugar
1	cup water
½	cup port or other sweet red wine
¼	teaspoon ground allspice
½	cup dried tart cherries
1	(12-ounce) package fresh cranberries
⅔	cup chopped walnuts, toasted
½	teaspoon grated orange rind
¼	teaspoon almond extract

Orange rind strips (optional)

1. Combine first 4 ingredients in a medium saucepan; bring to a boil. Add cherries, and cook 1 minute. Stir in cranberries; bring to a boil. Reduce heat, and simmer 10 minutes or until cranberries pop. Remove from heat. Stir in walnuts, grated rind, and extract. Garnish with orange rind strips, if desired. Cover and chill. **Yield:** 16 servings (serving size: ¼ cup).

CALORIES 108; FAT 3g (sat 0.2g, mono 0.7g, poly 2g); PROTEIN 1.5g; CARB 19.7g; FIBER 1.8g; CHOL 0mg; IRON 0.3mg; SODIUM 2mg; CALC 11mg

Cinnamon, ginger, and cloves boost the taste of this traditional whole-berry cranberry sauce. Vary the character by adding toasted nuts or other fruits.

Classic Cranberry Sauce

1½   cups sugar
¾   cup fresh orange juice (about 3 oranges)
½   teaspoon ground cinnamon
¼   teaspoon ground ginger
Dash of ground cloves
1   (12-ounce) package fresh cranberries
1   tablespoon grated orange rind

1. Combine first 6 ingredients in a medium saucepan; bring to a boil over medium-high heat. Reduce heat to medium; cook 12 minutes or until cranberries pop. Remove from heat; stir in rind. Cool completely. Serve chilled or at room temperature. **Yield:** 3 cups (serving size: 2 tablespoons).

CALORIES 59; FAT 0g; PROTEIN 0.1g; CARB 15g; FIBER 0.7g; CHOL 0mg; IRON 0.1mg; SODIUM 0mg; CALC 3mg

Tart marmalade is delicious on scones or breakfast breads. This recipe produces classic British-style bitter marmalade. If you prefer less bitterness, use only half the grapefruit rind called for in the recipe. Keep in mind that the mixture will thicken as it cools. Store marmalade in the refrigerator for up to three weeks.

Mixed Citrus Marmalade

2   large thin-skinned oranges
2   medium-sized red grapefruit (about 2 pounds)
1   lemon
2   cups sugar
2   cups water
⅛   teaspoon kosher salt

1. Carefully remove rind from fruit using a vegetable peeler; discard white pith. Cut rind from 1 orange, 1 grapefruit, and lemon into 1 x ¼–inch strips. Section fruit; cut into 1-inch pieces. Discard seeds; reserve juice.
2. Combine all ingredients in a large saucepan; bring to a boil. Reduce heat, and simmer 1 hour or until thick, stirring occasionally. Cool. Pour into airtight containers. Yield: 3 cups (serving size: 2 tablespoons).

CALORIES 77; FAT 0g; PROTEIN 0.2g; CARB 20.2g; FIBER 0.9g; CHOL 0mg; IRON 0.1mg; SODIUM 10mg; CALC 9mg

Caramelized Onion
Marmalade

This sweet-tart spread makes a delicious topping for bruschetta or pizza; it's also a nice complement to grilled flank steak, chicken, or pork.

Caramelized Onion Marmalade

1	tablespoon butter
3	tablespoons brown sugar
10	cups thinly sliced sweet onion (about 4 large)
4	garlic cloves, minced
2	tablespoons red wine vinegar
¾	teaspoon salt
⅛	teaspoon freshly ground black pepper

1. Melt butter in a large nonstick skillet over medium heat. Add sugar to pan; cook 1 minute or until sugar dissolves. Add onion and garlic to pan. Cover and cook 30 minutes or until onions are very tender, stirring occasionally. Uncover and add vinegar to onion mixture. Cook, uncovered, 10 minutes or until golden brown, stirring frequently. Stir in salt and pepper. **Yield:** 1½ cups (serving size: 2 tablespoons).

CALORIES 44; FAT 1g (sat 0.6g, mono 0.3g, poly 0.1g); PROTEIN 0.5g; CARB 8.8g; FIBER 0.7g; CHOL 3mg; IRON 0.2mg; SODIUM 157mg; CALC 16mg

This spiced fruit can be chopped and stirred into couscous or served with ham. For optimum texture and flavor, refrigerate the finished recipe for two weeks before using it.

Kumquats in Spiced Syrup with Cloves, Cinnamon, and Star Anise

2	pounds kumquats (about 8 cups)
4	cups water
2	cups sugar
9	whole cloves, divided
3	(3-inch) cinnamon sticks, divided
3	star anise, divided
1	vanilla bean, halved lengthwise and divided
1	cup brandy, divided

1. Pierce each kumquat several times with a wooden skewer.
2. Combine 4 cups water and sugar in a large saucepan; bring to a boil, stirring until sugar dissolves. Add 3 cloves, 1 cinnamon stick, and 1 star anise. Reduce heat, and simmer 5 minutes. Add kumquats, and simmer 20 minutes or until tender.
3. Using a slotted spoon, remove kumquats from pan, and divide evenly between 2 (1-quart) jars. Tuck 3 whole cloves, 1 cinnamon stick, 1 star anise, and half of vanilla bean into each jar.
4. Bring cooking liquid to a boil; cook 4 minutes. Remove from heat. Strain mixture, discarding solids. Pour 2 cups cooking liquid and ½ cup brandy into each jar. Seal jars; shake well. Store in refrigerator 2 weeks before using. **Yield:** 8 cups (serving size: ¼ cup).

CALORIES 87; FAT 0.2g (sat 0g, mono 0g, poly 0.1g); PROTEIN 0.5g; CARB 17g; FIBER 1.8g; CHOL 0mg; IRON 0.3mg; SODIUM 3mg; CALC 18mg

howto:

Make Cinnamon-Date-Pecan Rolls with Maple Glaze

1. Roll dough into a 15 x 10-inch rectangle, and brush with 2 tablespoons butter.

2. Sprinkle the brown sugar mixture over the dough, leaving a ½-inch border. Sprinkle the dates and pecans over sugar mixture.

3. Beginning with a long side, roll up the dough jelly-roll fashion, and pinch the seam to seal (do not seal ends of roll). Cut roll into 18 (½-inch) slices. Place slices, cut sides up, in a 13 x 9-inch baking pan coated with cooking spray. Cover; let rise in a warm place (85°), free from drafts, about 1 hour or until the rolls have doubled in size. Bake.

These frosted sweet rolls make a delectable breakfast or holiday brunch offering.

Cinnamon-Date-Pecan Rolls with Maple Glaze

Dough:
1 teaspoon granulated sugar
1 package dry yeast (about 2¼ teaspoons)
¾ cup warm water (100° to 110°)
⅓ cup granulated sugar
3 tablespoons butter, melted
½ teaspoon salt
1 large egg
14.5 ounces all-purpose flour (about 3¼ cups)
Cooking spray

Filling:
⅔ cup packed brown sugar
1 teaspoon ground cinnamon
1 teaspoon grated orange rind
2 tablespoons butter, melted
¾ cup chopped pitted dates
¼ cup chopped pecans, toasted

Glaze:
1 cup powdered sugar
2 tablespoons maple syrup
1 tablespoon fat-free milk

1. To prepare dough, dissolve 1 teaspoon granulated sugar and yeast in ¾ cup warm water; let stand 5 minutes. Combine ⅓ cup granulated sugar, 3 tablespoons butter, salt, and egg in a large bowl. Add yeast mixture; beat with a mixer at medium speed until blended.

2. Lightly spoon flour into dry measuring cups; level with a knife. Gradually add 3 cups flour to yeast mixture, beating mixture on low speed until a soft dough forms. Turn dough out onto a lightly floured surface. Knead until smooth and elastic (about 5 minutes); add enough of remaining flour, 1 tablespoon at a time, to prevent dough from sticking to hands. Place dough in a large bowl coated with cooking spray, turning to coat top. Cover and let rise in a warm place (85°), free from

366 cooking through the seasons

drafts, 1 hour or until doubled in size. Punch dough down; turn out onto a lightly floured surface.

3. To prepare filling, combine brown sugar, cinnamon, and rind in a small bowl. Roll dough into a 15 x 10–inch rectangle; brush with 2 tablespoons butter. Sprinkle brown sugar mixture over dough, leaving a ½-inch border. Sprinkle dates and pecans over sugar mixture. Beginning with a long side, roll up jelly-roll fashion; pinch seam to seal (do not seal ends of roll). Cut roll into 18 (½-inch) slices. Place slices, cut sides up, in a 13 x 9–inch baking pan coated with cooking spray. Cover and let rise in a warm place (85°), free from drafts, about 1 hour or until rolls have doubled in size.

4. Preheat oven to 375°.

5. Uncover dough. Bake at 375° for 20 minutes or until rolls are golden brown.

6. To prepare glaze, combine powdered sugar, syrup, and milk in a small bowl; stir with a whisk until smooth. Drizzle glaze over warm rolls. Serve immediately. **Yield:** 18 rolls (serving size: 1 roll).

CALORIES 226; FAT 4.9g (sat 2.2g, mono 1.6g, poly 0.6g); PROTEIN 3.2g; CARB 43.4g; FIBER 1.5g; CHOL 20mg; IRON 1.5mg; SODIUM 96mg; CALC 21mg

When preparing these cookies, be careful not to over-beat the egg whites; properly stiff peaks will have the consistency of marshmallow cream.

Chocolate-Dipped Almond Meringues

Meringues:

4   large egg whites
¼   teaspoon cream of tartar
¼   teaspoon salt
½   cup sugar
¼   teaspoon almond extract
2   ounces bittersweet chocolate, finely chopped

Chocolate Glaze:

½   cup semisweet chocolate chips

1. Preheat oven to 200°.
2. To prepare meringues, cover a baking sheet with parchment paper; secure to baking sheet with masking tape.
3. Beat egg whites with a mixer at high speed until foamy. Add cream of tartar and salt; beat until soft peaks form. Gradually add sugar, 1 tablespoon at a time, beating until stiff peaks form (do not overbeat). Gently fold in almond extract and chopped chocolate. Drop batter by rounded

tablespoonfuls onto prepared baking sheet. Bake at 200° for 2 hours or until dry. (Meringues are done when the surface is dry and meringues can be removed from paper without sticking to fingers.) Turn oven off; leave meringues in oven 1 hour or until cool and crisp. Remove from oven; carefully remove meringues from paper. Cool completely on a wire rack.

4. To prepare glaze, place semisweet chocolate chips in a medium microwave-safe bowl. Microwave at MEDIUM (50% power) 30 seconds or until melted, stirring until smooth. Dip half of each meringue in chocolate. Place on wire rack to dry. Store in an airtight container. **Yield:** 2 dozen (serving size: 1 meringue).

CALORIES 48; FAT 2.1g (sat 1.3g, mono 0.4g, poly 0g); PROTEIN 0.9g; CARB 7.6g; FIBER 0.4g; CHOL 1mg; IRON 0.2mg; SODIUM 34mg; CALC 2mg

americanfavorite

This cookie dough—with regular oats in the batter—needs to be chilled for several hours or overnight before baking.

—Allyn Stelljes-Young, Rochester, NY

Cranberry-Nut Chocolate Chip Cookies

3.4 ounces all-purpose flour (about ¾ cup)
3.5 ounces whole wheat flour (about ¾ cup)
¾ cup regular oats
½ teaspoon baking powder
¼ teaspoon baking soda
¼ teaspoon salt
¼ cup dried cranberries
2 ½ tablespoons finely chopped walnuts
2 ½ tablespoons semisweet chocolate minichips
¾ cup packed brown sugar
5 tablespoons butter, softened
2 tablespoons honey
¾ teaspoon vanilla extract
1 large egg
1 large egg white
Cooking spray

1. Lightly spoon flours into dry measuring cups; level with a knife. Combine flours, oats, baking powder, and next 5 ingredients in a large bowl.
2. Combine sugar and butter in a large bowl; beat with a mixer at medium speed until light and fluffy. Add honey, vanilla, egg, and egg white; beat well. Add flour mixture to sugar mixture; beat at low speed until well blended. Cover and refrigerate 8 hours or overnight.
3. Preheat oven to 350°.
4. Drop batter by tablespoonfuls onto a baking sheet coated with cooking spray. Bake at 350° for 10 minutes. Cool 2 minutes on pans. Remove from pans, and cool completely on wire racks. **Yield:** 36 cookies (serving size: 1 cookie).

CALORIES 75; FAT 2.6g (sat 1.3g, mono 0.7g, poly 0.4g); PROTEIN 1.4g; CARB 12.1g; FIBER 0.8g; CHOL 10mg; IRON 0.5mg; SODIUM 49mg; CALC 12mg

Molasses gives these brownielike squares deep, rich flavor. They are quick and easy to make and even lend a wonderfully fragrant aroma to your home while they're baking. Serve up a batch to your family or place them in a parchment paper-lined box for holiday gift-giving.

Gingerbread Squares

5.5 ounces all-purpose flour (about 1¼ cups)
1 teaspoon ground ginger
1 teaspoon ground cinnamon
½ teaspoon baking soda
½ cup granulated sugar
½ cup low-fat buttermilk
½ cup molasses
⅓ cup butter, melted
1 large egg, lightly beaten
Cooking spray
1 tablespoon powdered sugar

1. Preheat oven to 350°.
2. Lightly spoon flour into dry measuring cups; level with a knife. Combine flour, ginger, cinnamon, and baking soda, stirring with a whisk.
3. Combine granulated sugar and next 4 ingredients in a large bowl, stirring with a whisk. Stir in flour mixture. Pour batter into a 9-inch square baking pan coated with cooking spray.
4. Bake at 350° for 25 minutes or until a wooden pick inserted in center comes out clean. Cool in pan on a wire rack. Sprinkle gingerbread with powdered sugar. **Yield:** 25 servings (serving size: 1 [1¾-inch] square).

CALORIES 84; FAT 2.8g (sat 1.6g, mono 0.8g, poly 0.2g); PROTEIN 1.1g; CARB 14g; FIBER 0.2g; CHOL 15mg; IRON 0.7mg; SODIUM 61mg; CALC 22mg

Using light brown sugar yields sweet treats with caramel notes. These double easily; just bake each batch separately for the best results.

Brown Sugar Shortbread

5.5 ounces all-purpose flour (about 1¼ cups)
3 tablespoons cornstarch
¼ teaspoon salt
½ cup packed light brown sugar
7 tablespoons butter, softened
1½ teaspoons ice water
Cooking spray

1. Lightly spoon flour into dry measuring cups; level with a knife. Combine flour, cornstarch, and salt in a small bowl; stir with a whisk.
2. Place brown sugar and butter in a medium bowl; mix with hands until combined. Add flour mixture, and mix with hands until combined. Sprinkle dough with 1½ teaspoons ice water; knead dough lightly 4 times or just until smooth. Wrap in plastic wrap; refrigerate 30 minutes.
3. Preheat oven to 325°.
4. Place dough on a baking sheet coated with cooking spray; press dough into an 8 x 5–inch rectangle about ⅜-inch thick. Pierce entire surface liberally with a fork. Bake at 325° for 25 minutes or just until set and edges are golden. Cut shortbread into 24 pieces. Cool completely. **Yield:** 2 dozen (serving size: 1 cookie).

CALORIES 74; FAT 3.4g (sat 2.1g, mono 0.9g, poly 0.2g); PROTEIN 0.7g; CARB 10.4g; FIBER 0.2g; CHOL 9mg; IRON 0.4mg; SODIUM 50mg; CALC 6mg

Rich shortbread is easy to prepare and keeps for several days in an airtight container. Softened butter should be pliable but not easily spreadable. Because this mixture is already dark, it's hard to tell when the shortbread browns. Check your oven temperature using an oven thermometer, and bake just until the shortbread is set.

Chocolate Shortbread

4.5 ounces all-purpose flour (about 1 cup)
3 tablespoons unsweetened premium dark cocoa
¼ teaspoon salt
½ cup powdered sugar
5 tablespoons butter, softened
¼ cup canola oil
Cooking spray

1. Lightly spoon flour into a dry measuring cup; level with a knife. Combine flour, cocoa, and salt in a small bowl; stir with a whisk.

2. Place sugar, butter, and oil in a medium bowl; mix with hands until combined. Add flour mixture, and mix with hands until combined; wrap in plastic wrap. Refrigerate 30 minutes.

3. Preheat oven to 325°.

4. Place dough on a baking sheet coated with cooking spray; press dough into an 8 x 5–inch rectangle about ⅜-inch thick. Pierce entire surface liberally with a fork. Bake at 325° for 30 minutes or just until set. Cut shortbread into 24 pieces. Cool completely. **Yield:** 2 dozen (serving size: 1 cookie).

CALORIES 72; FAT 4.8g (sat 1.7g, mono 2.1g, poly 0.8g); PROTEIN 0.7g; CARB 7g; FIBER 0.3g; CHOL 6mg; IRON 0.3mg; SODIUM 42mg; CALC 2mg

Brown Sugar Shortbread and Chocolate Shortbread

When swirling the cheesecake and brownie batters in step 4, don't disturb the bottom brownie layer. Cool these bars completely before serving.

Peppermint Cheesecake Brownies

Cheesecake Batter:

1   (8-ounce) block ⅓-less-fat cream cheese
⅓   cup granulated sugar
¼   teaspoon peppermint extract
1   large egg
1   large egg white
1   tablespoon all-purpose flour

Chocolate Batter:

4.5 ounces all-purpose flour (about 1 cup)
½   cup unsweetened cocoa
½   teaspoon salt
1½ cups packed brown sugar
¼   cup canola oil
¼   cup buttermilk
2   teaspoons vanilla extract
2   large egg whites
1   large egg
Cooking spray

1. Preheat oven to 350°.
2. To prepare cheesecake batter, place cheese in a medium bowl; beat with a mixer at medium speed until smooth. Add granulated sugar and peppermint extract; beat well. Add 1 egg and 1 egg white; beat well. Add 1 tablespoon flour; beat mixture just until blended.
3. To prepare brownie batter, lightly spoon 4.5 ounces flour into a dry measuring cup; level with a knife. Combine flour, cocoa, and salt in a medium bowl, stirring with a whisk. Combine brown sugar and next 5 ingredients in a large bowl; beat with a mixer at medium-high speed until well blended. Add flour mixture to brown sugar mixture; beat at low speed just until blended.

4. Reserve ½ cup brownie batter. Pour remaining batter into a 9-inch square baking pan coated with cooking spray. Carefully pour cheesecake batter over top; spread evenly to edges. Dot cheesecake batter with reserved brownie batter. Swirl top two layers of batters together using the tip of a knife. Bake at 350° for 26 minutes or until top is set. Cool completely in pan on a wire rack. **Yield:** 16 servings (serving size: 1 bar).

CALORIES 213; FAT 7.5g (sat 2.6g, mono 2.3g, poly 1.1g); PROTEIN 4.4g; CARB 32.3g; FIBER 0.7g; CHOL 37mg; IRON 1.3mg; SODIUM 169mg; CALC 32mg

No holiday spread is complete without red velvet—cake or cupcakes. The frosting is just as important as the cake. The secret: Use part real butter and cream cheese.

—Nicolette Manescalchi, San Francisco, CA

Red Velvet Cupcakes

Cupcakes:

Cooking spray

10	ounces cake flour (about 2½ cups)
3	tablespoons unsweetened cocoa
1	teaspoon baking soda
1	teaspoon baking powder
1	teaspoon kosher salt
1½	cups granulated sugar
6	tablespoons unsalted butter, softened
2	large eggs
1¼	cups nonfat buttermilk
1½	teaspoons white vinegar
1½	teaspoons vanilla extract
2	tablespoons red food coloring (about 1 ounce)

Frosting:

5	tablespoons butter, softened
4	teaspoons nonfat buttermilk
1	(8-ounce) block cream cheese, softened
3½	cups powdered sugar (about 1 pound)
1¼	teaspoons vanilla extract

1. Preheat oven to 350°.

2. To prepare cupcakes, place 30 paper muffin cup liners in muffin cups; coat with cooking spray.

3. Lightly spoon cake flour into dry measuring cups; level with a knife. Combine cake flour, unsweetened cocoa, baking soda, baking powder, and salt in a medium bowl; stir with a whisk. Place granulated sugar and unsalted butter in a large bowl; beat with a mixer at medium speed until well blended (about 3 minutes). Add eggs, 1 at a time, beating well after each addition. Add flour mixture and 1¼ cups non-fat buttermilk alternately to sugar mixture, beginning and ending with flour mixture. Add white vinegar, 1½ teaspoons vanilla, and food coloring; beat well.

4. Spoon batter into prepared muffin cups. Bake at 350° for 20 minutes or until a wooden pick inserted in center comes out clean. Cool in pan 10 minutes on wire racks; remove from pan. Cool completely on wire racks.

5. To prepare frosting, beat 5 tablespoons butter, 4 teaspoons nonfat buttermilk, and cream cheese with a mixer at high speed until fluffy. Gradually add powdered sugar; beat until smooth. Add 1¼ teaspoons vanilla; beat well. Spread frosting evenly over cupcakes. **Yield:** 30 cupcakes (serving size: 1 cupcake).

CALORIES 205; FAT 7.3g (sat 4.5g, mono 2g, poly 0.3g); PROTEIN 2.3g; CARB 33.5g; FIBER 0.3g; CHOL 34mg; IRON 0.9mg; SODIUM 168mg; CALC 35mg

Cream cheese and peppermint candies yield a mildly sweet, tangy frosting, which complements the rich, chocolaty cupcakes.

Chocolate Cupcakes with Peppermint Frosting

Cupcakes:

1   cup packed brown sugar
6   tablespoons butter, softened
2   large eggs
5.5 ounces all-purpose flour (about 1¼ cups)
½   cup unsweetened cocoa
1   teaspoon baking powder
½   teaspoon baking soda
½   teaspoon salt
½   cup low-fat buttermilk
1   teaspoon vanilla extract

Peppermint Frosting:

2   cups powdered sugar
½   cup (4 ounces) tub-style light cream cheese
⅛   teaspoon peppermint extract
16 hard peppermint candies, finely crushed
    (about ⅓ cup)

1. Preheat oven to 350°.
2. To prepare cupcakes, place brown sugar and butter in a large bowl; beat with a mixer at medium speed 2 minutes or until well blended. Add eggs, 1 at a time, beating well after each addition. Lightly spoon flour into dry measuring cups; level with a knife. Combine flour, cocoa, baking powder, baking soda, and salt in a bowl, stirring well with a whisk. Add flour mixture to sugar mixture alternately with buttermilk, beginning and ending with flour mixture. Stir in vanilla extract.

3. Spoon batter into 18 muffin cups lined with paper liners. Bake at 350° for 12 minutes or until cupcakes spring back when touched lightly in the center. Cool in pan 10 minutes on a wire rack; remove from pan. Cool completely on wire rack.

4. To prepare frosting, combine powdered sugar, cream cheese, and peppermint extract in a bowl, stirring until smooth. Spread about 4 teaspoons frosting on each cupcake; sprinkle evenly with candies. **Yield:** 18 cupcakes (serving size: 1 cupcake).

CALORIES 214; FAT 6.2g (sat 3.7g, mono 1.3g, poly 0.3g); PROTEIN 3g; CARB 38.2g; FIBER 1g; CHOL 38mg; IRON 1.1mg; SODIUM 205mg; CALC 45mg

Peppermint

Peppermint's cool, refreshing quality is simpatico with December. It has a long history as a symbol of hospitality, so naturally the herb, and its extract, often find a place in holiday foods. Of the 30 species of mint, peppermint is the most pungent and, along with milder spearmint, the most widely available.

Fresh peppermint (look for bunches with no signs of wilting) is available year-round; use it to add bursts of mint flavor to a dish or as a garnish. Peppermint extract, a highly concentrated form of the plant's essential oils, is ideally suited for baking, when you want mint's bright flavor to suffuse an entire dish. Because extracts are so potent, a little goes a long way; start with a small amount, stir it in, and taste.

A seasonal version of the classic upside-down cake, this recipe is easy to make and yields impressive-looking results.

Upside-Down Cranberry-Ginger Cake

Cooking spray
¾ cup packed light brown sugar
2 tablespoons butter
1½ tablespoons grated peeled fresh ginger
3 cups fresh cranberries
6.75 ounces all-purpose flour (about 1½ cups)
2 teaspoons baking powder
¼ teaspoon salt
¼ cup butter, softened
1 cup granulated sugar
2 large egg yolks
½ cup fat-free milk
1 teaspoon vanilla extract
2 large egg whites
¼ teaspoon cream of tartar
⅔ cup frozen fat-free whipped topping, thawed

1. Preheat oven to 350°.
2. Heat a 9-inch round cake pan over medium heat; coat pan with cooking spray. Add brown sugar and 2 tablespoons butter to pan, stirring until melted. Stir in ginger; cook 1 minute, stirring constantly. Remove from heat; arrange cranberries on top of brown sugar mixture.

3. Lightly spoon flour into dry measuring cups; level with a knife. Combine flour, baking powder, and salt. Combine ¼ cup butter and granulated sugar in a large bowl; beat with a mixer at high speed until fluffy. Add egg yolks, 1 at a time, beating well after each addition. Add flour mixture and milk alternately to butter mixture, beginning and ending with flour mixture; mix after each addition. Beat in vanilla.
4. Beat egg whites and cream of tartar with a mixer at medium speed until stiff peaks form. Fold egg whites into batter; pour batter over cranberries in prepared pan. Bake at 350° for 55 minutes or until a wooden pick inserted in center comes out clean. Cool in pan 15 minutes; run a knife around outside edge. Place a plate upside down on top of cake pan; invert cake onto plate. Top each serving with whipped topping. **Yield:** 10 servings (serving size: 1 wedge and about 1 tablespoon whipped topping).

CALORIES 312; FAT 8g (sat 4.7g, mono 2.2g, poly 0.5g); PROTEIN 3.8g; CARB 57.3g; FIBER 2g; CHOL 59mg; IRON 1.5mg; SODIUM 185mg; CALC 96mg

Lemons

Whether you use the juice, the zest (rind), or the slices, the acidity of lemon adds to the balance of flavor in all types of food.

To select: Look for smooth, brightly colored skin (green means under-ripe), and lemons that feel heavy for their size.

To store: Store fresh lemons for two to three weeks in a plastic bag in the refrigerator.

To prepare: Microwaving the lemons on HIGH for approximately 30 seconds before squeezing them renders more juice. Use a handheld juice squeezer, and put the lemon half upside down in the press. This will extract the most juice and trap the seeds better.

To use: Lemon can be used to flavor, as a balancing agent, and as a salt or fat replacement.

Health benefits: Lemons are a good source of vitamin C, potassium, and fiber. They also contain several other nutrients, including vitamin B6, calcium, riboflavin, iron, and magnesium.

This rustic cake has a slight crunch from cornmeal; a mixture of winter fruits balances the tangy lemon flavor. The compote is best served at room temperature or slightly warm.

Lemon Polenta Cake with Winter Fruit Compote

Cake:

Cooking spray

5.5 ounces all-purpose flour (about 1¼ cups)

1 cup sugar

½ cup yellow cornmeal

½ teaspoon baking soda

¼ teaspoon salt

⅔ cup reduced-fat buttermilk

¼ cup extra-virgin olive oil

2 large eggs

2 teaspoons grated lemon rind

Compote:

1 cup unsweetened apple juice

½ cup golden raisins

½ cup fresh cranberries

1¾ cups finely chopped, peeled pear (about 2)

2 teaspoons fresh lemon juice

1. Preheat oven to 350°.
2. To prepare cake, coat an 8-inch round cake pan with cooking spray; line bottom of pan with parchment paper. Coat paper with cooking spray. Set aside.
3. Lightly spoon flour into dry measuring cups; level with a knife. Combine flour and next 4 ingredients in a large bowl, stirring well with a whisk. Make a well in center of mixture. Combine buttermilk, oil, eggs, and rind, stirring well with a whisk. Add buttermilk mixture to flour mixture, stirring until moist. Pour batter into prepared pan. Bake at 350° for 40 minutes or until wooden pick inserted in center comes out clean. Cool in pan 10 minutes on a wire rack; remove from pan. Cool completely on wire rack.
4. To prepare compote, combine apple juice and raisins in a small saucepan over medium-high heat; bring to a boil. Reduce heat, and cook until reduced to ⅔ cup (about 4 minutes). Add fresh cranberries to pan; cook 3 minutes or until cranberries pop. Add pear to pan, and cook 2 minutes or until pear is tender. Remove from heat; stir in lemon juice. Serve with cake. **Yield:** 12 servings (serving size: 1 cake wedge and about 2½ tablespoons compote).

CALORIES 243; FAT 6g (sat 1.1g, mono 3.7g, poly 0.7g); PROTEIN 3.8g; CARB 44.7g; FIBER 1.7g; CHOL 36mg; IRON 1.2mg; SODIUM 127mg; CALC 35mg

WINENOTE

With a modestly sweet dessert like this, try a classic **Madeira.** Serve it slightly chilled to contrast the warm cake. And don't worry about finishing the bottle; Madeira lasts almost indefinitely, even after it's been opened.

You will need an eight-inch springform pan for this rich and fudgy dessert. Dark chocolate and orange are a classic flavor combination. Garnish the center of the cake with curls of orange rind for a great finishing touch.

Dark Chocolate–Orange Cake

Cooking spray
¾ cup powdered sugar
3 large eggs
2 tablespoons cornstarch
3 tablespoons unsweetened cocoa
2 tablespoons fresh orange juice
1 tablespoon Triple Sec (orange-flavored liqueur)
1 tablespoon hot water
Dash of salt
2 ounces bittersweet chocolate, chopped
Powdered sugar (optional)
Orange rind strips (optional)

1. Preheat oven to 350°.
2. Coat an 8-inch springform pan with cooking spray; line bottom of pan with parchment or wax paper. Wrap outside of pan with aluminum foil.
3. Place ¾ cup sugar and eggs in a bowl; beat with a mixer at high speed 7 minutes.
4. Combine cornstarch and cocoa in a small bowl; set aside. Place juice, liqueur, water, salt, and chocolate in a small glass bowl; microwave at HIGH 1 minute or until almost melted, stirring every 20 seconds until smooth. Add cornstarch mixture; whisk until smooth.

5. Gently stir one-fourth of egg mixture into chocolate mixture; gently fold into remaining egg mixture. Scrape batter into prepared pan, and place pan in a 13 x 9–inch baking pan; add hot water to larger pan to a depth of 1 inch. Bake at 350° for 20 minutes or until top is set. Remove cake pan from water; cool 5 minutes on a wire rack. Loosen cake from sides of pan using a narrow metal spatula; cool to room temperature. Cover and chill at least 4 hours or overnight. Garnish with powdered sugar and rind just before serving, if desired. **Yield:** 6 servings (serving size: 1 slice).

CALORIES 175; FAT 6.1g (sat 3g, mono 1.3g, poly 0.4g); PROTEIN 4.3g; CARB 26.1g; FIBER 1.7g; CHOL 107mg; IRON 0.8mg; SODIUM 33mg; CALC 17mg

Jim Harrison, an artist specializing in rural Americana and the author of *American Christmas and Country Stores,* has fond memories of making and eating fruitcake with his family as a child in the '40s and '50s. You, too, can reminisce about Christmases past by preparing this all-American seasonal star. Substitute any type of nut for pistachios, if you prefer. Covering the cake locks in steam as it cooks, keeping it moist. It's crucial to allow the cake to "cure" for at least 24 hours in the refrigerator before eating it; this allows the rum to soak in and all the flavors to marry.

Christmas Fruitcake

Cooking spray
2   teaspoons all-purpose flour
1   cup raisins
⅔   cup dried currants
½   cup chopped pistachios
½   cup finely chopped dried apricots
½   cup finely chopped dried figs
1½   tablespoons all-purpose flour
4.5   ounces all-purpose flour (about 1 cup)
½   teaspoon baking soda
½   teaspoon ground cinnamon
¼   teaspoon salt
⅛   teaspoon ground nutmeg
½   cup butter
⅔   cup packed brown sugar
½   cup egg substitute
½   cup dark rum (such as Myers's), divided
1   teaspoon grated orange rind

1. Preheat oven to 325°.
2. Coat an 8 x 4–inch loaf pan with cooking spray; dust pan with 2 teaspoons flour. Set aside.
3. Combine raisins, dried currants, pistachios, dried apricots, dried figs, and 1½ tablespoons flour in a medium bowl; toss well to coat.
4. Lightly spoon 4.5 ounces flour (about 1 cup) into a dry measuring cup; level with a knife. Combine flour, baking soda, ground cinnamon, salt, and nutmeg in a small bowl, stirring with a whisk.
5. Melt butter in a large saucepan over medium heat. Remove from heat. Stir in sugar, egg substitute, ¼ cup rum, and rind. Add flour mixture to pan, stirring with a whisk until smooth. Gradually fold in fruit mixture. Spoon batter into prepared pan. Cover with foil.
6. Bake at 325° for 1 hour or until a wooden pick inserted in center comes out with a few moist crumbs. Pierce top of cake several times with a wooden pick, and brush remaining ¼ cup rum over top of warm cake. Cool completely in pan on a wire rack. Remove cake from pan. Wrap cake in plastic wrap, then wrap in foil. Refrigerate 24 hours before serving. **Yield:** 12 servings (serving size: 1 slice).

CALORIES 306; FAT 10.3g (sat 5.2g, mono 3.2g, poly 1.1g); PROTEIN 4.5g; CARB 48.4g; FIBER 3.6g; CHOL 20mg; IRON 2.2mg; SODIUM 190mg; CALC 54mg

You can prepare the ingredients ahead, spoon the batter into soufflé dishes, cover, and freeze until you're ready to cook them. They can go straight from the freezer to the oven. Make the sauce ahead, too, and simply warm it before serving. This recipe received our Test Kitchens' highest rating.

Double-Chocolate Soufflés with Warm Fudge Sauce

Soufflés:

Cooking spray

½   cup plus 2 tablespoons sugar, divided

3   tablespoons all-purpose flour

3   tablespoons unsweetened cocoa

⅛   teaspoon salt

1¼   cups fat-free milk

3   ounces bittersweet chocolate, chopped

1   teaspoon vanilla extract

1   large egg yolk

6   large egg whites

Sauce:

1   tablespoon butter

⅓   cup sugar

2   tablespoons unsweetened cocoa

1   tablespoon all-purpose flour

½   cup fat-free milk

½   ounce bittersweet chocolate, chopped

1. Position oven rack to lowest setting, and remove middle rack. Preheat oven to 425°.

2. To prepare soufflés, lightly coat 6 (8-ounce) soufflé dishes with cooking spray. Sprinkle evenly with 2 tablespoons sugar. Set aside.

3. Combine remaining ½ cup sugar, 3 tablespoons flour, 3 tablespoons cocoa, and salt in a medium saucepan over medium-high heat, stirring with a whisk. Gradually add 1¼ cups milk, stirring constantly with a whisk; bring to a boil. Cook 2 minutes or until slightly thick, stirring constantly with a whisk; remove from heat. Add 3 ounces chocolate; stir until smooth. Transfer mixture to a large bowl; cool to room temperature. Stir in vanilla and egg yolk.

4. Place egg whites in a large mixing bowl; beat at high speed with a mixer until stiff peaks form (do not overbeat). Gently fold one-fourth of egg whites into chocolate mixture; gently fold in remaining egg white mixture. Gently spoon mixture into prepared dishes. Sharply tap dishes 2 or 3 times on counter to level. Place dishes on a baking sheet; place baking sheet on the bottom rack of 425° oven. Immediately reduce oven temperature to 350° (do not remove soufflés from oven). Bake 40 minutes or until a wooden pick inserted in side of soufflé comes out clean.

5. To prepare sauce, melt butter in a small saucepan over medium-high heat. Add ⅓ cup sugar, 2 tablespoons cocoa, and 1 tablespoon flour; stir well with a whisk. Gradually add ½ cup milk, stirring well with a whisk; bring to a boil. Cook 1 minute or until slightly thick, stirring constantly with a whisk. Remove from heat; add ½ ounce chocolate, stirring until smooth. Serve warm with soufflés. **Yield:** 6 servings (serving size: 1 soufflé and about 2 tablespoons sauce).

CALORIES 315; FAT 9g (sat 5.1g, mono 1.8g, poly 0.3g); PROTEIN 9.1g; CARB 51.8g; FIBER 2.9g; CHOL 41mg; IRON 1.4mg; SODIUM 153mg; CALC 79mg

howto:

Make a Soufflé

Soufflés epitomize the art of French cooking. In fact, the French verb *souffler* means "to inflate" or "to breathe," hinting at the dish's fragile, fleeting nature. "Soufflé" is also a culinary term used in both French and English to refer to this sweet or savory dish.

The basic soufflé has acquired an undeserved reputation for being difficult. Success depends on two simple techniques: first, whip the egg whites properly, and second, fold the egg whites gently into a flavored base.

1. Use soufflé dishes with tall, straight sides. Lightly coat the entire soufflé dish with cooking spray. Add breadcrumbs or sugar, and roll the dish around until it's completely covered.

2. The base gives the soufflé its characteristic flavor. After you cook and cool the base, add the egg yolks and flavorings, such as vanilla or lemon juice, to enrich the dish.

3. Using a powerful stand mixer with a whisk attachment will incorporate the most air into egg whites; whip the egg whites to stiff satiny peaks, but be careful not to overbeat them.

4. Use a rubber spatula to gently fold the egg whites into the base, incorporating as much air as possible. "Cut" down the center and up the bowl's sides, making an S motion and rotating the bowl as you go.

5. The soufflé is done when it's puffed and set. To make sure it is completely cooked, insert a wooden pick or skewer horizontally into the side. If it comes out clean, the soufflé is ready.

The cranberries and pastry cream can be made up to three days ahead. Then, simply assemble and refrigerate the trifle up to 24 hours before you plan to serve it.

Cranberry-Orange Trifle

Cranberries:

¾   cup sugar

¾   cup fresh orange juice

¼   cup Grand Marnier (or other orange liqueur)

1   (12-ounce) package fresh cranberries

Pastry Cream:

½   cup sugar

5   tablespoons cornstarch

2 ½   cups 2% reduced-fat milk

2   large eggs, lightly beaten

2   teaspoons vanilla extract

⅛   teaspoon salt

Remaining Ingredients:

1   (10.75-ounce) loaf pound cake (such as Sara Lee), cut into ½-inch cubes

1   teaspoon orange rind

1. To prepare cranberries, combine ¾ cup sugar, orange juice, and Grand Marnier in a medium saucepan over medium-high heat; cook 3 minutes until sugar dissolves, stirring occasionally. Add cranberries to pan; bring to a boil. Reduce heat; simmer 8 minutes or until cranberries pop. Spoon mixture into a bowl; cover and chill.

2. To prepare pastry cream, combine ½ cup sugar and cornstarch in a medium, heavy saucepan over medium heat. Gradually add milk to pan, stirring with a whisk until blended; bring to a boil. Cook 1 minute, stirring constantly. Remove from heat. Gradually add half of hot milk mixture to eggs, stirring constantly with a whisk. Return milk mixture to pan; cook over medium heat 1 minute or until thick, stirring constantly. Remove from heat. Stir in vanilla and salt. Place pan in a large ice-filled bowl until custard cools to room temperature (about 25 minutes), stirring occasionally.

3. Arrange half of cake cubes in bottom of a 2-quart trifle dish. Spoon 1½ cups cranberry mixture over cake; top with 1½ cups pastry cream. Repeat layers. Garnish with rind. Cover loosely with plastic wrap, and chill at least 4 hours. **Yield:** 12 servings (serving size: about ¾ cup).

CALORIES 265; FAT 6.2g (sat 3.2g, mono 1.9g, poly 0.4g); PROTEIN 4.6g; CARB 46.5g; FIBER 1.7g; CHOL 75mg; IRON 0.5mg; SODIUM 155mg; CALC 84mg

Moroccan-Spiced Oranges

2 ½ cups orange sections, cut into ½-inch pieces (about 6)
¼ cup slivered almonds
2 ½ tablespoons chopped pitted dates (about 4)
1 tablespoon powdered sugar
1 tablespoon fresh lemon juice
¼ teaspoon ground cinnamon
Ground cinnamon (optional)
Grated orange rind (optional)

1. Combine first 6 ingredients in a medium bowl, tossing to combine. Cover; chill 20 minutes. Garnish with cinnamon and rind, if desired. **Yield:** 4 servings (serving size: about ½ cup).

CALORIES 167; FAT 3.6g (sat 0.3g, mono 2.2g, poly 0.9g); PROTEIN 3g; CARB 35g; FIBER 5.3g; CHOL 0mg; IRON 0.7mg; SODIUM 0mg; CALC 81mg

Oranges

Whether sectioned, sliced, juiced, or zested, these juicy fruits are a kitchen staple.

To select: Choose firm oranges that have smooth skins and are not moldy. Don't worry about brown patches on the skin; this does not indicate poor quality.

To store: Store oranges at room temperature up to one week or in the refrigerator up to three weeks.

To prepare: To section an orange, peel it with a paring knife. Be sure to remove the white pith. While holding the orange over a bowl to catch the juices, slice between membranes and one side of one segment of the orange. Lift the segment out with the knife blade.

To use: For the best flavor, use oranges raw. If they are cooked, cook them only briefly.

Health benefits: Along with vitamin C, oranges contain calcium, antioxidants, magnesium, and potassium.

howto:

Seed a Chile Pepper

Hot chiles like serranos or jalapeños can add depth to a recipe, but they can also set your taste buds on fire. To modify their scorch, follow these tips for removing the seeds and veins—the source of capsaicin, the chemical that gives peppers their kick. You can control the heat by removing as many or as few of the seeds as you'd like. Since capsaicin can stick to your hands, be sure to wear gloves.

1. Use a paring knife to cut off the stem and slice the chile in half lengthwise.

2. Next, cut each half lengthwise to create four separate strips.

3. Lay the strips skin sides down, and slide the knife against the pepper to cut away the vein and seeds.

Cranberry-
Jalapeño Granita

This simple compote of pears, apples, and cranberries smells wonderful while it bakes. The applesauce adds body to the syrup.

Baked Compote of Winter Fruit

½   cup applesauce

1½ cups fresh cranberries

½   cup ruby port or other sweet red wine

½   cup apple cider

⅓   cup sugar

1   (1-inch) slice lemon rind strip

4   cups sliced peeled Golden Delicious apple (about 1¼ pounds)

2   cups firm Anjou pears, cored and cut into ¼-inch-thick wedges (about ¾ pound)

Cooking spray

3   cups vanilla low-fat ice cream

1. Preheat oven to 400°.

2. Spoon applesauce onto several layers of heavy-duty paper towels; spread to ½-inch thickness. Cover with additional paper towels; let stand 5 minutes. Scrape into a bowl using a rubber spatula.

3. Combine cranberries, wine, cider, sugar, and rind in a small saucepan; bring to a simmer over medium heat, stirring occasionally. Remove from heat; stir in applesauce.

4. Combine apple and pears in an 11x 7–inch baking dish coated with cooking spray. Pour cranberry mixture over apple mixture. Cover and bake at 400° for 25 minutes. Uncover and bake an additional 10 minutes or until fruit is tender, basting occasionally with liquid from dish. Remove rind. Serve compote with ice cream. **Yield:** 6 servings (serving size: 1 cup compote and ½ cup low-fat ice cream).

CALORIES 260; FAT 2.5g (sat 1.1g, mono 0.7g, poly 0.2g); PROTEIN 3.6g; CARB 57.6g; FIBER 5g; CHOL 5mg; IRON 0.4mg; SODIUM 49mg; CALC 115mg

Remove the jalapeño seeds if you prefer a milder dessert. You could also use this spicy-sweet ice to top oysters on the half shell.

Cranberry-Jalapeño Granita

2   cups cranberry juice cocktail

⅓   cup sugar

4   (5-inch) fresh mint sprigs (about ½ ounce)

1   jalapeño pepper, sliced

2   tablespoons fresh lime juice

1. Combine first 4 ingredients in a small saucepan; bring to a boil. Cover and remove from heat; let stand 15 minutes. Strain cranberry mixture through a fine mesh sieve into an 11 x 7–inch baking dish; discard solids. Cool to room temperature; stir in lime juice. Cover and freeze about 45 minutes. Stir cranberry mixture every 45 minutes until completely frozen (about 3 hours). Remove mixture from freezer; scrape entire mixture with a fork until fluffy. **Yield:** 4 servings (serving size: ½ cup).

CALORIES 135; FAT 0.1g (sat 0g, mono 0g, poly 0.1g); PROTEIN 0.1g; CARB 34.5g; FIBER 0.1g; CHOL 0mg; IRON 0.3mg; SODIUM 3mg; CALC 7mg

Nutritional Analysis

How to Use It and Why

Glance at the end of any *Cooking Light* recipe, and you'll see how committed we are to helping you make the best of today's light cooking. With chefs, registered dietitians, home economists, and a computer system that analyzes every ingredient we use, *Cooking Light* gives you authoritative dietary detail like no other magazine. We go to such lengths so you can see how our recipes fit into your healthful eating plan. If you're trying to lose weight, the calorie and fat figures will probably help most. But if you're keeping a close eye on the sodium, cholesterol, and saturated fat in your diet, we provide those numbers, too. And because many women don't get enough iron or calcium, we can also help there, as well. Finally, there's a fiber analysis for those of us who don't get enough roughage.

Here's a helpful guide to put our nutritional analysis numbers into perspective. Remember, one size doesn't fit all, so take your lifestyle, age, and circumstances into consideration when determining your nutrition needs. For example, pregnant or breast-feeding women need more protein, calories, and calcium. And men older than 50 need 1,200mg of calcium daily, 200mg more than the amount recommended for younger men.

In Our Nutritional Analysis, We Use These Abbreviations

sat	saturated fat	**CHOL**	cholesterol
mono	monounsaturated fat	**CALC**	calcium
poly	polyunsaturated fat	**g**	gram
CARB	carbohydrates	**mg**	milligram

Daily Nutrition Guide

	Women Ages 25 to 50	Women over 50	Men over 24
Calories	2,000	2,000 or less	2,700
Protein	50g	50g or less	63g
Fat	65g or less	65g or less	88g or less
Saturated Fat	20g or less	20g or less	27g or less
Carbohydrates	304g	304g	410g
Fiber	25g to 35g	25g to 35g	25g to 35g
Cholesterol	300mg or less	300mg or less	300mg or less
Iron	18mg	8mg	8mg
Sodium	2,300mg or less	1,500mg or less	2,300mg or less
Calcium	1,000mg	1,200mg	1,000mg

The nutritional values used in our calculations either come from The Food Processor, Version 8.9 (ESHA Research), or are provided by food manufacturers.

Metric Equivalents

The information in the following charts is provided to help cooks outside the United States successfully use the recipes in this book. All equivalents are approximate.

Cooking/Oven Temperatures

	Fahrenheit	Celsius	Gas Mark
Freeze Water	32° F	0° C	
Room Temp.	68° F	20° C	
Boil Water	212° F	100° C	
Bake	325° F	160° C	3
	350° F	180° C	4
	375° F	190° C	5
	400° F	200° C	6
	425° F	220° C	7
	450° F	230° C	8
Broil			Grill

Liquid Ingredients by Volume

¼ tsp	=	1 ml					
½ tsp	=	2 ml					
1 tsp	=	5 ml					
3 tsp	=	1 tbl	=	½ fl oz	=	15 ml	
2 tbls	=	⅛ cup	=	1 fl oz	=	30 ml	
4 tbls	=	¼ cup	=	2 fl oz	=	60 ml	
5⅓ tbls	=	⅓ cup	=	3 fl oz	=	80 ml	
8 tbls	=	½ cup	=	4 fl oz	=	120 ml	
10⅔ tbls	=	⅔ cup	=	5 fl oz	=	160 ml	
12 tbls	=	¾ cup	=	6 fl oz	=	180 ml	
16 tbls	=	1 cup	=	8 fl oz	=	240 ml	
1 pt	=	2 cups	=	16 fl oz	=	480 ml	
1 qt	=	4 cups	=	32 fl oz	=	960 ml	
				33 fl oz	=	1000 ml	= 1 l

Dry Ingredients by Weight

(To convert ounces to grams, multiply the number of ounces by 30.)

1 oz	=	¹⁄₁₆ lb	=	30 g
4 oz	=	¼ lb	=	120 g
8 oz	=	½ lb	=	240 g
12 oz	=	¾ lb	=	360 g
16 oz	=	1 lb	=	480 g

Length

(To convert inches to centimeters, multiply the number of inches by 2.5.)

1 in	=				2.5 cm	
6 in	=	½ ft		=	15 cm	
12 in	=	1 ft		=	30 cm	
36 in	=	3 ft	=	1 yd	=	90 cm
40 in	=				100 cm	= 1m

Equivalents for Different Types of Ingredients

Standard Cup	Fine Powder (ex. flour)	Grain (ex. rice)	Granular (ex. sugar)	Liquid Solids (ex. butter)	Liquid (ex. milk)
1	140 g	150 g	190 g	200 g	240 ml
¾	105 g	113 g	143 g	150 g	180 ml
⅔	93 g	100 g	125 g	133 g	160 ml
½	70 g	75 g	95 g	100 g	120 ml
⅓	47 g	50 g	63 g	67 g	80 ml
¼	35 g	38 g	48 g	50 g	60 ml
⅛	18 g	19 g	24 g	25 g	30 ml

recipe index

subject index